CASSELL

Dictionary of English Grammar

CASSELL

Dictionary of
English Grammar

JAMES AITCHISON

CASSELL

This edition first published in the UK 1996 by
Cassell
Wellington House
125 Strand
London WC2R 0BB

British Library Cataloguing-in-Publication Data
A catalogue record for this book is available from the British Library

ISBN 0–304–34690–X

Designed by Geoff Green
Typeset by Gem Graphics, Trenance, Cornwall
Printed and bound in Great Britain by
Biddles Ltd, Guildford and King's Lynn

Introduction

Grammar is a systematic account of how certain features of a language function in the writing and speech of users of that language. Until the 1950s English grammar was partly modelled on Latin grammar and was usually taught in a prescriptively rule-bound way, which stated how language ought to work rather than how it actually works. The Latin-based, prescriptive model sometimes obscured the real nature of the English language, which is fundamentally different from Latin.

Since the 1950s, academic grammarians and linguists have largely rejected the old model in favour of a variety of descriptive approaches to English grammar. Some of these approaches include a much closer interest in the grammar and other linguistic features of speech and the ways in which the grammar of spoken English differs from that of written standard English.

In the same period, linguists have taken account of other subject areas that offer insights into language and grammar. Logic and anthropology, the traditional areas of interest, are still important, but the interest now extends to the social sciences of psychology and sociology, to some branches of the new generation of physical sciences, including microelectronics and artificial intelligence, and the medical neurosciences. But the most obvious development in grammar in the last fifty years is that the subject itself has divided, multiplied and divided again.

The result of these processes is a fascinating set of diverse, inter-related fields of study, but the sheer diversity can be a source of confusion. Grammar today is, in effect, several grammars, that is, a number of grammatical theories, systems and terminologies, some of which contradict others.

One of the main aims of the *Cassell Dictionary of English Grammar* is to clarify this confusion. Current theories and systems of grammar are assessed and explained, and grammatical terminologies both old and new are clearly defined. Several entries in the dictionary trace the historical development of English grammar; other entries, notably those on word classes and types of clauses and sentences, show a continuity between the pre-1950s model and some current models.

Grammar, for some linguists, is an end in itself. The *Cassell Dictionary of English Grammar* takes a more pragmatic approach in the belief that the realization as well as the source of grammar lies in the writing and speech of the language user.

Abbreviations

a.	adjective
adv.	adverb
a./n.	adjective and/or noun
a./n./adv.	adjective and/or noun and/or adverb
a./v.	adjective and/or verb
n.	noun
n./a.	noun and/or adjective
n./v.	noun and/or verb
v.	verb
v./a.	verb and/or adjective
v./n.	verb and/or noun
*	indicates an unacceptable or incorrect form
/ /	phonemes are set within oblique strokes

Words and phrases in SMALL CAPITALS have their own entries. Headwords cross-referenced to another article appear in **bold** type within that article, while *italic* type is used to highlight examples of the word class under discussion.

a

abbreviation *(n.)*
A shortened form of a word or phrase. Words can be reduced to their initial letters:

C: carbon, Celsius, centigrade, century

to the initial letters of words in a compound word:

cm: centimetre; HQ: headquarters

or to the initial and last letters:

St: Saint, Street.

Phrases can be reduced to the initial letters of the words in the phrase:

AIDS/Aids: Acquired Immune Deficiency Syndrome

DOA: dead on arrival.

Abbreviations that, like AIDS, can be treated as single words are known as ACRONYMS. *See also* BLEND; CLIPPING; DIMINUTIVE.

ablative case
The form, or INFLECTION, taken by nouns and pronouns in Latin and other languages to show that their grammatical function and meaning are *by*, *from* or *with*. Latin *initium*, for example, is inflected to *initio* in *ab initio*, from the beginning. *See also* CASE.

ablaut *(n.)*
A vowel change that marks a change in the grammatical functions of closely related words, notably strong verbs:

sing, sang, sung

take, took, taken

Also known as vowel **gradation**.

1

absolute *(adj./n.)*

An alternative term for POSITIVE (2).

absolute construction

A word, phrase or clause whose meaning is self-contained and partly independent of the sentence in which it appears.

Disgusted, he resigned from the committee.

British weather being as it is, the fans were drenched in the thunderstorm.

abstract noun and concrete noun

Abstract nouns denote phenomena that have no physical or visible substance. They include human emotions, qualities and characteristics:

courage, intelligence, love

conditions and states:

childhood, happiness, poverty

systems and philosophies:

Buddhism, Christianity, democracy

intellectual concepts and intellectual activity:

irony, relativity, deception, ideation.

Although abstractness is expressed mainly through nouns, it can also be expressed through adjectives, adverbs and verbs:

intelligent, lovable (adjectives)

happily, democratically (adverbs)

to deceive, to impoverish (verbs)

All language is abstract in a fundamental sense because words are different, abstracted, from the things to which they refer. The word 'guitar' is nothing like a guitar.

Concrete nouns are words that signify physical, material realities:

book, computer, forest, stone

Concreteness, like abstractness, can be expressed through words from classes other than nouns:

wooden, greasy, reptilian (adjectives)

to afforest, to stone, to grease (verbs)

Abstractness and concreteness are not absolute or exclusive categories. A railway is concrete, but a railway system is an abstract concept as well as a physical reality; a mathematical formula chalked on a blackboard is the concrete expression of an abstraction.

accent *(n.)*

1 A pattern of pronunciation that indicates a speaker's regional origin or identity, or social background or status.

> a Birmingham accent
>
> an educated accent
>
> RECEIVED PRONUNCIATION

or a speaker's regional and social identity:

> an educated Birmingham accent.

See also DIALECT; SOCIOLECT.

2 The stress or emphasis placed on one or more syllables of a word.

> *pho*tograph, pho*to*grapher, photo*graph*ic.

The audible stress of the spoken word is normally shown in writing by placing a primary stress mark, like a single inverted comma, immediately before the stressed syllable:

> 'photograph, pho'tographer, photo'graphic.

acceptable *(adj.)*

1 A use of language that is regarded as appropriate or normal in a given situation. Expressions that are commonly viewed as acceptable in informal English:

> Know what I mean?
>
> Get away!

may not acceptable in more formal speech or in written standard English.

2 In written standard English, a text that observes the norms, or standards, of spelling, syntax and punctuation.

See also APPROPRIATENESS; FORMAL LANGUAGE AND INFORMAL LANGUAGE; STANDARD AND NON-STANDARD ENGLISH; USAGE.

accidence *(n.)*

An alternative term for INFLECTION.

accusative case

An alternative term for OBJECTIVE CASE.

acoustic confusion

A listener's uncertainty about the nature of an acoustic signal. A common example of acoustic confusion is to mishear the speech sounds for the numbers 13, 14, 15, 16, 17, 18 and 19 as 30, 40, 50, 60, 70, 80 and 90, and vice versa.

acoustic cue

A feature of an acoustic signal that allows the listener to differentiate one acoustic stimulus from another. In speech the acoustic stimuli are PHONEMES, and acoustic cues allow the listener to distinguish between, say, *fan* and *van* or *than* and *then*.

acoustic phonetics *see* PHONETICS.

acoustics *(n.)*

The study of the physical properties of sound, its generation, transmission and reception. In the study of speech, acoustics is sometimes regarded as a branch of PHONETICS.

acquisition of language

The informal learning of language and the development of the capacity for language. In the case of children, this takes place in their first four or five years, normally in the family home. The word 'acquisition' is preferred to 'learning' because the process is normally spontaneous and unstructured. *See also* INNATENESS; LANGUAGE ACQUISITION DEVICE; SPECIES-SPECIFIC.

acrolect *(n.)*

A regional form of a standard language that has evolved from a CREOLE or BASILECT form of the language.

acronode *(n.)*

The highest node on a TREE DIAGRAM. The term 'acronode' is preferred to the polysemous and ambiguous ROOT, which is sometimes used to refer to the topmost node of a tree diagram.

acronym *(n.)*

A word formed from the initial letters of the words in a phrase.

laser (from *l*ight *a*mplification by the *s*timulated *e*mission of *r*adiation)

Some acronyms have been fully assimilated into English and are used as common nouns:

laser, radar, scuba.

Other acronyms remain recognizable as the initial letters of phrases:

GATT: General Agreement on Tariffs and Trade.

Acronyms abbreviate the longer forms and partly simplify the more complex meanings; they are also a means of WORD FORMATION in English. *See also* ABBREVIATION.

action *(n.)*

The process, condition or state denoted by a verb. Action verbs include verbs of acting and doing:

eat, listen, speak, walk

and also verbs that denote a state of being:

She *seems* self-confident but she *suffers* from anxiety and *has* few friends.

active vocabulary *see* VOCABULARY (2).

active voice and passive voice

Voice is one of the grammatical categories that expresses the mode of action of a verb. The voice of a verb affects the syntax of a sentence by determining the relationship of the subject, verb and object. A verb with an active voice is always a main verb, and its subject is always the ACTOR – a noun, noun phrase or pronoun – responsible for the action denoted by the verb. In the sentence:

A member of the audience interrupted the chairman

the subject, *A member of the audience*, is the actor and is responsible for the action denoted by the verb *interrupted*. The voice of the verb is **active**.

A verb with a **passive voice** is always a VERB PHRASE consisting of the appropriate form of the verb *be* functioning as an AUXILIARY VERB, and the past participle, or -ED FORM, of the MAIN VERB:

The chairman was interrupted by a member of the audience.

The subject of the second sentence, *The chairman*, is not the actor but instead is 'acted on' by the real actor, *a member of the audience*. The voice of the verb phrase *was interrupted* is passive. The transformation from the active sentence:

A member of the audience interrupted the chairman

to the passive sentence:

The chairman was interrupted by a member of the audience

is accompanied by the change in syntax. The subject of the active sentence, *A member of the audience*, becomes the object of the passive sentence; the object of the active sentence, *the chairman*, becomes the subject of the passive sentence.

Passivity is often indicated by the presence of the preposition *by* immediately before the AGENT in the object of a passive sentence, as in *by a member of the audience*. Some passive sentences do not contain an agent or *by*:

Two penalty kicks *were saved*, and the game *was won*.

Passive constructions that make no reference to an agent are known as agentless passives.

In informal English passives can be formed by using the verb *get* and the *-ed* form of the main verb instead of *be* and a main verb:

They got injured at work.

They are getting compensated for their injuries.

This construction is known as the **get passive**.

The terms 'active' and 'passive' can be applied to clauses or sentences in which active or passive verbs appear.

A **semi-passive** construction is one that functions as a passive verb and also as a participial adjective:

They were distressed to hear of his illness and are pleased to learn of his recovery.

Such constructions can usually be written in active form:

To hear of his illness distressed them, and to learn of his recovery pleased them

but they also have some of the properties of adjectives. They are gradable:

more distressed, most distressed; more pleased, most pleased

and they can be premodified by adverbs:

deeply distressed, highly pleased.

actor *(n.)*

A noun, noun phrase or pronoun that is the subject of an active verb or the object of a passive verb and is thus the source of the action denoted by the verb.

Archaeologists excavated an Iron Age site.

The noun *Archaeologists* is the actor. In this sentence:

Opposition Members of Parliament voted for the bill

the noun phrase *Opposition Members of Parliament* is the actor.

When the verb is passive, the actor is the object of the verb:

An Iron Age site was excavated by archaeologists.

The noun *archaeologists* has changed its position in the sentence but has not changed its function as the actor. In passive sentences, the actor is also known as the AGENT.

address, forms of

1 The words, normally nouns or pronouns, that are used to refer directly to someone. The form of address can be formal:

Sir, Mr, Madam

informal:

Mike, pal, mate

a term of endearment:

darling, dear, love

or a term of abuse:

fool! rat! scum!

2 When someone is appealed to or addressed directly in written standard English, a comma often needs to be inserted to indicate the directness:

Please reply to my letter, Gordon.

The comma indicates that the noun *Gordon* is in the VOCATIVE case.

adjacency principle

The general principle that linguistic units that are interrelated semantically should normally be placed together, or be adjacent, in a clause or sentence; also known as the **minimum distance principle**.

The car, fitted with false number plates, was driven by the third member of the gang.

*The car was driven by the third member of the gang fitted with false number plates.

See also AMBIGUITY.

adjectival noun

An adjective that functions as a noun:

the rich, the poor, the sick.

adjective *(n.)*

A large, varied and open class of CONTENT WORDS, whose main function is to modify nouns and pronouns. Adjectives usually appear immediately before the nouns they modify and thus premodify the nouns. A premodifying adjective is known as **attributive** because it usually denotes an attribute of the noun:

>the *compact* disc, *loud* music, a *practical* joke.

When a noun is premodified by two or more adjectives, an adjective denoting an INHERENT quality is usually placed immediately before the noun, with non-inherent adjectives farthest from the noun:

>a tall, grey, concrete tower

not

>*a concrete, grey, tall tower

and

>a long, cool, non-alcoholic drink

not

>*a non-alcoholic, cool, long drink.

Inherent adjectives are also known as intrinsic, and are contrasted with non-inherent or extrinsic adjectives.

Nationality adjectives form a separate class of inherent adjectives. They have no comparative or superlative forms, and they are always spelled with a capital letter:

>*French* cheese, *Italian* wine;

>*Frencher cheese, *Italianest wine.

A few adjectives appear after the nouns they modify and thus postmodify the nouns. When an adjective functions as a postmodifier it can be classed as a POSTPOSITIVE ADJECTIVE, positive in this instance meaning 'posited' or 'placed'.

A **predicative adjective** is one that appears in the predicate of a sentence and functions as the subject complement or the object complement of a COPULA or linking verb, that is, a verb such as *be, seem, appear*:

>The music seemed loud.

The adjective *loud* modifies the noun phrase *The music*, and because *The music* is the subject of the sentence, *loud* is the subject complement. In the sentence:

>He found the concert enjoyable

the adjective *enjoyable* modifies the noun phrase *the concert*, which is the object of the sentence, and so *enjoyable* is described as the object complement.

Some linguists apply the term 'predicative' only to adjectives that are the complements of linking verbs and do not immediately follow the nominals that they modify:

> Although he had been wide awake when he arrived, he soon grew tired and fell asleep.

The predicative adjective phrase *wide awake* is the complement of the verb *had been*, the predicative adjective *tired* is the complement of *grew*, and the predicative adjective *asleep* is the complement of *fell*. Other adjectives that are used predicatively include:

> afraid, alive, alone, apart, content, glad, ill, well.

Some predicative adjectives are usually followed by prepositions:

> He became *resigned to* working alone because he was *incompatible with* his colleagues and proved *incapable of* friendship.

Predicative adjectives are sometimes contrasted with attributive adjectives.

Adjectives that can function in three of the ways outlined above – as attributes, subject complements or object complements – are known as **central adjectives**:

> He seems a *happy* man. (attributive)
>
> The man seems *happy*. (subject complement)
>
> Success made the man *happy*. (object complement)

An adjective appears as the headword or main word in an **adjective phrase**, and in some adjective phrases the adjective is premodified by an adverb:

> more *expensive*, highly *effective*, much too *ambitious*, almost *extinct*.

A **participial adjective** is the present participle, or -ING FORM, of a verb, or the past participle, or -ED FORM, of a verb functioning as an adjective:

> a *limping* man, the *televised* debate.

Adjectives formed from past participles can also function as semi-passive verbs:

> I *was dismayed* when I heard the news.
>
> She *has been interested* in music for many years.

Most adjectives are **gradable** or **comparative**, that is, they can be compared to show differences of degree. The three levels, or grades, of intensity are described by the terms positive, comparative and superlative:

positive	comparative	superlative
fat	fatter	fattest
beautiful	more beautiful	most beautiful

Adjectives that cannot be compared in that way are **non-gradable** or **ungradable**, usually because they denote an absolute condition or an ultimate degree that is beyond comparison:

complete, dead, final, perfect, unique.

Gradable adjectives that take the inflections *-er* and *-est* or the premodifiers *more* and *most* are known as **regular** adjectives. **Irregular** adjectives are those that do not have the inflection *-er* or the premodifier *more* for the comparative forms, nor the inflection *-est* or the premodifier *most* for the superlative forms. Adjectives that express gradability by changing their internal forms are:

bad, worse, worst; good, better, best.

See also SEMI-PASSIVE *under* ACTIVE VOICE AND PASSIVE VOICE; MODIFICATION; REGULAR AND IRREGULAR.

adjective clause

The traditional term for a RELATIVE CLAUSE.

adjective phrase *see* ADJECTIVE.

adjunct *(n.)*

1 A general term for a word or a phrase that extends the meaning of the subject, verb or predicate of a sentence.

2 An ADVERB, ADVERBIAL PHRASE or PREPOSITIONAL PHRASE that modifies, or extends the meaning of, the verb in a sentence.

Miriam practised the sonata thoroughly.

The adverb *thoroughly* is an adjunct modifying the verb *practised*.

She played with great skill.

The prepositional phrase *with great skill* is an adverbial adjunct modifying the verb *played*.

After the concert, Miriam went for a late supper.

The prepositional phrases *After the concert* and *for a late supper* are adjuncts modifying the verb *went*.

adnominal *(n./adj.)*

A general term for a word, phrase or clause that describes a NOUN. The word is usually an ADJECTIVE, the phrase is usually an adjective phrase or a PREPOSITIONAL PHRASE, and the clause is usually a relative, or adjective, clause.

> She drinks black coffee.

The adjective *black* is an adnominal of the noun *coffee.*

> He prefers his coffee with milk and sugar.

The prepositional phrase *with milk and sugar* is an adnominal of the noun *coffee.*

> Fire destroyed the café in which they used to meet.

The subordinate relative clause *in which they used to meet* is an adnominal of the noun *café.*

See also NOMINAL.

adverb *(n.)*

A large, open and flexible class of words, the main function of which is to modify verbs and, occasionally, adjectives or other adverbs.

> Traffic moved slowly.

The adverb *slowly* modifies the verb *moved.*

> Exhaust fumes were exceptionally dense.

The adverb *exceptionally* modifies the adjective *dense.*

> Some drivers behaved remarkably badly in the traffic jam.

The adverb *remarkably* modifies the second adverb *badly.* INTENSI-FIERS, that is, words like *remarkably* that indicate a degree of intensity, are normally adverbs. Common intensifiers include:

> always, astonishingly, extremely, intensely, highly, never, rather, surprisingly, very.

Some adverbs at the beginning of a sentence or clause have a double grammatical function: they modify verbs but they also act as conjunctions, linking the clauses or sentences.

> Small boats remained in the harbour *until* the storm ended. *While* the storm raged, most yachtsmen remained ashore.

Adverbials with this double function can be called adverbial conjunctions.

Adverbs, like adjectives, are **gradable** or **comparative**: that is, they can be compared to show differences of degree. Regular adverbs are compared:

positive	comparative	superlative
fast	faster	fastest

Adverbs that cannot be compared in that way are **ungradable** or **non-gradable**, usually because they denote an absolute or unalterable condition that is beyong comparison:

firstly, finally, eternally, uniquely.

Irregular adverbs are compared in various ways:

positive	comparative	superlative
well	better	best
little	less/lesser	least

Adverbs can be compared to show equivalence:

Frank fought as strongly as Dave

and to make a negative comparison:

Mike fought less strongly than Frank and Dave.

Some words:

early, late, quick, slow

function as adverbs or adjectives, depending on the context. The simplest distinction between the two word classes is that adjectives modify nouns, and adverbs normally modify verbs. In the sentence:

He arrived early because he caught the early plane

early is used first as an adverb modifying the verb *arrived* and then as an adjective modifying the noun *plane*. Another method of identifying adverbs, adverbial phrases and adverbial clauses is to apply the *Wh-?* test, that is, ask if the adverbial answers the questions *when? where? why?* or *how? See also* REGULAR AND IRREGULAR.

adverbial *(n./adj.)*

A word, phrase or clause that can form a major component of a sentence and functions like an adverb. An adverbial is not an obligatory component of a sentence unless it is required to clarify the meaning of the verb, for example, verbs of movement or position, such as, *come, go, lie, run, sit, stand, stay, walk*:

go *away*, stand *in a straight line*.

See also ADVERBIAL PHRASE; SUBORDINATE ADVERBIAL *under* CLAUSE.

adverbial clause *see* CLAUSE.

adverbial conjunction *see* CONJUNCTION.

adverbial phrase
A group of words that functions like an adverb. An adverbial phrase may have an adverb as its headword:

> Emily decided, almost immediately, to spend the prize money on a holiday.

The two adverbs in the adverbial phrase *almost immediately* modify the verb *decided*. Some phrases have an adverbial function even when they do not include adverbs:

> After her holiday, Emily returned to university.

The phrase *After her holiday* consists of a preposition, *after*, a personal pronoun, *her*, and a noun, *holiday*, but the phrase also has an adverbial function because it modifies the verb *returned*. The phrase *to university* (preposition + noun) also modifies the verb *returned*.

adversative *(adj./n.)*
A linguistic unit, for example, an AFFIX, a word, a phrase or a clause, that expresses OPPOSITION or ANTITHESIS. *See also* ANTONYM; CHIASMUS; OPPOSITE.

affected participant *see* PARTICIPANT (2).

affective language *see* EMOTIVE LANGUAGE; EXPRESSIVE LANGUAGE.

affective meaning *see* MEANING.

affirmative *(adj./n.)*
A verb, clause or sentence that is not marked for negative or interrogative; a verb, clause or sentence that makes an assertion; in some contexts, affirmative is an alternative term for **positive** (1). *See also* DECLARATIVE.

affix *(n.)*
A small verbal element that, when added to the ROOT word, can change the word's grammatical function, its meaning or its word class. English affixes are either **prefixes**, which are added in front of the word, or **suffixes**, which are added to the end of the word. For example, when the prefix *un-* is added to the adjective *happy*, the result is another adjective, *unhappy*, but with a different meaning.

Suffixes often change the word class as well as the meaning of the words to which they are added. When *-ness* is added to *happy* to produce *happiness*, the word class changes from adjective to noun.

Suffixes can be classed as inflectional or derivational. An inflectional suffix is an INFLECTION added to a word, for example, *-s* for plural nouns and *-ed* for the past tense of verbs.

A derivational suffix is one that is used to form a derived word from the base word:

child*hood* (noun), loath*some* (adjective), harmon*ize* (verb).

Some roots can take a prefix and a suffix: *dis*grace*ful*. Affixes are widely used in WORD FORMATION:

*de*select, gentri*fication*, *post*femin*ism*.

The process of adding affixes is known as affixation. *See also* DERIVATION.

affricate *(adj./n.)*

A phonetic term for the sounds /ch/ as in *chicken* and /j/, /ge/ or /dge/ as in *jam*, *charge* and *grudge*.

agent *(n.)*

The nominal that follows a passive verb and the word *by*.

A new album was produced by the rock group, Positron.

Passive constructions that omit the agent are known as agentless passives:

New speed limits have been imposed.

The term 'agent' can also be applied to the SUBJECT of an active verb; the agent then functions as the ACTOR.

The term 'agentive' can be applied to the agent subjects of sentences such as:

Fred paid the bill by credit card.

Some linguists state that, just as an agent is a particular kind of subject, so agentive is a particular form of the SUBJECTIVE CASE. *See also* ACTIVE VOICE AND PASSIVE VOICE.

agglutinative language *see* ANALYTIC, SYNTHETIC AND AGGLUTINATIVE LANGUAGES.

agrammatism *(n.)*
The loss of the ability to speak or write grammatically, usually as a result of a cerebral injury, disease or mental illness. Victims normally retain their vocabularies but cannot use the words grammatically.

agraphia *(n.)*
Partial or complete loss of the ability to write, usually as a result of brain damage.

agreement *(n.)*
A grammatical rule, also known as **concord**, that nouns, noun phrases, or pronouns must correspond in NUMBER (singular or plural) with verbs in a sentence.

> A whale was stranded in the bay. Dozens of holidaymakers were watching it.

The singular noun *whale* must have the singular form of the verb *was stranded*. The plural noun phrase *Dozens of holidaymakers* must have the plural verb *were watching*. It is a grammatical rule that nouns must correspond in number, PERSON and GENDER with the equivalent PERSONAL PRONOUN in a sentence.

> Jean drives her car to work.

The proper noun *Jean* is singular, and so the verb *drives* takes the singular form. And because *Jean* is grammatically third person and feminine gender, the personal pronoun must be the third person, feminine, singular *her*.

There has been a change in the rule that once required agreement in number of indefinite pronouns and personal pronouns in the same sentence. The indefinite pronouns *anybody, anyone, everybody, everyone, nobody* and *no one* are singular because *body* and *one* are singular, but English grammar now accepts either the singular pronoun or the plural pronoun *their* with a singular indefinite pronoun:

> Everyone has a right to their privacy.

The verb *has* rather than *have* shows that singular indefinite pronouns still require a singular verb.

The verb that follows a COLLECTIVE NOUN can take the singular or the plural form. This option, known as **optional agreement** or **concord** or **notional agreement** or **concord**, allows emphasis to be given to the unity and singularity of the collective noun:

> A squad of workers *has arrived* on the site

or to the multiplicity or diversity of the collective noun:

A convoy of lorries *travel* to and from the site.

alexia *(n.)*

Loss of the ability to read or understand written words, especially as a result of a brain injury or brain haemorrhage. *See also* ANOMIA; APHASIA; DYSLEXIA.

alienable possession and inalienable possession

An **alienable possession** is a property or object that can be exchanged as a gift or a purchase, for example, a pair of shoes or a house. An **inalienable possession** is a quality or feature that cannot be exchanged, for example, a person's physical appearance or temperament. In some languages possessions are marked for alienable and inalienable; in English, the distinction is made by nouns and verbs. In general, inanimate nouns and nouns denoting animals are alienable:

camcorder, computer, cat;

nouns denoting persons and personal qualities are inalienable:

husband, son, laziness.

The verbs *own* and *possess* are more often used with alienable rather than inalienable possessions:

She owns a house and a car.

*She owns three children.

*She possesses brown eyes.

aliterate *(adj./n.)*

Unwilling to learn to read, although able to do so. *See also* ILLITERATE; NON-LITERATE.

alliteration *(n.)*

A sound effect, or phonological device, that uses repetition of the initial letters of two or more words in a sequence, or the repetition of letters with similar sounds or the repetition of stressed syllables in single words.

*S*occer *s*upremo *s*acked

The *f*rail, elderly patient took her *f*irst *f*altering steps after the operation.

The verb 'to alliterate' is a back-formation of alliteration.

Alliteration is one of several common phonological devices. *See also* ASSONANCE; CONSONANCE; CACOPHONY; ONOMATOPOEIA; PHONAES-THEME.

allograph *(n.)*

1 One of two or more forms of a GRAPHEME. A grapheme is a letter of the alphabet, a punctuation mark or other minimal unit in a writing system. An upper case, or capital, A and a lower case a are allographs of the grapheme that is the first letter of the alphabet. Other allographs of the same grapheme can be produced by different fonts or styles of type:

> A, a, *A, a*

2 One of two or more letters of the alphabet, or combinations of letters, that represent a single PHONEME. A phoneme is the smallest unit of sound in a language. The phoneme for the *u* sound in *pure* is represented not only by /u/ but by the /ou/ of *your*, the /ew/ of *yew* and by *ewe*. The characters /u/, /ou/, /ew/ and *ewe* are allographs of the same vowel sound. *See also* GRAPH.

allomorph *(n.)*

One of two or more forms of a MORPHEME. A morpheme is a minimum morphological, or physical, unit of language. The *-ed* past participle of regular verbs:

> talked, listened, recorded

and the *-en* past participle of some irregular verbs:

> spoken, written, chosen

are allomorphs of the same morpheme.

The *-en* of *children*, the *-im* of *seraphim* and the *-ves* of *wolves* are allographs of the morpheme of plural nouns. *See also* MORPHOLOGY.

allophone *(n.)*

One of two or more sounds that represent a PHONEME. Allophones are most obvious when one regional or national form of a spoken language is compared with another. In Scotland, for example, the letter /r/ is generally rhotic, that is, pronounced with a roll or trill; in Received Pronunciation /r/ is not rhotic. In the United States the letter /t/ is sometimes pronounced like /d/, so that Received Pronunciation *wettest* is sounded as *weddest*. *See also* PHONETICS.

alphabet *(n.)*

A writing system in which each sign, also known as a CHARACTER, SYMBOL or LETTER, represents one or more sounds, or PHONEMES, in a language. The English alphabet of twenty-six characters consists of the classical **Latin alphabet**, also known as the **Roman alphabet** of twenty-three characters, with the addition of j, v and w.

The Latin alphabet replaced the Old English runic, a Germanic system of twenty-four characters, or runes, adapted from Greek and Latin and used in inscriptions on wood and stone. It also replaced the ogham, or ogam, alphabet of the Celtic peoples of Britain. The Latin alphabet was adapted from the Greek alphabet, and Greek from Phoenician, a language from what is now west Lebanon.

Although alphabets are essentially phonetic systems, few alphabets are wholly phonetic. The English alphabet cannot exactly represent all the sounds of all the words in the constantly changing English language. Even so, most alphabetic writing systems are easier to learn and thus easier to read and write than systems in which the signs represent syllables, words or pictures. *See also* LOGOGRAM; PICTOGRAM; SYLLABARY.

alternative question *see* QUESTION.

ambiguity *(n.)*

Speech or writing that has more than one meaning. Speech is more tolerant of ambiguity than writing because a speaker can repeat or rephrase the ambiguous words, and can use emphasis and intonation to clarify the meaning of the utterance. There are several common forms of ambiguity in writing.

1 Failure to formulate an idea fully into thought and language:

> This makes it easier for them to sympathize with her.

A reader may not understand such a sentence unless the pronouns *This*, *them* and *her* are clearly identified.

2 Omissions:

> A car left in a city car park is stolen twice a day

for

> [On average] there are two incidents of car theft from city car parks every day.

> Police were ordered to stop sleeping in shop doorways.

for

> Police were ordered to stop [homeless people from] sleeping in shop doorways.

3 Syntax and the ADJACENCY PRINCIPLE:

> MI5 has taken over the hunt for terrorists from Scotland Yard's Special Branch

for

> MI5 has taken over from Scotland Yard's Special Branch the hunt for terrorists.

4 Polysemy, words with two or more meanings, two or more grammatical categories or two or more word classes:

> I'll ring the old bat

where *ring* can mean to telephone or to fit a leg-ring, and *bat* can mean the flying mammal or an unpleasant woman. In

> Fish talks after skippers clash

fish, a noun, is used as an adjective, and *talks*, a verb, is used as a noun.

5 The -ING FORM as a noun, an adjective or a present participle:

> Racing cars can be dangerous

and the MISRELATED PARTICIPLE:

> Rowing across a loch, an osprey caught an eel

for

> Rowing across a loch, the old poacher saw an osprey catch an eel.

See also GERUND.

ambilingual *(adj./n.)*

Descriptive of a bilingual person who is equally skilled in both languages; also known as a balanced BILINGUAL. The condition of being ambilingual is known as ambilingualism.

amelioration *(n.)*

The development of a more favourable meaning that replaces, or partly replaces, a pejorative meaning of a word or phrase; sometimes contrasted with PEJORATION.

In Samuel Johnson's *Dictionary* of 1755, a definition of the verb 'to hack' is 'to turn hackney or prostitute', but that meaning does not appear in the latest edition of the *Shorter Oxford English Dictionary* (OED). Similarly, Johnson defined 'job' as 'a low word' meaning 'a low mean lucrative busy affair' and 'petty, piddling work', but job now means employment generally or a specific piece of work. 'A jogger', wrote Johnson, is 'one who moves heavily and dully,' but the OED's first definition of jogger is 'a person who runs at a gentle pace for physical exercise'.

The processes of amelioration and pejoration show that language is subject to continuous change.

American English

A use of English language particular to the United States of America and not normally found in BRITISH ENGLISH. American English includes differences in vocabulary:

> a flat, gas, a trunk;

spelling differences:

> color, theater, tire (tyre);

grammatical differences:

> dove (dived), gotten (got), snuck (sneaked);

and distinctive WORD FORMATION:

> bartender, disc jockey, newscaster.

There are also many distinctively American IDIOMATIC expressions and innumerable differences in pronunciation.

The existence of American English shows that a language evolves differently in different SPEECH COMMUNITIES.

American borrowings in British English include *city desk* for British newspapers' *news desk*, *movie* for *film*, *serial killer* for *mass murderer*, *lookalike* for *double*, and colloquial and idiomatic expressions such as *laid-back* for *relaxed* and *uptight* for *anxious*.

anachronism *(n.)*

Assigning or relating things to the wrong period of time, either too early or too late. Shakespeare's reference to the clock in *Julius Caesar*, the cannons in *Macbeth* and billiards in *Antony and Cleopatra* are literary examples of anachronism, or prochronism (too early). For a time the UK television soap opera *Coronation Street* was anachronistic, or parachronistic (too late), in that it presented a picture of a society that had ceased to exist. *See also* ARCHAISM.

anacoluthon *(n.)*

An abrupt change of thought that breaks the syntax so that one part of a sentence does not logically or grammatically follow another.

> Ladies and gentlemen, I am grateful for this opportunity to – Who let him into the meeting?

analect *(n.)*

A selection of writings by one author. Analects sometimes consist of short passages that may be peripheral to an author's main work.

analogy *(n.)*

1 A new word or phrase modelled on an existing form. The words *meritocract* and *meritocracy*, *technocrat* and *technocracy* are modelled on *bureaucrat* and *bureaucracy*. The phrases *alternative comedy*, *alternative press* and other *alternative* phrases are modelled on *alternative society*, a phrase from the mid-1960s.

An historic example from Middle English is the replacement, with a few exceptions, of the *-en* suffix for plural nouns by the *-s* suffix of the more dominant London–East Midlands dialect.

2 A figure of speech, for example, METAPHOR, PERSONIFICATION and SIMILE, that compares one thing with another, usually to show that they are analogous but occasionally to show a contrast between the two.

3 Generally, a correspondence between one item or system and another. A computer's artificial intelligence is an analogy for human intelligence to the extent that a computer is an analogy for the human brain.

analysis *(n.)*

1 (a) The breaking up of a simple SENTENCE into its grammatical components, normally the SUBJECT (S), VERB (V) OBJECT (O), COMPLEMENT (C) and ADVERBIAL (Adv). *See also* TREE DIAGRAM.

(b) The breaking up of a complex sentence or a compound-complex sentence into its main and subordinate CLAUSES.

2 (a) The scrutiny of a piece of writing to identify its main linguistic features, for example, VOCABULARY and SYNTAX; also known as text linguistics or textual analysis.

(b) The scrutiny of a piece of writing to identify its main literary and stylistic features, for example, characterization in a novel, and the use of rhyme and rhythm in a poem.

See also BRACKETING; COMPONENTIAL ANALYSIS.

analytic, synthetic and agglutinative languages

An **analytic language** is one in which few words, or none, are inflected and in which grammatical and semantic relationships are indicated by syntax rather than by morphology, that is, by the order of words in sentences rather than by the forms of the words.

Analytic languages are also known as **isolating**, or root, languages. Modern English, which has few INFLECTIONS, is an analytic language.

A **synthetic language** is one that is highly inflected and in which meaning is indicated by MORPHOLOGY rather than syntax. A synthetic language is also known as an **inflected, inflecting** or **inflectional**

language. Latin and Finnish are synthetic languages. Old English has fewer inflections than Latin, but because meaning in Old English is more often dependent on inflections than word order, Old English, too, can be classed as a synthetic language.

An **agglutinative language** is one in which words are formed by uniting other words and elements. Turkish is such a language.

The study of language types is known as **typology**, or typological linguistics. The study of word forms is known as morphology.

analytic proposition and synthetic proposition

An **analytic proposition** is one that is necessarily true because of the nature of the subject denoted by the PROPOSITION or because of the truth of its semantic components. The proposition:

> Anna's husband is the man she married

is an analytic, or necessary, truth.

A **synthetic proposition** is one whose truth or falseness is determined by factors beyond the proposition and the language. The proposition:

> Anna's husband is the only man she loves

can be proved or disproved only by information that is not present in the proposition. *See also* CONTINGENCY AND NECESSITY; ENTAILMENT.

anaphora *(n.)*

1 A word, usually a pronoun, that refers to a word or words, usually a noun or a noun phrase, that occur earlier in a text or an utterance.

> As soon as the manager arrived he began to discuss tactics.

The pronoun *he* refers anaphorically to the noun *manager*. In the sentences:

> Polluted beaches are dangerous. You should avoid *them*

the pronoun *them* is an anaphoric reference to the noun phrase *Polluted beaches*. The noun phrases *the manager* and *Polluted beaches* are ANTECEDENTS of *he* and *them*.

2 The deliberate repetition of a word, phrase or clause.

> 'I see,' said the prosecutor. 'You just happened to go for a walk at midnight. You just happened to find the antique chairs lying in the street. And you just happened to meet an old friend in his transit van.'

See also CATAPHORA.

Anglo-Saxon *(adj./n.)*

A term for the peoples from mainland Europe who began to settle in England from around the year 450. Angles, a people from what is now the most northern part of Germany, settled along the east coast of England from Norfolk to Northumberland. Saxons, from an area of north Germany to the west of Hamburg, settled in the south and west of England, roughly from the Isle of Wight to Exeter. Jutes from what is now Denmark settled in the southeast of England.

The term 'Anglo-Saxon' is also used for the culture and sometimes for the language of these peoples, but the language is usually called OLD ENGLISH.

animate and inanimate *(adj./n.)*

An **animate** word, usually a noun, denotes a living, animate thing, human or non-human, as distinct from a lifeless, or **inanimate**, thing.

> musician, horse (animate);
>
> trumpet, saddle (inanimate).

anomalous sentence or anomalous statement

A way of showing that even when a sentence observes the norms of morphology, syntax and spelling, the sentence may still have an irregularity, or anomaly, of semantics or idiom that makes it unacceptable.

> *Ambitious clouds merrily ate the falling sleep.

anomia *(n.)*

Loss of the ability to remember names, usually as a result of brain lesions. *See also* ALEXIA; APHASIA; DYSLEXIA.

antecedent *(adj./n./adv.)*

A noun, noun phrase or pronoun to which a following RELATIVE PRONOUN refers.

> Overtime payments, which were fairly generous, were made to those who worked on Sundays.

The relative pronoun *which* refers to the antecedent noun phrase *Overtime payments*, and the relative pronoun *who* refers to its antecedent pronoun *those*.

anticlimax *(n.)*

A statement that, intentionally or unintentionally, falls from the serious to the ludicrous.

> Police forces, the fire and ambulance services, the coast guard and some
> bird watchers will be affected by the new legislation.

antithesis *(n.)*

A sentence or clause that expresses an OPPOSITE argument – the anti
thesis – to the argument in the immediately preceding sentence or
clause.

> The opposition says that payment should be given as a right. The
> government says that payment is a privilege that must be earned.

See also ANTONYM; CHIASMUS.

antonym *(n.)*

A word whose meaning is OPPOSITE to the meaning of another word.

Antonyms can be divided into two types, **gradable** and **ungradable**,
also known as **non-gradable**. Gradable antonyms, for example, *short*
and *long*, can be compared:

> short, shorter, shortest; long, longer, longest.

Ungradable antonyms usually denote an absolute condition or a condition that cannot be compared:

> alive/dead, human/non-human, past/present.

This property of oppositeness is known as antonymy. The condition of
being gradable is known as GRADABILITY.

aphaeresis and aphesis *(n.)*

Historically, **aphaeresis** is the loss of a letter or syllable from the
beginning of a word, which results in the formation of a new word.

> stress (distress), fence (defence), van (caravan).

Aphesis is the loss of an unstressed vowel from the beginning of a word,
and thus the formation of a new word.

> cute (acute), lone (alone), mend (amend).

The terms 'aphaeresis' and 'aphesis' have been displaced by other
terms – CLIPPING, CONTRACTION and ELISION – for this kind of
reduction.

See also apocope and syncope.

aphasia *(n.)*

A general term for the loss of language ability, usually as a result of brain
lesions. Aphasia takes many forms, depending on which area of the brain
is damaged. The condition can be partial or complete, and it can affect

the ability to speak and to interpret the speech of others, and the ability to read and write. Much of our understanding of the LANGUAGE CENTRES and language functions of the brain comes from pathological studies by neurosurgeons, and this has led to a specialized branch of language studies known as NEUROLINGUISTICS.

apocope and syncope *(n.)*

Apocope is the loss of one or more letters or syllables from the end of a word and, as a result, the formation of a new word.

> maths (mathematics), mike (microphone), lab (laboratory).

Historically, the loss of inflections in the evolution from Old English to Modern English is a long process of apocope.

Syncope is the shortening of a word, especially a spoken word, by omitting one or more letters or syllables from the middle of the word.

Syncopation is most obvious in place-names:

> Glou(ce)ster, Lei(ce)ster, Wo(rce)ster.

It is also commonplace even in formal speech:

> categ(o)ry, int(e)r(e)sting, I s(u)ppose, usef(u)lly.

The terms 'syncope' and 'syncopation' have been replaced by the term ELISION. *See also* ANALYTIC, SYNTHETIC AND AGGLUTINATIVE LANGUAGES for apocope; APHAERESIS AND APHESIS.

aposiopesis *(n.)*

A form of words that is incomplete but offers enough information for the reader or listener to draw a conclusion.

> He struck a match, dropped it on the petrol-soaked rags and ...

The incomplete statement can end with an ellipsis, as above, or with a dash.

apostrophe *(n.)*

1 The punctuation mark that indicates that one or more letters of the alphabet have been omitted from a word or phrase. Common examples are the colloquial blends of pronoun and verb:

> he's: he is; he'll: he will; we're: we are.

Missing numbers can be indicated in the same way:

> the '90s (for the 1990s).

There is no need for an apostrophe between the 0 and the s because '90s and 1990s are plural forms, not possessives.

2 The same punctuation mark applied in the POSSESSIVE, or genitive, case of nouns in order to indicate ownership or possession. If the noun in the possessive case is singular, an apostrophe and the letter *s* are added to form the possessive case:

Mike's computer, a bus's windscreen, Jones's cottage.

If the possessive noun is plural and ends with an *s*, as most English plural nouns do, an apostrophe is added after the *s*:

players' entrance, cities' parks.

If the plural form of the noun does not end with an *s*, then an apostrophe and *s* are added:

women's rights, geese's eggs.

Expressions such as

the Joneses' cottage, the Hugheses' car

which are grammatically correct but which look and sound awkward, can be rephrased as

the Jones family's cottage, the Hughes family's car

3 An exclamatory piece of figurative language in which the writer or speaker directly addresses or appeals to an absent person. Literary examples of this are William Wordsworth's 'Milton! thou shouldst be living at this hour' and John Betjeman's appeal to the friendly bombs to fall on Slough. The apostrophe can also be directed towards inanimate things; a common example is a driver speaking to his or her car, especially when the car develops a fault.

appellative *(adj./n.)*

1 (a) A word or words denoting a person's name, designation or title, especially when the person is being ADDRESSED.

(b) A noun that denotes a general type or common class rather than a specific person or thing:

Here comes the doctor

instead of

Here comes Dr Summers

2 A common noun that is similar or identical to a proper noun, for example, the name of a person or place; an alternative term for EPONYM.

cardigan, sandwich, wellington

applied linguistics

A wide field of study in which LINGUISTIC principles and methods are brought to bear on, or applied to, a variety of language activities, including the study of the teaching of reading and writing; teaching, learning and translating foreign languages; lexicography; speech analysis; computerized language processing.

apposition *(n.)*
The placing of a descriptive word or phrase, usually a noun phrase, alongside another noun phrase so that a person or thing is more fully identified. Apposition is a form of MODIFICATION. In the sentence:

> Deirdre Miller, the club secretary, has resigned

the noun phrase *the club secretary* is in apposition to, and also modifies, the equivalent noun phrase *Deirdre Miller*.

When more than two phrases are in apposition the result is known as **multiple apposition**:

> December Dawn,/an eight-year-old grey,/winner of last year's Cheltenham Gold Cup/and favourite for the race this year,/is trained by George Partridge.

The oblique lines show the division into four apposition phrases.

appropriateness *(n.)*
A use of language that is suitable for a particular audience in a given circumstance or suitable for the discussion of a particular subject. Specialist terminology, for example, is appropriate in a workplace discussion but not in general conversation; formal standard English is appropriate in a letter of complaint but not in a birthday card. *See also* ACCEPTABLE.

arbitrariness *(n.)*
The fact that words do not express the real nature of the things the words represent; the lack of identity or similarity between a word and the physical or abstract reality to which the word refers. There is no correspondence, for example, between the word *tree* and the material reality of a tree, or between the word *idea* and the mental state that forms the idea. The same quality of arbitrariness exists between signs in other communication systems and the things the signs refer to.

Exceptions are ONOMATOPOEIC words, such as *bang, clatter, crash,* which partly echo the sounds they represent, some forms of ICONICITY and some gestures that simulate an activity by mime: *give me food, come here, go away. See also* NON-VERBAL COMMUNICATION; PHONAES-THEME; REFERENCE (1).

archaism *(n.)*

A form of words that is no longer current in the language. Changes in technology led to the word *wireless* being replaced by *radio* and to *gramophone* being replaced successively by *record player, music centre* and *radio cassette recorder*. Languages evolve irrespective of changes in physical reality. The differences between the archaic:

> Prithee, maiden, whence comest thou?

and

> Excuse me miss. Where have you come from?

are the result of social changes and change in the use of language rather than physical, material change. *See also* ANACHRONISM; OBSOLETE.

argot *(n.)*

Originally a term for the secret language of London thieves and now a term for forms of SLANG used by criminal underclasses or groups on the edges of society. Argot, a borrowing from French, entered the English language in the mid-nineteenth century, probably by way of J.C. Hotten's *Slang Dictionary*. The word is similar in form and meaning to another French loan word, JARGON (1), which first appeared in Middle English with the meaning 'the warbling and twittering of birds' and 'meaningless talk or writing', but its meaning gradually extended to specialist or secretive talk or writing. *See also* CANT (1).

argument *(n.)*

1 A series of connected statements, reasons or explanations designed to establish a position or present a case.

2 More narrowly, the term for the items that are connected in a logical PROPOSITION. Grammatically, these items are usually nominals. In

> Jake met Anna

there are two arguments, *Jake* and *Anna*. In the sentence:

> Anna bought lunch for Jake

there are three arguments, *Anna*, *lunch* and *Jake*. In linguistics, the grammatical terms NOUN PHRASE, OBJECT and SUBJECT are more appropriate and precise than 'argument'.

article *(n.)*

A word that precedes a noun phrase and indicates whether the noun is definite or indefinite; also known as DETERMINER. The **definite article** is *the*:

the party, the political party.

The **indefinite article** is *a*, or *an* before a vowel:

a politician, an opposition party.

Articles usually precede common nouns but can precede proper nouns that refer to entire classes of persons or things:

the Rolls Royce, a Scotsman, an Englishman.

The can refer to singular nouns: *the city*, to plural nouns: *the cities*, and to uncountable nouns: *the money*; *a* and *an* refer only to singular nouns: *a village*, and to countable nouns: *a litre of oil*.

The omission of an article is sometimes known as a ZERO ARTICLE.

articulation *(n.)*

The production of speech sounds by the upper VOCAL TRACT, particularly the tongue, lips, teeth and hard palate.

articulatory phonetics *see* PHONETICS.

artificial intelligence (AI)

1 A computer system that simulates, or attempts to simulate, aspects of human intelligence such as learning, problem-solving, planning and decision-making.

2 The branch of computer science that deals with these topics. A major research field of artificial intelligence is the synthetic production and interpretation of human language. Artificial intelligence is, of course, the product of human intelligence. *See also* ARTIFICIAL LANGUAGE; SYNTHETIC SPEECH.

artificial language

1 A language that has been designed by one or more persons as distinct from a natural language that has evolved over millennia. Also known as **synthetic language**.

Esperanto ('one who hopes') was synthesized from several European languages in 1887 by the Polish physician, Dr L.L. Zamenhof, who hoped his invention would be adopted as a universal language. Although Esperanto attracted some support at the beginning of the twentieth century, it failed to gain wide recognition because it had no natural speech community, was not the first language of any country and was overwhelmed as an international language by English.

Another such artificial universal language is Novial, an acronym formed from *nov*, the prefix meaning new, and *I*nternational *A*uxiliary

*L*anguage. Novial was designed in 1928 by the eminent Danish philologist, Otto Jesperson (1860–1943).

2 A language designed for use on a computer. **Computer languages** are programs of instructions in the form of a series of numbers or coded patterns of digits that are converted into machine code instructions and then interpreted by the computer's central processor. A distinction is made between low-level computer languages, in which each instruction has a machine code equivalent, and high-level languages, in which each instruction has several machine code equivalents.

High-level languages allow computer users to write in a standard language or code, for example, the English language in COBOL, an acronym for *C*ommon *B*usiness-*o*rientated *L*anguage, and scientific and mathematical data in FORTRAN, *For*mula *Tran*slation. Other high-level scientific and mathematical computer languages are ALGOL (*Algo*rithmic *L*anguage), and a derivative of ALGOL known as Pascal, which is named after the French scientist and philosopher, Blaise Pascal (1623–62). A language that is widely used in personal computers is BASIC, *B*eginner's *A*ll-purpose *S*ymbolic *I*nstruction *C*ode.

Computer languages, like natural languages, can be adapted into dialects by computer programmers for specific purposes. *See also* SYNTHETIC SPEECH.

aspect *(n.)*

A form of a verb that indicates the duration of the action, condition or state denoted by the verb; a form of a verb that relates the completion of an action, condition or state to the present time. Aspect, like TENSE, refers to time, but aspect is concerned with time in terms of duration and completion.

Duration, that is, the length of time over which an event occurred or a condition or state existed, is indicated by the CONTINUOUS FORM of a verb, also known as the **progressive form**.

Continuous aspect, so-called because it indicates that an event or condition is or was continuing for a time, is expressed by a two- or three-word verb that includes the appropriate form of the verb *be* as an auxiliary verb, and the -ING FORM, or present participle, of the main verb. Continuous aspect also implies the temporary nature of the event or condition.

Present continuous: They *are visiting* friends in Edinburgh.

Past continuous: Their friends *were waiting* at the station.

Present perfect continuous: Anna *has been practising* the solo all week.

Past perfect continuous: Last year she *had been considering* a career in journalism rather than music.

The completion of an action, condition or state is indicated by the use of the PERFECT form of a verb, perfect in this context meaning completed or accomplished. **Perfect aspect**, also known as **perfective aspect**, is expressed by a two-word verb: *have* or *has* functioning as an auxiliary verb, followed by the -ED FORM, or past participle, of the main verb.

Present perfect aspect refers to something that began at an unspecified point in past time and extends to the present:

He *has worked* in London for ten years.

It can also refer to an event that occurred in the past but is still valid in the present:

They *have won* the championship.

Past perfect aspect is expressed by a two-word verb: *had*, the PAST TENSE of *have*, and the -*ed* form of the main verb. The past perfect, occasionally known as the pluperfect, refers to a circumstance that is farther back in time than the present perfect:

He *had lived* and [*had*] *worked* in York before he went to London.

They *had been* champions two years before.

aspirate *(adj./n.)*
A plosive consonant, that is, a consonant pronounced with a puff of breath, for example /h/, /k/, /p/ and /t/. The pronunciation of an aspirate can be called aspiration.

assertive and non-assertive *(adj.)*
An **assertive** linguistic unit is one that makes a declaration, or assertion, that something is true. Assertion usually takes the form of an affirmative statement:

Three centimetres of rain fell yesterday.

Assertion can also be expressed in a single word, usually an adverb:

absolutely, assuredly, certainly, definitely.

In some contexts, assertion can be expressed in sentences that are syntactically negative or interrogative but that are nevertheless assertive in meaning:

We haven't had so wet a day for months.

The weather was nasty yesterday, wasn't it?

A **non-assertive** linguistic unit is one that expresses indefiniteness or indecision. The MODAL AUXILIARY VERBS *could, may* and *might* are often used:

> We *may* be able to stop him.

A degree of indecision is expressed when the modal verb is preceded by the word *perhaps* and the dummy *it*:

> *Perhaps it would* be better to wait.

The indefinite pronouns *one, someone, somebody* and *anyone*, the indefinite DETERMINERS *some* and *any* and the indefinite adverbs *somehow, somewhere* and *sometimes* also express non-assertion. *See also* INDETERMINACY.

assimilation *(n.)*

The fusion or partial fusion of two adjacent speech sounds into one. Assimilation is normal practice because speech consists mainly of fused clusters of words rather than individually pronounced words. For example, the /t/ of *fast* is clearly pronounced in

> He eats food fast

but the /t/ is assimilated by the following /f/ in

> He eats fas(t) food.

Similarly, the /n/ of *can* is pronounced in

> Can you guess?

but the /n/ is assimilated by the following /g/ in

> You ca(n) guess.

assonance *(n.)*

The sound effect produced by the repetition of similar vowel sounds in a sequence of words.

> large tracts of barren land.

Assonance, like other phonological devices, can be found in poetry, political speeches, newspaper headlines and advertising copywriting. *See also* ALLITERATION; CACOPHONY; CONSONANCE; ONOMATOPOEIA; PHONAESTHEME.

asterisk *(n.)*

A symbol used in linguistics to show that a form of words is unacceptable or ungrammatical.

> *him are here, *the muchest share.

asyndeton and polysyndeton *(n.)*

Asyndeton is the omission of conjunctions, usually to achieve the effect of speed or urgency through the compressed syntax.

> She felt angry, awkward, embarrassed.

> Police arrived, surrounded the building, sealed off the street.

Polysyndeton is the repeated, sometimes excessive, use of conjunctions in a piece of writing. The result can seem repetitive:

> We travelled by car *but neither* Bridget *nor* I enjoyed it *because* traffic was dense *and because* there were patches of fog, *but* we've arrived safely *and* we're happy to be here.

See also PARATAXIS AND HYPOTAXIS.

asyntactic *(adj.)*

A piece of writing that is loosely structured and does not observe normal standards of syntax in its sentence structure.

attitudinal past *see* PRESENT TENSE.

attributive adjective *see* ADJECTIVE.

auditory phonetics *see* PHONETICS.

auxiliary language

A language used by speakers of one language in order to communicate with speakers of other languages. An auxiliary language is normally a SECOND LANGUAGE or a LINGUA FRANCA, and is used for business, education and some professions.

auxiliary verb

A VERB that cannot function as the only verb in a clause or sentence but must be followed by a MAIN VERB; a verb that is subordinate to a main verb; a verb that, partly or wholly, indicates the TENSE, ASPECT, MOOD and VOICE of the main verb; a verb that is essential in the formation of negative and interrogative sentences.

Auxiliaries can be divided into two sub-classes, the MODAL AUXILIARY VERBS:

> will, would, can, could, shall, should, may, might, must

and the three PRIMARY VERBS:

> be, do, have.

A modal auxiliary indicates the mood, or modality – for example, fact, possibility or obligation – of the main verb:

> You *can complete* the task. (possibility)
>
> You *should complete* the task. (likelihood or obligation)
>
> You *must complete* the task. (necessity)

Primary auxiliaries, which can also function as main verbs, can indicate the tense, aspect, voice and sometimes the PERSON of main verbs:

> The botanist is examining the plant.

The primary verb *is* is third person singular and present tense; the verb phrase *is examining* is present continuous in aspect and active in voice.

> The plant has been examined by the botanist.

The verb phrase *has been examined* is present perfect in aspect and passive in voice.

Auxiliary verbs are also essential for the formation of negative and interrogative sentences. A declarative sentence:

> The botanist has examined the plant

becomes a negative sentence by placing the particle *not* between the auxiliary and the main verb:

> The botanist has not examined the plant.

And the declarative is transformed to the interrogative by reversing the word order of the auxiliary verb and the subject of the sentence:

> Has the botanist examined the plant?

See also SEMI-AUXILIARY VERB; SEMI-MODAL AUXILIARY VERB.

b

back-formation *(n.)*

A type of WORD FORMATION in which the new word appears to be the root word but has in fact been derived from another word. The process of back-formation removes an AFFIX from the longer word, often a noun, to produce the new, back-formed word, often a verb. The verb *to automate* is a back-formation from the noun *automation*; both words entered the English language in the mid-twentieth century, but *automation* is the earlier word. Another mid-twentieth century verb, *to transduce*, is a back-formation from the noun *transducer*. The earlier twentieth-century verb *to escalate* is a back-formation of *escalator*. The verb *back-formed* is a back-formation from *back-formation*.

backshift *(n.)*
The systematic changes in the tenses of verbs required when DIRECT SPEECH is transformed to indirect, or reported, speech.

bahuvrihi *(n.)*
An exocentric compound adjective or noun; that is, a compound adjective or noun whose meaning is not the same as any of its constituents. The term has come to be used mainly to describe a metaphorical type of insult or nickname:

> blackleg, yellow-belly, roughneck, square-eyes.

barbarism *(n.)*
A use of language that may be grammatically correct but is unacceptable or inappropriate in a particular context. Examples of barbarism are the use of specialist jargon in a book aimed at non-specialist readers, the use of regional dialect when the audience or readership is not of that region, or the use of slang on a formal occasion. Barbarism is essentially a question of ACCEPTABLE USAGE.

bare infinitive
The simplest, uninflected, non-finite form of the verb.

> approach, steal, row

> We saw them *approach* the river. What they did then was *steal* a boat. We watched them *row* to the other side.

The bare infinitive is similar in function to the INFINITIVE with the particle *to*:

> to approach, to steal, to row.

base form
The same uninflected form of the verb as the BARE INFINITIVE but with two differences in grammatical function. The base form is finite, that is, it always has a subject, and it is always in the present tense.

> The three fugitives approach the river.

The verb *approach* is the base form, and the subject is the noun phrase *The three fugitives*.

We watch them as they row to the other side.

The pronoun *We* is the subject of the base form *watch*; and the pronoun *they* is the subject of the base form *row*. *See also* FINITE AND NON-FINITE FORMS OF VERBS.

Basic English

A drastically simplified form of English consisting of only 850 words. Basic English was designed by Charles Kay Ogden (1889–1957) assisted by Ivor Armstrong Richards (1893–1979) as a simple system of English for international use. Basic English attracted little support, partly because its formation coincided with the adoption of the natural English language as the main international language. *See also* ARTIFICIAL LANGUAGE (2).

basilect *(n.)*

The lowest form, that is, the form furthest removed from the standard or prestige form, of a CREOLE system of language. *See also* ACROLECT.

BBC English

A form of RECEIVED PRONUNCIATION (RP) associated with the British Broadcasting Corporation (BBC), founded in 1927. The first BBC news readers and announcers – Godfrey Adams, T.C. Farrar, Freddy Grisewood, Stuart Hibberd and John Snagge – spoke the non-regional, educated, prestige form of BRITISH ENGLISH. They also spoke from written scripts, which added to the formality of their speech, and the speech pattern was further reinforced by the BBC's Advisory Committee on Spoken English. The combination of RP and a written script is still the norm for network, that is, national and non-regional, news readers in the BBC and other broadcasting media.

The term NETWORK ENGLISH is now more appropriate than BBC English. *See also* ACCENT (1); KING'S ENGLISH.

behaviourism *(n.)*

In linguistics the view that the ACQUISITION OF LANGUAGE in childhood is determined by objective stimuli in the form of speech heard by the child and that language can be analysed in terms of stimulus and response. The behaviourist theory of language, which is associated with the American psychologist Burrhus Frederick Skinner (1904–90), was challenged by Noam Chomsky (b.1928), whose theories of the

INNATENESS of language and a LANGUAGE ACQUISITION DEVICE are now widely accepted. Other features of language acquisition by children, for example, TELEGRAMMATIC (2) speech and OVER-GENERALIZATION, confirm Chomsky's views to some extent.

bidialectal *(adj.)*

Able to speak or write two DIALECTS of the same language. The practice of bidialectalism, also known as bidialectism, is widespread. Many countries have higher and lower forms of the same language. In Britain regional dialects exist alongside the prestige form of spoken English and written standard English. It is common for people to practise bidialectalism by switching codes from one dialect to another. *See also* DIGLOSSIA; HIGH VARIETY AND LOW VARIETY; VERNACULAR.

bilingual *(adj./n.)*

Of a person, able to speak or write two languages; of a country, acknowledging two languages for use in national government, the law, higher education and national news media.

Most countries of the world are bilingual or MULTILINGUAL because of their mixed populations, their close contacts with neighbouring countries or their adoption of English or some other international language as a SECOND LANGUAGE. Although bilingualism is comparatively rare in Britain, there is some bilingual education in Welsh and English in Wales and in Gaelic and English in Scotland. Some British people of Asian descent speak Hindi, a NATIONAL LANGUAGE of India, or Urdu, the national language of Pakistan, in the home and use English in wider contexts. *See also* AMBILINGUAL; MONOLINGUAL.

binary *(adj./n.)*

Grammatical categories or linguistic features that are mutually exclusive. The grammatical categories singular/plural and active/passive and the semantic categories abstract/concrete and animate/inanimate are examples of binaries. *See also* OPPOSITE.

binding *see* GOVERNMENT-BINDING THEORY.

binomial *(n./adj.)*

1 A phrase containing two words of the same class linked by *and*. A binomial is often a fixed expression:

> black and white, kith and kin, short and sweet.

2 Originally, the Latin botanical nomenclatures formulated by Linaeus and Bernard Jussieu in the eighteenth century:

> *Malus sylvestris* (crab apple), *Pyrus communis* (common pear)

Black English

In Britain, and especially in London, a use of non-standard English particular to people of Afro-Caribbean descent. Black English is used not only in informal conversation but also in West Indian English poetry, in alternative newspapers and magazines, and in some television and radio programmes. The survival of this distinctive use of English so long after the arrival of the first Afro-Caribbean immigrants in Britain shows that there are cohesive Afro-Caribbean English SPEECH COMMUNITIES, and to that extent cohesive cultures, in London and some other cities.

Different DIALECTS of Black English, sometimes known as Black English Vernacular, are spoken in black speech communities throughout the United States.

blend or blending *(n.)*

The abbreviation of two words and the fusion of the two abbreviated forms into a single new word. The resulting blend normally consists of the first part of the first word and the latter part of the second word: *advertorial* from *advertising* and *editorial*, *bit* from *binary digit*, *quasar* from *quasi-stellar* and *televangelist* from *tele(vision) evangelist*.

When a new word is formed by using the first letters of two or more words, the result is normally classified as an ACRONYM rather than a blend. *Modem*, from *modulator/demodulator*, is an acronym, but *camcorder* from *camera* and [*video*] *recorder* is a blend. *See also* PORTANTEAU WORD; WORD FORMATION.

block language

The use of language in posters, billboards, traffic signs, newspaper headlines, labelled packaging and other short public notices designed to catch the eye. Despite their brevity, block language statements can summarize complex messages and are occasionally amusing:

> Get Mower Horse Power with a Shire Power Mower

> Love all as tennis stars wed.

The term 'block language' is probably taken from the related term 'block letters', which are normally capital letters in a simple type face.

body language

An alternative term for NON-VERBAL COMMUNICATION.

borrowing (n./v.)

A word that enters the English language from another language; also known as a **loan word**. Most of the borrowings in English denote things that did not exist in Britain or other English-speaking countries at the time of borrowing. English has borrowed words from all parts of the world, from Inuit, or Eskimo, in the north: *anorak, parka*, to Australian Aboriginal in the south: *budgerigar, kangaroo*; from Japanese in the east: *bonsai, origami*, to Native American in the west: *tomahawk, wigwam*. Some borrowings remain obviously foreign in form and pronunciation: *entrepreneur* from French, *graffiti* from Italian, *perestroika* from Russian; others are completely anglicized: *catamaran* from Tamil, *robot* from Czech, *tank* from Gujarati, *tulip* from Persian.

Direct borrowing of whole words is less common than derivation. When the two processes, borrowing and derivation, are considered jointly, it is clear that the greatest numbers of new words have come from French, Latin and Greek, as many of the headword derivations in this dictionary show. *See also* LOAN SHIFT; LOAN TRANSLATION; WORD FORMATION.

bound morpheme *see* MORPHEME.

bracketing (n.)

A way of illustrating the internal structure and the relationship of linguistic units in a clause or sentence.

When the sentence 'The angler caught a trout in Loch Lomond' is bracketed:

[[The angler] [caught] [a trout] [in Loch Lomond]]

the brackets show the division into a noun phrase, *The angler*, a verb, *caught*, a noun phrase, *a trout*, and an adverbial in the form of the prepositional phrase, *in Loch Lomond*. Additional bracketing:

[[[The] [angler]] [caught] [[a] [trout]] [[in] [Loch Lomond]]]

can be used to show the interrelationships of specific classes of words: definite article, *the*; noun, *angler*; verb, *caught*; indefinite article, *a*; noun, *trout*; preposition, *in*; noun phrase, *Loch Lomond*.

In longer sentences such detailed bracketing may obscure rather than clarify the contents. Another method of illustrating internal structures and relationships is the TREE DIAGRAM.

brackets *see* PUNCTUATION.

British English

A use of English that is particular to Britain. The term is imprecise because there are many varieties of English in the British Isles, but the term can be used to distinguish broad differences between, say, British English and American English or Australian English. The main differences are outlined under AMERICAN ENGLISH.

broad transcription *see* TRANSCRIPTION.

broadening and narrowing (*n./v.*)

Broadening is the process by which a word's meaning is gradually extended to cover a wider range of items. The process is also known as EXTENSION (1). When *screen* first appeared in Middle English the word meant a piece of furniture, an upright panel; now the word is used in electronics, meteorology, printing, photography, cinema, television, computing, cricket and other areas. Similarly, when *module* entered the English language in the late sixteenth century, the word meant a person's range or scope in terms of physical ability. Now the word is widely used in science, technology, education, administration and weaponry.

Many words extend their meanings metaphorically; for example, the anatomical items *head, hand* and *foot* are used figuratively in hundreds of different contexts. A few proprietary words extend their meanings when they come to be used as GENERIC terms: *biro* (Laszlo Biro 1899–1985) for ball-point pens, *hoover* (W.H. Hoover 1849–1932) for vacuum cleaners, and *sellotape*, a specific brand name, for all cellulose adhesive tapes.

Narrowing is the process in which a word's meaning is gradually restricted to cover a smaller range of items or one item only. The word *deer* once denoted any four-legged creature but now denotes a particular type of animal, a horned ruminant. *Hound* once meant dog but now means a hunting dog, as in *deer-hound, fox-hound, wolf-hound. Meat* once meant food generally but now means the flesh of animals. *Wife* once meant woman, and then a woman who sells a commodity, as in *ale-wife*, but now means a married woman.

C

cacography *(n.)*
Writing that is unacceptable because it includes errors of grammar, spelling or syntax, or because the handwriting or mechanical printing is difficult to read.

cacophony *(n.)*
Harsh, discordant sound or writing that is designed to create the effect of harshness of sound.

> They heard the squealing shriek of the brakes and then the rasping screech of metal being ripped apart.

cadence *(n.)*
1 A falling or lowering of PITCH, sometimes accompanied by a slowing of tempo of rhythm, at the end of an utterance, or a similar effect in written language.

> I set off with great hopes, but, after an hour, well, I just … I just … gave up.

See also INTONATION; TONE.

2 A combination of sound and tempo that creates a melodic, rhythmic effect; a varied pattern of melody and rhythm in speech or writing.

> Half-asleep beneath a sycamore tree, he heard the new leaves moving in the wind like children whispering in another room.

See also TONE.

calque *(n.)*
An alternative term for LOAN TRANSLATION.

cant *(n.)*
1 The particular language, or JARGON (1), of a specific occupational or social group.

2 A dogmatic statement, or the statement of a merely fashionable opinion, made without explanation and sometimes without understanding.

> I turned to crime because I had a deprived childhood.

capital letter

A letter of the ALPHABET of a larger size and sometimes bolder style than non-capital letters. Historically, the first letter, or head letter, of a printed work and sometimes the whole of the first word was set in capitals. This led to the norm of using a capital letter as the first letter of the first word in every sentence and, by extension, as the first letter of the first word quoted in direct speech.

He said, 'My father was astonished when I passed my driving test.'

Capital letters are also required for proper nouns, that is, the names of specific persons, places and organizations:

Rebecca Fainlight, Wembley Stadium, Ben Nevis.

Days of the week and months of the year, but not seasons of the year, are treated as proper nouns:

fine autumn weather

the second Monday in October.

Capitals are used for most abbreviations, BBC, NATO, MP and so on, but not for abbreviated weights and measures, cm, kg.

The alternative term for capitals, **upper case** letters, dates from the time when typesetting was done by hand; the capital letters were kept in a box at a higher level – the upper case – than the small, non-capital, or **lower case**, letters.

cardinal *see* NUMERAL.

case *(n.)*

A grammatical category of a NOUN or PRONOUN that indicates the relationship of the noun or pronoun to its immediate context in a clause or sentence. English has a simple system of cases. In effect, nouns have only two cases, the standard, unmarked or uninflected, form, and the POSSESSIVE or genitive form, indicated by an apostrophe and the letter s or the letter s and an apostrophe:

the student's computer (possessive singular)

the students' computers (possessive plural)

When a noun is the subject of a verb, the noun is in the nominative or SUBJECTIVE CASE; when a noun is the object of a verb or a preposition, the noun is in the accusative or OBJECTIVE CASE. The noun changes case without changing its form:

Passengers boarded the aircraft.

The aircraft carried the passengers.

In the first sentence *Passengers* is in the subjective case because it is the subject of the verb *boarded*; *aircraft* is in the objective case because it is the object of the verb *boarded*. In the second sentence *Aircraft* is subjective and *passengers* is objective.

The terms 'subjective' and 'objective' usually indicate the syntax, or word order in a sentence, as well as case: a subjective noun or pronoun usually precedes a verb; an objective noun or pronoun follows a verb or a preposition.

Personal pronouns have three cases: subjective, objective and possessive:

subjective	objective	possessive
I	me	mine
you	you	yours
he	him	his
she	her	hers
we	us	ours
you	you	yours
they	them	theirs

A fourth case, known as VOCATIVE, is the case of nouns or pronouns used to address or invoke a person, thing or condition. English has no vocative inflection, but a comma must normally be used to indicate the difference between the vocative and other cases:

Look up, John (vocative)

Look up John (objective).

case grammar *see* GRAMMAR.

cataphora *(n.)*
A word, usually a pronoun, that refers to a following word or words, usually a noun or noun phrase, in a sequence.

As soon as *he* arrived *the manager* began to discuss tactics.

The pronoun *he* is a cataphoric reference to the noun phrase *the manager*. The word 'cataphora' was coined in the late twentieth century to contrast with ANAPHORA.

category *(n.)*
A class of linguistic items with the same grammatical feature or features; also known as property. The term is usually applied to such features as

VOICE, MOOD and TENSE of verbs or CASE and NUMBER of nouns and pronouns.

Category is sometimes contrasted with function. In the sentence:

> The girls are studying music

the category of the noun *girls* is female in gender and plural in number, but the function of *The girls* is to act as the subject of the sentence. The words *are studying* are categorized as plural in number and present continuous in ASPECT, but the words function as the verb phrase in the sentence. The category of *music* is abstract, uncountable noun, but its function is to act as the object of the sentence.

catenative verb

A verb that appears immediately before a non-finite form of another verb.

> She hopes to work.

The verb *hopes* is the catenative verb and *to work* is the non-finite form. In this example:

> She wants to begin working again

wants is the catenative verb; *to begin* (infinitive) and *working* (present participle) are the non-finite verbs. The catenative verb and the non-finite verb or verbs that follow it are MAIN VERBS. *See also* FINITE AND NON-FINITE FORMS OF VERBS.

causative verb

A verb that denotes causation, that is, the bringing about of a particular state or condition. In one group of verbs the causative element is explicitly indicated by the *-en* ending:

> waken, weaken, gladden, sadden.

In other causative verbs the form of the verb sometimes indicates the condition it causes:

> infuriate: to make furious or to cause fury
>
> glorify: to make glorious
>
> victimize: to make a victim of.

Many other verbs, especially those denoting action, can be classed as causative:

> abduct, create, demolish, inspire, uproot.

cause *(n.)*

An ADVERBIAL that indicates reason or cause; an adverbial that expresses a connection between a cause and an effect. Cause is often expressed through an adverbial phrase beginning with the word 'because':

> Play was abandoned *because of the rain.*

Other adverbs of cause include *as, for* and *since.*

A subordinate adverbial clause of cause, or reason, usually begins with the word *because, since, as* or *for*:

> Spectators left The Oval because rain had stopped play.

> At the end of the debate he abstained for he felt the issue was a matter of conscience.

Adverbials of cause often answer the question 'why'? *See also* ADVERBIAL CLAUSE *under* CLAUSE; CAUSATIVE VERB.

ceneme *(n.)*

An alternative form for KENEME.

central adjective *see* ADJECTIVE.

central determiner *see* DETERMINER.

change *(n./v.)*

The ENGLISH LANGUAGE, like all living natural languages, is in a state of continuous evolution, its grammar and vocabulary constantly being modified. After 1,500 years of change, English is now so different from its origins, the Old English of the Anglo-Saxons, that Old English strikes the reader as a foreign language.

Here are some of the comments by Ælfric, master of the monastic school at Cerne Abbas, Dorset, in the late tenth century, in the preface to his translation of the Book of Genesis from Latin to Old English. The Old English is followed by first a literal translation and then a translation in current standard English.

> Ic cweþe nu þæt ic ne dearr ne ic nylle nane boc æfter þisse of Lædene on Englisc awendan; and ic bidde þe, leof ealdormann, þæt þu me þæs na leng ne bidde, þylæs þe ic beo þe ungehiersum.

> I say now that I neither dare nor I wish not no book after this from Latin to English to translate; and I beg you, dear nobleman, that you me this not for a long time do not ask, lest I be to you disobedient.

I say now that I neither dare nor wish to translate any book after this from Latin into English; and I beg you, dear nobleman, not to ask me to do this for a long time in case I disobey you.

The original passage and the translations show some of the main changes from Old English to Modern English. Two letters of the Old English alphabet, *æ*, known as *ash*, and *þ*, known as *thorn*, have disappeared; *þ* and another Old English letter, *ð*, known as *eth*, have been replaced by *th*. Some Old English words, *ic* for *I*, *þe* and *þu* for *you*, *boc* for *book*, have changed their forms. The words *awendan*, meaning *translate*, and *ungehiersum*, *disobedient*, have been replaced by two of the hundreds of thousands of words that have entered the language since Ælfric's time.

Although we cannot know exactly how Old English sounded as a spoken language, it is clear that the whole pattern of pronunciation has changed. Grammar, too, has been transformed. Old English nouns and pronouns had four cases, subjective, objective, possessive and dative, and all nouns had grammatical as well as biological gender; *boc*, for example, is feminine. The definite article *the*, the demonstrative pronoun *this* and all adjectives were inflected to agree with nouns in case, gender and number; agreement in Modern English is much simpler. The multiple negative construction *I neither dare nor I wish not no book* disappeared in Middle English; double negative constructions survived into Shakespeare's time but are not now acceptable.

The literal translation of the passage shows the differences in internal syntax, the word order within a sentence, between Old and Modern English. On the wider question of syntax in continuous prose, the current preference is for comparatively short, firmly structured sentences and paragraphs. With the change in prose style came changes in punctuation, notably less use of the semicolon and greater use of the full stop.

One feature of Modern English that resists change is SPELLING. Spelling was standardized by the time Johnson's *Dictionary* was published in 1755, and there are fixed spellings for all but a few of the many thousands of words that have entered the language since then. *See also* VOCABULARY.

character *(n.)*

A graphic sign, or symbol, denoting a sound, a syllable, a word or an idea in a writing system. In the English language, a letter of the alphabet.

chiasmus *(n.)*

An antithetical rhetorical device in which the same words are used in a different order in two or more parts of a statement.

> The glutton thinks of nothing but food; the philosopher feeds on nothing but thought.

Two examples from the world of politics are:

> This is not the end. It is not even the beginning of the end. But it is, perhaps, the end of the beginning.   Winston Churchill, 1942

> And so, my fellow-Americans, ask not what your country can do for you. Ask what you can do for your country.   John F. Kennedy, 1961

chunking *(n./v.)*

A colloquial term for the way in which words, especially in speech, and the information expressed by the words, are organized in small units and then coordinated into longer units by the speaker. *See also* REDUC-TIONISM.

circumlocution *(n.)*

A roundabout way of speaking or writing; using more words than are necessary to express a meaning.

> I travelled in a northerly direction until such time as my progress was halted by adverse weather conditions

for

> I travelled north until I was stopped by bad weather.

See also PERIPHRASIS (2); PLEONASM; REDUNDANCY (2).

citation form

The form of a word, phrase or other linguistic unit that is specified, or cited, for discussion; the form of a linguistic item that is the identifying word, or headword, phrase, AFFIX or other linguistic unit for a dictionary entry.

class of words

A group of words with the same or similar syntactical qualities and grammatical categories; an alternative term for **word class**; also known as PART OF SPEECH.

The classes are: NOUNS, ADJECTIVES, VERBS and ADVERBS; MODAL AUXILIARY VERBS, PRONOUNS, DETERMINERS, CONJUNCTIONS, PRE-POSITIONS and INTERJECTIONS. Nouns and adjectives are the largest classes of words, with tens of thousands of examples of each; verbs and adverbs are large classes. These four, nouns, adjectives, verbs and adverbs, are known as **open classes** of content words (*see* CONTENT WORD AND FUNCTION WORD) in the sense that the class is open for new additions and each word has a semantic content.

Modal auxiliary verbs, pronouns, determiners, conjunctions, prepositions and interjections are small classes, with only a few examples in each class. They are known as **closed classes** of function words because it is almost impossible to add new words to these classes and because the grammatical function of these words is sometimes more significant than their meaning.

Assigning words to classes in this way exposes anomalies. For example, full verbs form an open class of content words, but verbs have more grammatical functions than any other class of words. Function words are sometimes known as form words, but in other contexts form is contrasted with function. Words can change their class in different syntactic structures:

> He walked *up* the street (preposition)
>
> Life has its *ups* and downs (noun)
>
> The dealer *upped* the price (verb)
>
> The batsman played an *uppish* stroke (adjective)
>
> He stood *up* (adverb)

classifier *(n.)*

1 An AFFIX or INFLECTION that indicates the class of words to which a particular word belongs. The suffix -*ness*, for example, usually indicates that the word is a noun that denotes a quality or condition:

> freshness, kindness, weariness.

2 An affix or inflection that partly indicates the meaning of a word or phrase. The prefix *non*-, for example, indicates negation:

> nonconformist, non-existent, nonsense.

3 An attributive ADJECTIVE that modifies, or classifies, a noun:

> a *dangerous* journey, a *happy* conclusion.

clause *(n.)*

A sequence of words that normally includes a subject and a verb. Clauses are classified as main clauses, subordinate clauses and non-finite clauses.

A **main clause**, also known as an **independent clause** or a **principal**

clause, is usually said to be superordinate to, that is, more important grammatically and semantically than, a subordinate clause in the same sentence. If it is isolated from the subordinate clause, the main clause can often function as a complete sentence:

> When the alarm was raised, two rescue helicopters flew to the scene.

The main clause *two rescue helicopters flew to the scene* meets the grammatical and stylistic requirements of a sentence, but the subordinate clause *When the alarm was raised* does not.

A sentence can consist of main clauses only:

> The climbers were enthusiastic/but they had little experience of the Scottish mountains/and they under-estimated the difficulty of the climb.

The oblique lines show the division into three main clauses.

Subordinate clauses, also known as **dependent clauses**, can be sub-divided into three types: nominal, relative and adverbial clauses.

A **nominal clause**, sometimes known as a **noun clause** or, in some contexts as a **nominal relative clause,** is a subordinate clause that functions like a noun or noun phrase as the subject, the object or the complement of the main clause in a SENTENCE.

> *What you say* bewilders me. (subject)
>
> You can remember *where we met before*? (object)
>
> The question is *whether I should believe you*. (complement)

A nominal clause can also follow a preposition:

> Your credibility will be determined *by* how you answer this question.

A particular type of nominal clause is the nominal relative clause, which is introduced by a relative pronoun, *who, whom, whose, whoever, that, what, whatever.*

> *Whoever you met* may have looked like me.
>
> I know *that I have never seen you before*.

Nominal clauses usually answer the question *Who?* or *What?*

A **relative clause**, which is traditionally known as an **adjective clause** or adjectival clause, modifies, or relates to, a noun, noun phrase or pronoun in the main clause or another clause in a sentence. A relative clause usually begins with a relative pronoun, *who, whom, whose, that, which.*

> Mountaineering is a sport *in which errors can be fatal*.

The subordinate relative clause *in which errors can be fatal* modifies the noun *sport* in the main clause. A distinction can be made between **defining** and **non-defining** relative clauses. A defining relative clause is a subordinate clause that defines, identifies or explains a noun, noun phrase or pronoun in another clause in the same sentence:

> Club members *who are eligible for a discount* should apply to the club secretary.

The subordinate relative clause *who are eligible for a discount* is a defining clause because it defines the noun phrase *Club members* in the main clause *Club members should apply to the club secretary*. The implication is that there are club members who are eligible, as distinct from others who are not eligible, for a discount. A defining relative clause is also known as a **restrictive relative clause** because it restricts the meaning of the noun that it modifies. In the following sentence, by contrast:

> Club members, *who are eligible for a discount*, should apply to the club secretary.

the subordinate relative clause is non-defining because it is clear that all members are eligible. Non-defining, or **non-restrictive**, relative clauses, like the one immediately above, are usually punctuated by commas, but defining clauses are not.

An **adverbial clause** functions like an adverb and modifies a verb, an adjective or an adverb in another clause. All adverbial clauses have similar syntactic functions, but, depending on the kind of information they offer, they can be subdivided into clauses of time (*see* TIME ADVERBIAL), PLACE, CAUSE or reason, PURPOSE or intention, MANNER, comparison or degree, RESULT, condition (*see* CONDITIONAL CLAUSE) and CONCESSION.

> *When the alarm was raised*, two rescue helicopters flew to the scene. (Time)

> A rescue team on foot was searching *where the climbers had last been seen*. (Place)

> The helicopters returned to base *because darkness made the search impossible*. (Cause or reason)

> The climbers had set off at seven in the morning *so that they could have a full day on the mountain*. (Purpose or intention)

> All morning Harry Martin climbed *as well as he had ever done*. (Manner)

> The first part of the climb was easier *than he had imagined*. (Comparison or degree)

> Harry and his fellow-climbers were so confident *that they underestimated the last stage of the ascent*. (Result)

> *If they had been better prepared* they would not have lost their way. (Condition)

> *Although the climbers suffered exposure and hypothermia*, none of them was injured. (Concession)

Subordination, that is, the structuring of sentences with one or more main clauses and one or more subordinate clauses, is a key element in prose style.

Non-finite clauses, which are also known as **participial clauses**, contain non-finite forms of verbs.

> We saw him *leave the main road*. (*leave*, bare infinitive)

> He began *to climb the long hill*. (*to* infinitive)

> We could see him *walking slower and slower*. (-ING FORM or present participle)

> *Exhausted by the long climb*, he sat down on a rock. (-ED FORM or past participle)

cleft sentence

A simple SENTENCE that is broken, or cleft, and restructured as a complex sentence by using the construction *It* and the appropriate form of the verb *be*.

> He volunteered

can be cleft into the complex sentence:

> It was he who volunteered

in which *It was he* is the main clause, and *who volunteered* the subordinate clause. The effect of cleaving a sentence in this way is to add emphasis to the main clause:

> It was he [and no one else] who volunteered.

cliché *(n.)*

A stereotypical idiomatic expression, normally avoided in formal or original speech and writing but acceptable in informal contexts.

> Let's hear it for Thelma.

> She's the flavour of the month.

> We have a window of opportunity here.

These are late twentieth-century clichés. There are, as film producer Sam Goldwyn is alleged to have said, 'old clichés':

> Police left no stone unturned

> They're selling like hot cakes

> Avoid clichés like the plague.

clipping (*n./v.*)

A colloquial type of WORD FORMATION in which the new word is produced by abbreviating, or clipping, a piece from the end of a longer word.

> ad (advertisement), sarge (sergeant), taxi cab (taximeter cabriolet), telly (television).

See also DIMINUTIVE.

clitic *see* ENCLITIC AND PROCLITIC.

closed class *see* CLASS OF WORDS.

closed question

An alternative term for yes/no question. *See* QUESTION.

cloze test

A language comprehension test in which the candidate is required to supply words that have been omitted from a text. By its nature, a cloze test can be used as a test of spelling and grammar as well as vocabulary. The irregular spelling of 'cloze' has become standardized.

code (*n.*)

1 A secret system of language or communication.

2 A system of language designed to be read or processed by a computer or machine.

3 A set of procedures for transforming one system of language or communication into another.

All languages and most other forms of communication are codes in the sense that the signals – a set of signs, symbols, gestures or electronic pulses – represent something other than themselves. For example, our sense impressions about another person can be **encoded** into thought, further encoded into speech and encoded yet again into writing, which a reader may then **decode** into thought and feeling.

code-switching

1 Changing from one language to another, as in BILINGUALISM.

2 Changing from one dialect of a language to another, as in BIDIALECTALISM.

3 Changing from one level of formality in a language to another in order to meet the requirements of ACCEPTABILITY and APPROPRIATENESS.

4 Changing from one system of communication to another, for example, from speech to shorthand symbols, or from shorthand to written English.

See also DIGLOSSIA; ELABORATED CODE AND RESTRICTED CODE; FORMAL LANGUAGE AND INFORMAL LANGUAGE; LEVEL (2).

cognate *(adj./n.)*
1 Descriptive of languages that are of the same language family; a language that has evolved from the same parent language as another.

Old Norse was cognate with Old English, both having evolved from Germanic. French, Spanish, Portuguese, Italian and Romanian are cognate languages, all having evolved from the same parent language, Latin. *See also* FAMILY OF LANGUAGES.

2 A word derived from the same original word or root as another. English *father*, Spanish and Italian *padre*, German *Vater*, French *père*, Greek and Latin *pater* and Sanskrit *pitr* all derive from an INDO-EUROPEAN root. *See also* FALSE COGNATE; ROOT.

cognition *(n.)*
A general term for a range of conscious mental activities, including almost all conscious forms of language activity: thinking, reasoning, planning, forming concepts, problem-solving and decision-making. *See also* IDEATION.

coherence *(n.)*
The logical and grammatical consistency that is required to make a series of spoken or written statements intelligible and acceptable.

When he bought a new camera he gave his old one to his young brother

but not:

*When he bought a new camera *she* gave his old one to his young brother.

cohesion *(n.)*
The structural unity that is required to give the continuity that makes a series of spoken or written statements intelligible. A chronological or sequential narrative such as a biographical statement or the itinerary for a journey must be cohesive. On some occasions, notably casual conversations, the cohesion is implicit or assumed. The question:

Are you going to the concert tonight?

could prompt the implicitly cohesive reply:

> My mother's just gone into hospital.

In spoken communication, cohesion and coherence partly depend on the listener's ability or willingness to interpret the meaning. In written communication, the responsibility is the writer's.

coinage *(n.)*

1 A new word; an invented word.

2 The process of inventing a new word.

By these definitions, coinage is the same as NEOLOGISM. The verb for the process of coinage is coin. *See also* WORD FORMATION.

collective noun

A noun that denotes a group, or collection, of people or things.

> a *board* of directors
>
> an *archipelago* of islands
>
> a *squad* of footballers.

Although the collective noun is itself grammatically singular:

> a *cast* (singular) of actors (plural)

the practice of notional AGREEMENT allows the collective noun to be followed by a singular or plural verb, depending on whether the writer wishes to indicate the unity and singularity of the collective noun, or the variety and multiplicity of the items in the collection:

> The board of governors has approved the salary increase. (singular)
>
> After three successive defeats the squad have lost their confidence. (plural)

collocation *(n.)*

1 The necessary or appropriate association of particular words in a given context. The collocation *filled in*, for example, can be used in the sense of *completed* in the sentence:

> He filled in his application form

but not

> *He filled in a marathon.

The same principle of collocation applies in the phrases:

> to repair a car, to cure a patient, to correct an error.

2 The frequent association of one word with another, or a group of words with another group. The elements, or coordinates, in the collocation may form a neutral, almost automatic, association:

> oranges and lemons; red, white and blue;

one coordinate may prompt the other because they are contrasting pairs:

>   north/south, fission/fusion;

or the collocation may be a form of cliché:

>   the intrepid traveller, the silent majority.

The examples above are **lexical collocations**, that is, forms of SEMANTIC RESTRICTION that limit the nature and the number of collocations in which a word or phrase can be used. Lexical collocations are sometimes contrasted with **grammatical collocations**, which require that one linguistic form be followed by another. MODAL AUXILIARY VERBS, for example, cannot function alone but must be followed by main verbs. *See also* RANGE.

colloquialism *(n.)*
An informal expression in speech or writing. The commonest colloquialisms are contractions of pronouns and verbs:

>   she'd/she would, you'll/you will

The colloquial:

>   OK, mate. See you at the match

contrasts with the formal:

>   Very well, my friend. I shall see you at the football match.

colon *see* PUNCTUATION.

comitative *(adj./n.)*
A word or phrase that denotes company, companionship or association. Some languages have a comitative case to express this idea. In English, the association of two or more people is expressed by such words and phrases as:

>   alongside, along with, together, together with, in association with, in partnership with, in the company of, accompanied by, partnered by.

See also RECIPROCAL.

comma *see* PUNCTUATION.

comma splice
Using a comma as a punctuation mark when the syntax of the sentence requires either a different punctuation mark or a different construction. A comma splice produces a **run-on sentence**:

    *She went to university, there she edited *Shrews*.

That faulty sentence could be rewritten as:

    She went to university where she edited *Shrews*.

    She went to university and there she edited *Shrews*.

    The following versions are syntactically correct but could be rejected on grounds of style:

    She went to university; there she edited *Shrews*.

    She went to university. There she edited *Shrews*.

command *(n.)*
A verb that expresses an order or instruction. *See also* IMPERATIVE; MOOD.

comment *see* TOPIC AND COMMENT.

commissive speech act *see* SPEECH ACT.

common noun and proper noun
A **common noun** denotes a general class of persons, things or conditions.

    athlete, piano, beauty.

Common nouns can be abstract:

    ambition, boredom, intellect, zest

or concrete:

    car, pineapple, sofa, tree.

    A **proper noun** denotes one particular person, place or institution, and to mark this individuality proper nouns are always spelled with initial capital letters:

    Harry Stark, Ludlow Castle, United Nations Organization.

Some proper nouns, the titles of poems, newspapers, books, films and other created works, are additionally punctuated. As a general rule, the titles of shorter works such as poems, short stories and newspaper articles are punctuated with inverted commas as well as initial capitals:

    'The Elephant's Child' by Rudyard Kipling.

The titles of longer works, such as novels, collections of poems or stories, films, newspaper and magazines, are spelled with initial capitals and set in italic type or underlined:

    The Long Revolution by Raymond Williams.

Proper nouns, like common nouns, can be abstract, Christianity, or concrete, Mount Everest. *See also* ABSTRACT NOUN AND CONCRETE NOUN; NOUN.

communication *(n.)*

The exchange of INFORMATION by speech, writing or other means. The information is encoded in the brain of the sender and transmitted in an agreed CODE by a MEDIUM to the receiver, who then decodes the information.

communicative competence

A person's ability to communicate appropriately in social situations. Communicative competence, like language itself, is acquired in a process that may be conscious or unconscious. In informal contexts, such as casual conversation, a speaker's management of particular factors in communicative competence – when and how to agree or disagree, how to alternate with another speaker, how to end the conversation – may be partly intuitive. In formal contexts, such as structured meetings and interviews, the participant is more likely to be conscious of the factors in communicative competence. *See also* COMPETENCE AND PERFORMANCE.

comparative *(adj./n.)*

1 The form of an ADJECTIVE, adjective phrase, ADVERB or ADVERBIAL PHRASE that is used to express an intermediate level or degree of intensity. *See also* GRADABILITY.
2 A subordinate adverbial CLAUSE that expresses comparison or degree.

comparative adjective

An alternative term for gradable adjective. *See* ADJECTIVE.

comparative adverb

An alternative term for gradable adverb. *See* ADVERB.

comparative clause *see* ADVERBIAL CLAUSE *under* CLAUSE.

comparative linguistics

The branch of LINGUISTICS that compares features of different languages, especially those originating from the same parent language. Comparative linguistics has replaced the older term 'comparative philology'.

comparison *see* COMPARATIVE.

competence and performance *(n.)*

The theory proposed by Noam Chomsky that **competence**, a person's understanding of his native language, allows him to interpret and formulate an infinite number of sentences in the language. Chomsky contrasts competence with **performance**, a person's actual, and sometimes faulty, use of language. Competence and performance are similar to the concepts of LANGUE AND PAROLE proposed by Ferdinand de Saussure (1857–1913).

complement *(n.)*

A word, phrase or clause that follows the verbs *be* and *become*, or a verb with a similar meaning and function, in order to complete the action of the verb and thus complete the meaning of the SENTENCE; one of the five major components of a sentence. In the sentence:

Traffic was dense

the adjective *dense* complements the SUBJECT *Traffic*, and so *dense* is a **subject complement** in that sentence. Similarly, in the sentence:

She became prime minister

the phrase *prime minister* is the complement of the subject *She*. The subject complement is normally an attribute of the subject, as in the first example above, or is effectively in apposition to the subject, as in the second example. In this example:

Passengers consider Alex an erratic driver

the noun *Alex* is the OBJECT of the verb *consider*, and since the phrase *an erratic driver* is the complement of *Alex*, the phrase is an **object complement**. In the sentence:

Alex continued to alarm his passengers

the words *to alarm his passengers* form an infinitive clause that complements the verb *continued*.

The term 'complement' can also be applied to a noun phrase that follows a preposition:

towards *the setting sun*

over *the horizon*.

complementarity *see* OPPOSITE.

complex preposition *see* PREPOSITION.

complex sentence *see* SENTENCE.

complex stem *see* STEM.

complex transitive verb *see* TRANSITIVE VERB AND INTRANSITIVE VERB.

complex word
A word that can be broken down into two or more parts, or MORPHEMES, each of which expresses some meaning. The noun *childishness*, for example, can be broken down to the noun *child*, the adjective suffix, *-ish* and the noun suffix *-ness*.

component *(n.)*
1 A set of factors in a GENERATIVE GRAMMAR. The **syntactic component** is a set of rules that provide information about the structures of clauses and sentences. The **phonological component** accounts for the transformation of syntactic structures into sounds. The **semantic component** provides information about the meanings of the words and phrases in clauses and sentences.

2 In COMPONENTIAL ANALYSIS (2) a semantic element, or component, that forms part of the meaning of two or more words. The semantic component *immature*, for example, is present in the words:

> calf, child, cub, foal, kitten.

componential analysis
1 Breaking down a piece of writing into its component parts.

2 More specifically, an approach to semantics based on the theory that universal human experience – of family and kinship, for example – leads to universal concepts and that these concepts in turn lead to universal **semantic primitives**, that is, fundamental components of meaning. The words *man*, *father* and *boy* share the component of masculinity.

compound-complex sentence *see* SENTENCE.

compound sentence *see* SENTENCE.

compound stem *see* STEM.

compound word
1 A word that is formed from two or more other words. The words may be fully compounded, as in:

frogman, hovercraft, laptop, meltdown;

or they may be hyphenated:

brother-in-law, happy-go-lucky, soul-destroying.

2 A semantic unit, that is, a single identifiable thing, consisting of two or more elements:

brain waves, wave power, scanning electron microscope.

computer language *see* ARTIFICIAL LANGUAGE (2).

concept *(n.)*
A mental representation of a class of things; an idea of the shared attributes or properties of a class. The terms *concept, conception* and *conceptual thought* can be applied to concrete things, for example, the concept of *chair*, but the terms are more frequently applied to abstractions.

Examples of concepts in grammar are agreement, synonymy, tense and transitivity (*see* TRANSITIVE VERB AND INTRANSITIVE VERB).

concession *(n.)*
A subordinate adverbial clause that seems to oppose the proposition in the main clause but is, in fact, part of an overall expression of compliance or concession; also known as a concessive clause.

Although he was late he did not apologize.

The words that introduce clauses of concession are known as adverbial conjunctions:

although, though, despite, however, nevertheless, and yet, even so.

See also CLAUSE.

concord *(n.)*
An alternative term for AGREEMENT.

concrete noun *see* ABSTRACT NOUN AND CONCRETE NOUN.

conditional clause
A subordinate adverbial clause that expresses a requirement or condition that must be met in order to realize the proposition in the main clause.

I won't go to the concert *unless you come with me.*

We shall go hillwalking *if the weather is fine.*

A conditional clause is also known as a clause of condition and, less often, as a **contingent clause**. *See also* CLAUSE; CONTINGENCY AND NECESSITY.

conjoining *(n.)*
An alternative term for COORDINATION.

conjugate *(v.)*
To identify the various inflections of a VERB and thus identify the verb's various grammatical categories: NUMBER, PERSON, TENSE, MOOD and VOICE. Old English, an inflecting language, had seven verb classes, each of which was conjugated differently. In Modern English, regular verbs have a total of only four inflections, and irregular verbs have only five.

conjunct *(adj./n.)*
An adverbial that links one clause or sentence to' another. Conjuncts often have the additional function of focusing or re-focusing the attention of the reader or listener on a change of emphasis in a topic.

> Police examined the damaged car. *In addition*, they took statements from the driver, the injured pedestrian and two eye-witnesses. *As a result*, the police concluded that no crime had been committed.

The main difference between a conjunct and a CONJUNCTION is that a conjunct always has an adverbial function as well as its connective function.

conjunction *(n.)*
A small closed class of function words that link words, phrases or clauses in the same sentence, or link two or more sentences in a sequence. One type of conjunction, the **coordinating conjunction**:

> and, but, or, yet, and yet

is used to link words, phrases, clauses or sentences of equal grammatical value. Some coordinating conjunctions:

> both … and, either … or, neither … nor, not only … but also

are also known as **correlative conjunctions** because they indicate a correlation of linguistic units. A few words:

> where, when, why, how, however, nevertheless

operate as conjunctions and as adverbs, and can be called **adverbial conjunctions** or **conjunctive adverbs**.

A complex conjunction is one that consists of two or more words:

in order that, in order to, so as to, so that.

The coordinating conjunctions *and* and *but* can be used as the first words in sentences. Repeated use of such sentence structures could be censored for reasons of style but not usually for grammatical reasons. *See also* COORDINATION.

conjunctive adverb *see* CONJUNCTION.

connective *(adj./n.)*

A general term for a word or phrase that links linguistic units; also known as a connector. Connectives include CONJUNCTIONS, CONJUNCTS and the COPULA *be*.

connotation *(n.)*

Words, ideas, images or emotions associated with, or suggested by, another word or phrase. Connotation is an imprecise process, a loose form of association that can occur at a personal or national level and at intermediate levels. The word *syringe*, for example, will prompt different connotations – a dentist's or doctor's surgery, hospital, pain relief, anaesthesia, immunization, illicit drug use, AIDS – in the minds of different people. At a national level the words *maple leaf* or the image of a maple leaf are likely to prompt stronger connotations in the minds of Canadians than people of other nationalities. Connotations often evoke affective, or emotional, associations. *See also* DENOTATATION; EMOTIVE LANGUAGE; AFFECTIVE MEANING *under* MEANING.

connotative meaning

An alternative term for affective meaning. *See* MEANING.

consonance *(n.)*

1 The repetition of consonant sounds before and after different vowel sounds, especially as a phonological device.

A west wind ruffles the surface and whips the ripples into waves.

2 A melodic or pleasant combination of sounds.

See also ASSONANCE; DISSONANCE; PHONAESTHEME.

consonant *(n.)*

A speech sound produced by a closure or partial closure of the vocal tract and normally accompanied by a sudden release of air or by vocal friction. Consonants can be subdivided into AFFRICATES, FRICATIVES, LIQUIDS, NASALS and PLOSIVES. They are sometimes contrasted with VOWELS.

consonant cluster

An unbroken group, or cluster, of consonants in a word. A cluster of consonants at the beginning of a word is an **initial cluster**:

> *chr*onicle, *phr*ase, *sch*eme.

A cluster in the middle of a word is a **medial cluster**:

> a*ltr*uism, o*ffspr*ing, u*pst*art.

A consonant cluster at the end of a word is a **final cluster**:

> fi*rst*, hea*lth*, sho*rts*.

constant word

An alternative term for invariable word. *See* VARIABLE WORD AND INVARIABLE WORD.

constituent *(n.)*

A general term for a linguistic unit that is part of a larger linguistic unit. The scope of the term ranges from the smallest linguistic units, MORPHEMES and PHONEMES, to the largest, CLAUSES and SENTENCES.

constituent analysis

Breaking down a sentence into its separate but related parts, or constituents, and identifying the parts.

> A pack of journalists surrounded the disgraced politician outside the court

can be analysed into its sentence components:

> A pack of journalists (subject)
>
> surrounded (verb)
>
> the disgraced politician (object)
>
> outside the court (adverbial).

The same sentence can be analysed into its **immediate constituents** or major constituents:

> A pack of journalists (noun phrase)
>
> surrounded (verb)
>
> the disgraced politician (noun phrase)
>
> outside the court (prepositional phrase functioning as an adverbial)

These immediate constituents can be further analysed into smaller, or **ultimate constituents**:

> A (indefinite article)
>
> pack (noun)

of journalists (prepositional phrase, or *of* preposition, *journalists* (noun)

surrounded (verb)

the (definite article)

disgraced (adjective)

politician (noun)

outside (preposition)

the (definite article)

court (noun)

Constituent analysis is sometimes shown graphically by BRACKETING or as a triangular TREE DIAGRAM.

construction *(n.)*
A general term for a phrase, clause or sentence formed, or constructed, from smaller linguistic units.

content analysis
Identifying the significant features of a written text or of a speech or broadcast material. The significant features may be stylistic: the vocabulary and rhetorical devices in a speech; they may be visual: the use of images in magazines or television; they may be thematic: the topics, ideas, appeals or promises in a political speech. The analysis can also be a statistical one that counts the incidence or frequency of certain words, ideas or images. *See also* DISCOURSE ANALYSIS.

content word and function word
A **content word** is one whose meaning can be stated. The open CLASSES OF WORDS – NOUNS, ADJECTIVES, full VERBS and ADVERBS – are content words. Content words are also known as **lexical words** or **full words**.

A **function word** is one whose significance lies as much in its grammatical function as its meaning. The closed classes of words: MODAL AUXILIARY VERBS, CONJUNCTIONS, PREPOSITIONS, DETER-MINERS, NUMERALS and INTERJECTIONS, are function words. Function words are also known as **grammatical words** and **form words**.

The distinction between content words and function words, tradi-tionally known as **major** and **minor parts of speech**, is not absolute; all words have some semantic value, and almost all words in sentences have some syntactic function.

context *(n.)*

The words that surround a particular word or phrase and partly determine the meaning, or sense, of the word or phrase. The word *piping*, for example, may appear in a context that includes the words *pibroch*, *lament* and *Flowers o' the Forest*; or a context that includes the words *water*, *cistern* and *ballcock*; or *cloth*, *seam* and *hem*; or *icing*, *cake* and *Happy Birthday*. The particular meaning of *piping* would be determined by the particular context.

context-dependent *(adj.)*

Descriptive of a linguistic unit whose meaning is determined partly or entirely by the surrounding linguistic units or CONTEXT. The SENSE of most synonyms and polysemous words and the sense of some hyponyms are context-dependent:

> The accusation did not stick.
>
> The glue would not stick.
>
> The stick broke in his hands.
>
> I shall stick to the task.

context-free rule and context-sensitive rule

A **context-free** rule is one that applies in any circumstance or context. For example, the rewrite rule 's→ NP VP', that is, a sentence (S) consists of a noun phrase (NP) and a verb phrase (VP), can be applied to all sentences, irrespective of context.

A **context-sensitive rule**, by contrast, is one that applies only in certain contexts. The rule 'add *-ed* to form the past tense and past participle form of a verb' applies only to regular verbs; context-sensitive rules are needed for *-en* forms of verbs:

> forbade/forbidden, forsook/forsaken;

for other irregular verbs such as:

> sang/sung, drank/drunk;

and for verbs that have precisely the same form in both present and past tenses:

> burst, hurt, spread.

contextual meaning *see* CONTEXT; LINGUISTIC MEANING *under* MEANING.

contingency and necessity *(n.)*

Contingency is a state or condition that is non-essential or is subject to chance, choice or accident. Contingency is also descriptive of a condition whose truth is determined by surrounding or external factors. Some linguists use the term with reference to dynamic verbs, alienable possessions and some adverbials. In this sentence, for example:

> The train will leave only if the signal is green

the PROPOSITION of the main clause, *The train will leave*, is contingent on the proposition in the adverbial clause.

Necessity is a condition in which a proposition is intrinsically or necessarily true because of the semantic and syntactic rules of the language. For example, if this proposition is true:

> Anna married Jake

then the following propositions are necessarily true:

> Jake married Anna
>
> Anna is Jake's wife
>
> Jake is Anna's husband.

The words 'necessity' and 'necessary' can be applied to stative verbs that denote a long-lasting or permanent condition and to inalienable possessions. *See also* ANALYTIC PROPOSITION AND SYNTHETIC PROPOSITION; DYNAMIC VERB AND STATIVE VERB; ENTAILMENT.

contingent clause

An alternative term for CONDITIONAL CLAUSE. *See also* CONTINGENCY AND NECESSITY.

continuous form

The present participle of a VERB, the -ING FORM (1), preceded by the appropriate form of the verb *be* or *have* to indicate the ASPECT or TENSE of the verb; also known as **progressive form**. For example:

> is walking (present continuous)
>
> was walking (past continuous)
>
> has been walking (present perfect continuous)
>
> had been walking (past perfect continuous)
>
> will be walking (future continuous)

See also FUTURE TENSE; PAST TENSE; PRESENT TENSE.

contraction (n.)

The shortening of a word or phrase. The commonest contractions are the fusions of pronoun and verb:

> I'll, you're, they'd.

In informal speech or writing, longer linguistic units, including sentences, can be contracted:

> Seen Gordon? (Have you seen Gordon?)
>
> Like the show? (Did you like the show?)
>
> Coffee? (Would you like some coffee?)

See also ABBREVIATION.

contradictory (adj./n.)

A general term for a linguistic unit whose meaning is OPPOSITE that of another linguistic unit. The application of the term ranges from AFFIXES:

> *pro*-Europe, *anti*-Europe

to sentences:

> He swore he had never been inside the bank before. Later, he said his last visit to the bank had been to open an account.

contrastive stress *see* STRESS.

conventional implicature *see* IMPLICATURE.

conventional metaphor *see* METAPHOR (2).

convergence (n.)

1 In a bilingual or multilingual society, or on either side of a language boundary, the process by which two or more languages come together and share certain linguistic features, most obviously vocabulary and phonology.

2 The process by which two or more dialects come to share certain features.

3 The process by which a non-standard form of a language adopts some of the features of the standard form.

Convergence, which is also known as **merging**, occurs when two or more speech communities interact. *See also* DIVERGENCE.

conversational implicature *see* IMPLICATURE.

converseness *see* OPPOSITE.

conversion *(n.)*

A type of WORD FORMATION in which an existing word changes its word class, usually from noun to verb.

> Traffic was *channelled* into one lane when a lorry *jack-knifed* on the motorway.

> The BBC will *network* the programme.

Conversion is common practice among newspaper sub-editors. In the headline:

> Sex-in-the-shower scandal MP named

the compound nonce-word *Sex-in-the-shower*, despite its two noun components, *sex* and *shower*, functions as an adjective; the noun *scandal* functions as a noun and an adjective. The process is also known as **functional change** or **functional shift**, **reclassification** and **redesignation**.

coordinate clause or coordinating clause

A clause that is linked to another by means of a coordinating CONJUNCTION. In the sentence:

> He was offered a place on the training course but he rejected the offer

the coordinate clauses are *He was offered a place on the training course* and *he rejected the offer*; the coordinating conjunction is *but*. Similarly, in the sentence:

> She closed the book and put it back on the shelf

the two coordinate clauses are linked by the coordinating conjunction *and*.

coordinating conjunction *see* CONJUNCTION.

coordination *(n.)*

A balanced combination of words, phrases or clauses, usually linked by a coordinating CONJUNCTION; also known as **conjoining**.

> Newspapers, magazines and books were on sale at the airport.

The coordinates are the single words *Newspapers*, *magazines* and *books*; the coordinator is the conjunction *and*. In this example:

> Airport security staff must attend a safety demonstration on Monday morning or on Wednesday afternoon

the coordinates are the prepositional phrases *on Monday morning* and *on Wednesday afternoon*, and the coordinator is *or*. In the compound sentence:

> International flights were delayed but most domestic flights were on time

the coordinates are the two main clauses *International flights were delayed* and *most domestic flights were on time*; the coordinator is *but*.

copula *(n.)*
The verb *be* when it functions as the link between the SUBJECT and the COMPLEMENT of a sentence. Other verbs that can function in the same way include:

> appear, become, look, seem, feel, remain.

A copula is also known as a **copular verb** and a **linking verb**.

copular verb
An alternative term for COPULA.

co-reference *(n.)*
A referent that is denoted by two or more linguistic units.

> The *bowler* was furious with *himself* when *he* was hit for six.

See also PRO-FORM.

correctness *(n.)*
Conforming to agreed standards of language USAGE.

Absolute conformity is attainable in spelling because almost every word in English has a fixed spelling, and the few exceptions, for example, *inflection/inflexion*, have agreed optional spellings. On questions of grammar there is some agreement among linguists, but there is often disagreement between these specialists and educated non-specialists. Disputed areas include split infinitives, beginning a sentence with a conjunction and ending a sentence with a preposition. A possible barrier to public understanding is that the terminology, the jargon, of grammar has grown more complicated, partly because the traditional, PRESCRIPTIVE terminology has sometimes been replaced by descriptive terminology, and partly because of the different, occasionally conflicting, approaches to the study of grammar as an academic discipline since the 1950s.

On questions of syntax there is agreement on what is not correct – for example, *Finished I have not yet this book* – but because of the innumerable possible permutations of correct word order in sentences and paragraphs there is no known limit to correctness in syntax. Punctuation, too, is variable; for example, a parenthetical statement can be punctuated by round brackets, commas or dashes.

Apart from pronunciation, the feature that raises most questions of correctness is vocabulary. Some people cannot accept language change. They use an etymological argument, sometimes known as the etymological fallacy, that an early definition of an existing word is more correct, or even purer, than a new definition; and their response to neologisms is to reject them as incorrect. Sometimes the rejectors are right; of the thousands of new words that enter the English language every year – new derivations, conversions of existing words and new scientific and technological terms – some will disappear and others will never be standardized but will remain slang or colloquial or jargon words and thus incorrect in standard English.

Concepts of correctness are inevitable when a language is standardized, because the standard forms come to be seen not as neutral points of reference but as mandatory; forms that diverge from the standard are sometimes regarded as substandard rather than non-standard. Professional linguists usually assume the role of neutral observers of, and commentators on, language. Other professional users of language, for example, editors, publishers and some teachers, must adopt a more prescriptive approach. *See also* ETYMOLOGY; NORMATIVE; STANDARD AND NON-STANDARD ENGLISH.

correlative conjunction *see* CONJUNCTION.

countable noun and uncountable noun

Countable, or count, nouns are nouns that can be identified and counted as separate, individual entities. They can appear in singular or plural form:

city/cities, harvest/harvests, writer/writers.

Singular countable nouns can be preceded by the definite or indefinite article:

the tree, a shoe, an elephant.

Plural countable nouns can be preceded by plural forms:

many journalists, those photographers.

Countable nouns, singular or plural, cannot be preceded by the words *less* or *much*. The forms:

*less elephants, *much photographers

should be written:

> fewer elephants, many/most photographers.

Uncountable, or **non-count**, nouns do not have plural forms:

> *ignorances, *wealths.

They cannot normally be preceded by the indefinite article:

> *a fame, *an information,

and they cannot normally be preceded by plural forms:

> *many traffics, *these agricultures.

Uncountable nouns cannot be preceded by the word *fewer*. The forms:

> *fewer optimism, *fewer information

should be written:

> less optimism, less information.

Uncountable nouns include a sub-group known as **mass nouns**, which denote substances in the forms of undifferentiated masses:

> sand, petrol, oxygen.

Some nouns can function as countable or uncountable, depending on the context. For example, the nouns in this sentence are countable:

> There was *a time* when *the anxiety* was caused by *a change* in *the work* he did.

When the same nouns are used in a more general, fully abstract, way they are uncountable:

> *Change* at *work* can cause *anxiety*, but *time* will heal.

creole *(adj./n.)*
A language that has evolved from a PIDGIN language to become the first language, or natural language, of a SPEECH COMMUNITY. The evolution from a pidgin to a creole involves an extension of vocabulary and a development of grammar.

critical period
The theory that a young person can acquire a language, learn a foreign language and develop the language faculty of the brain more easily during the period up to mid-adolescence than at a later period in life.

An extension of the theory is that, if the LANGUAGE CENTRES OF THE BRAIN are not developed before the end of the critical period, the centres may not develop normally, a condition known as **functional atrophy**. Studies of feral children, that is, children who grew up with little or no contact with other humans, tend to support the critical period theory. *See also* ACQUISITION OF LANGUAGE; INNATENESS; LANGUAGE ACQUISITION DEVICE.

dangling participle *see* MISRELATED PARTICIPLE.

dash *see* PUNCTUATION.

dative case
In an inflecting language, for example, in Latin or Old English, the form, or inflection, of a noun, pronoun or adjective to express the meaning *to* or *for*. *See also* CASE.

dead language
A language that has no natural SPEECH COMMUNITY; a language that has ceased to be the natural medium of spoken or written communication in any community.

Old English and Latin are dead languages; so too are the Cornish and Manx versions of the Celtic language, and the hundreds of indigenous languages throughout the world whose speakers have ceased to exist or have adopted other languages. Many of these languages, in North and South America, for example, died without ever being recorded in written form.

declarative *(adj./n.)*
A sentence, clause or verb that expresses a statement, an opinion or a promise.

> Teachers voted against strike action. The education secretary welcomed their decision. She said, 'I guarantee that your conditions of service will not deteriorate.'

Some linguists say that the declarative function is a MOOD of verbs and an alternative term for INDICATIVE mood, as distinct from IMPERATIVE or SUBJUNCTIVE MOOD.

declarative knowledge *see* KNOWLEDGE.

declarative speech act *see* SPEECH ACT.

declension *(n.)*
1 In an inflecting language, the form, or INFLECTION, of a noun, pronoun or adjective that shows the word's grammatical case and thus its precise function and meaning in a sentence.

2 A class of nouns with the same pattern of inflection. To decline a noun is to study, or recite, its different CASES in an agreed order.

decode *see* CODE.

decontextualize *(v.)*
To interpret part of a text without reference to the CONTEXT. In an extreme form, decontextualization is an interpretation based on the denotative or referential MEANING of words.

deep structure and **surface structure**
Theories of grammar developed by the American linguistic philosopher, Noam Chomsky. The **surface structure** of a grammar is the sequence of words that we see in written language or the sequence of sounds we hear in spoken language. These sequences can be identified by CONSTITUENT ANALYSIS, but constituent analysis cannot account for our recognition of ambiguity in ambiguous sentences:

The tourist asked the policeman with a smile on his face.

On whose face was the smile: the tourist's or the policeman's? The reader can see that there are two possible meanings in the one surface structure. Similarly, the reader recognizes a single meaning expressed in two different sentences:

The tourist asked the policeman

and

The policeman was asked by the tourist.

Chomsky argues that language has a **deep structure**, a level at which the various interrelated aspects of structure and meaning are interpreted. The interpretation takes place, of course, in the mind of the reader; the depth of structure is an aspect of the human brain rather than of grammar. It is possible, then, that beneath the surface structure of a sentence lies not a deep linguistic structure but sub-linguistic or pre-linguistic mental activity, a complex and sophisticated – but not necessarily linguistic – way of recognizing and interpreting different orders of reality. It is this mental capacity that decodes the surface structure in order to recognize the ambiguity of a single sentence and the single meaning of two different sentences. The recognition can then be re-encoded into different words. *See also* IDEATION; TRANSFORMATION; UNDERLYING STRUCTURE AND DERIVED STRUCTURE.

deficit theory and difference theory

Deficit theory, also known as the deficit hypothesis, is the argument that some children do not acquire the level of spoken or written language skills expected at their age.

The theory suggests that the deficiency is partly a result of a social background in which little value is attached to conversation, reading or writing; or that the deficiency is partly the result of a minority culture in which the language is not the national language.

Difference theory, also known as the difference hypothesis, argues that a deficiency in one dialect or language may be counterbalanced by language skills in another dialect or language, and that any dialect or language can express the level of thought expected of children at a given age. *See also* ELABORATED CODE AND RESTRICTED CODE.

defining relative clause *see* CLAUSE.

defining vocabulary *see* VOCABULARY (4).

definite article *see* ARTICLE.

degree *(n.)*

1 The stage of comparison – positive, comparative, superlative – of an ADJECTIVE or ADVERB. *See also* GRADABILITY.

2 A subordinate adverbial CLAUSE of comparison or degree.

deictic language

A word or phrase that refers pointedly to a specific context in terms of time:

> now, then, before, after,

or place:

> here, there, inside, outside,

or in terms of the participants:

> you; me; you, sir; and you, madam.

The grammatical category is known as deixis.

delexical verb

A verb in a clause or sentence in which the action is denoted by the noun that is the object of the verb rather than by the verb itself.

> Councillors put a ban on the rock festival

can be rewritten with a full, or lexical, verb:

> Councillors banned the rock festival.

Similarly, the sentence:

> Have a taste of this pudding

can be rewritten as:

> Taste this pudding.

See also FULL VERB.

demonstrative adjective

The words *this*, *that*, *these* and *those* when placed immediately in front of a noun; an alternative for the more usual term, demonstrative DETERMINER.

> this supermarket, that shopping trolley, these customers, those free-range eggs.

demonstrative pronouns

The words *this*, *that*, *these* and *those* used instead of nouns.

> Whose disc is this?

> These are mine.

demotic *(adj./n.)*

A less formal version of a language; the language of the common people as distinct from a high variety or **hieratic** version of a language.

In Scotland, for example, an urban demotic form of English, roughly midway between English and Scots language, is widely used in the street and the workplace, while standard English is the language of education, commerce, law and most sectors of the communications media. *See also* HIGH VARIETY AND LOW VARIETY; VERNACULAR.

denominal *(adj.)*

An alternative term for DENOMINATIVE.

denominative *(adj./n.)*

A word that is formed or derived from a noun. Adjectives formed from nouns include:

> lifelike (life), wooden (wood).

Denominative verbs include:

> magnetize (magnet), metricate (metrication).

The compound nouns *wavelength* and *weedkiller* are formed from their two component nouns.

Denominative words are also known as **denominals**.

denotation *(n.)*

A reference that is limited to a thing itself as distinct from any CON-NOTATION that may be evoked by the reference. A strictly denotative use of language is not always attainable in normal speech or writing, partly because most nouns, adjectives and verbs in English are POLYSEMES, that is, they have more than one meaning, and partly because ordinary speech often includes IDIOM and METAPHOR. By contrast, the languages of science are almost entirely denotative. *See also* DENOTATIVE, REFERENTIAL *under* MEANING.

denotative, referential meaning *see* MEANING.

deontic *see* EPISTEMIC AND DEONTIC.

dependency grammar *see* GRAMMAR; VALENCY.

dependent and independent *(adj./n.)*

A **dependent** linguistic unit is one that is subordinate to, and thus depends on, another, usually SUPERORDINATE, linguistic unit. A subordinate CLAUSE, for example, is usually dependent on a main clause, or occasionally on another subordinate clause. Words in a phrase can be said to be dependent on the headword in the phrase.

An **independent** linguistic unit is one that can stand alone. The main clause of a sentence and the headword of a phrase are independent units.

The distinction between dependency and independence is not an absolute one; linguistic units in a sentence are usually interdependent.

dependent clause

An alternative term for subordinate CLAUSE.

derivation *(n.)*

1 The formation of a word from an earlier word by adding an AFFIX to the root. The LATIN prefix *sub-* (under, beneath, close to) produces hundreds of derived words in the ENGLISH LANGUAGE, from *subabdominal* to *subway*. The GREEK suffix *-ology* produces many nouns denoting subjects of study and branches of knowledge. The Old English suffix *-ness* produces hundreds of nouns denoting a condition, quality or property.

The majority of derived words in English are from FRENCH, Latin, Greek and English itself. Precise ETYMOLOGY is not always possible, but the main patterns of derivation are from Greek to Latin to French to English, and from Latin to French to English. Throughout most of the period of Modern English, the majority of derivations have been from Greek and Latin. Greek and Latin derivations are an important type of WORD FORMATION in general English, and the most important type in scientific English.

2 Tracing a word back to its root. *Frogman*, for example, is derived from two Old English words, *frog* and *man*. *Polytonality* is derived from Greek *poly* (many), Latin *tonalis* from Greek *tonos* (tone), and Latin *-itas* or *-itatis* (a state or condition).

derived structure *see* UNDERLYING STRUCTURE AND DERIVED STRUCTURE.

descriptive grammar *see* GRAMMAR.

determiner *(n.)*

A closed class of frequently used function words (*see* CONTENT WORD AND FUNCTION WORD). Determiners are usually placed immediately before nouns in order to specify, or determine, the scope of the noun. The classification, determiner, is often used as a general term for several word classes:

indefinite and definite ARTICLES: a, an, the;

DEMONSTRATIVE PRONOUNS: this, that, these, those;

POSSESSIVE adjectives: my, your, his, her, our, their.

There are two other types of determiner: **relative determiners**, which take the same forms as relative pronouns:

whose, which, whichever, what, whatever;

and **indefinite determiners** such as:

a, an, any, all, each, few, half, many, more, most, much, several, some.

Determiners can also be classified as predeterminers, central determiners and postdeterminers.

A **predeterminer** appears before the determiner in a noun phrase:

all those people

half the population.

A **central determiner** follows a predeterminer and precedes a postdeterminer:

all *her* many virtues

the *next* few years.

The **postdeterminers** in the examples above are *many* and *few*.

determinism *see* SAPIR-WHORF HYPOTHESIS.

deverbal *(adj./n.)*

A word derived from, or modelled on, a verb. Nouns from verbs include:

boxer (box), utterance (utter), wreckage (wreck).

Adjectives from verbs include:

drowsy (drowse), passable (pass), prevalent (prevail)

deviant *(adj./n.)*

A general term for a linguistic unit that does not observe the norm established by other units of the same type.

A sentence without a verb, for example, deviates from the norm. *See also* NORMATIVE.

diachronic linguistics and synchronic linguistics

Diachronic linguistics is the study of the historic development of a language, its evolution through time, as distinct from **synchronic linguistics**, which is the study of the state of a language at any one time, past or present.

dialect *(n.)*

A way of speaking or writing that is particular to a specific geographical region or to a specific social class. Until the standardization of English vocabulary, grammar and spelling, a process that was under way by around the year 1450, all writing was in regional dialect form. The dominant East Midlands dialect, the language of London, Oxford and

Cambridge, and the language of Chaucer, became the basis of Modern English and the prototype of standard English.

Spoken **regional dialects** have existed since the beginning of the English language; the Anglo-Saxons who began to settle in England from around the year 450 spoke different dialects of West Germanic. Regional dialects survived the unification of England, and then of Britain, because groups of people who live in geographical or social isolation from each other develop differently. Distinctive regional dialects, that is, patterns of accent, vocabulary and grammar, will persist as long as there are regional speech communities and as long as succeeding generations of speakers acquire language in the regional family home.

The examples that follow show some of the varieties of vocabulary and grammar in British regional dialects.

> He's oop rek behint intek wi' tethera yows. (He's up the fell track behind the enclosure with three ewes.) Cumbrian

> Have youse drove all the way doon fae Inverness? (Have you [plural] driven all the way down from Inverness?) Scottish

> All de time she howlin' 'nough fe wake de dead. (All the time she was howling [loud] enough to wake the dead.) Afro-Caribbean English

A **social dialect**, also known as a SOCIOLECT, for example, the prestige form of spoken English, RECEIVED PRONUNCIATION, is a use of language that reflects the speaker's social background, social status, profession or occupation. A dialect may be both social and regional, for example, Midlands and working class, or Northumbrian and middle class.

dialect continuum

A process of gradual change from one dialect to another, or from one language to another, across a geographical area; also known as a **speech continuum**.

Dialects do not change abruptly at the line of the ISOGLOSS; the change is a continuous process, or continuum, within which speakers who live in proximity to each other use the same or a similar dialect. Two different languages may be modified so that they are mutually intelligible to speakers on either side of a national boundary.

dialectology *(n.)*

The study of DIALECTS. Dialectology covers the study of regional dialects, including urban and rural; it also covers social dialects and such factors as the social background, occupation, education, age and gender of the language user. *See also* SOCIOLECT.

diction *(n.)*

1 In written English and sometimes in spoken English, the choice of words from the wider vocabulary of the speaker or writer. The diction could then be defined more precisely, for example, as emotive diction, colloquial diction, scientific diction or formal diction, depending on the content. *See also* REGISTER (2).

2 The way in which a speaker enunciates his or her words. *See also* PRONUNCIATION.

dictionary *(n.)*

A reference book that explains the meanings of words of one or more languages, and may also indicate the words' pronunciations, spellings, word classes and etymologies. English/Latin and Latin/English dictionaries were published from the mid-fifteenth century, but the first English dictionary was Robert Cawdrey's *A Tale Alphabeticall* in 1604. Cawdrey's *Tale* contained fewer than 3,000 words; Samuel Johnson's *A Dictionary of the English Language* of 1755 contained around 40,000 words; a modern two-volume English dictionary will have over 500,000 definitions.

The best modern dictionaries are products of considerable scholarship and represent a vast accumulation of knowledge, but without the kind of idiosyncrasy that enlivens some of Johnson's entries:

> *penguin.* A bird. This bird was found with this name, as is supposed, by the first discoverers of America; and *penguin* signifying in Welsh a white head, it has been imagined, that America was peopled from Wales; whence Hudibras: *British Indians named from penguins.* Grew gives another account of the name, deriving it from *pinguis*, Lat. *fat*; but is, I believe, mistaken.

A dictionary is also known as a lexicon, the compiler as a lexicographer, and the task of compilation as lexicography.

difference theory *see* DEFICIT THEORY AND DIFFERENCE THEORY.

diffusion *(n.)*

The spread of a language, or a feature of a language, from a source to a different or wider area. Diffusion takes several forms. In the age of empires, imperial nations, notably Britain, France, Spain and Russia, imposed their national languages on the subject nations of their empires. Other nations, wilfully or not, exercise forms of economic and cultural imperialism that help to diffuse their languages. When the imperial language or dialect is regarded as a prestige form, then it may be willingly adopted by non-native speakers and thus further diffused. The dominance of the United States' entertainment and communications industries, along with the international presence of US tourists and, for a time, US military bases, helped to diffuse American English and even American accents to different parts of the world.

In British schools throughout much of the twentieth century there were conscious, systematic attempts to diffuse regional versions of the standard form of spoken English and to eliminate regional dialect from the classroom.

diglossia *(n.)*

The use of two different forms or dialects of a language; the use of two different languages for different social and professional purposes. Where two dialects are used, the forms are sometimes known as HIGH VARIETY AND LOW VARIETY. The high variety is usually taught in schools and universities and is the medium of education; it is also used in contexts that are socially or intellectually formal: law, national politics and national news media. The low form is used in informal contexts: the street, the workplace, folk publications and folk broadcasting. *See also* BIDIALECTAL; DEMOTIC.

digraph *(n.)*

1 Two letters of the alphabet representing a single sound.

    rou*gh*, *ph*antom; *qu*estion, s*ch*eme.

2 Two letters of the alphabet that are fused together; also known as a ligature. This second form of digraph disappeared from English during the twentieth century. Spellings such as *ægis* and *æsthetic* have been replaced by *aegis* and *aesthetic*. Changes in English spelling are very rare.

diminutive *(n./adj.)*

A suffix, or occasionally a word, indicating that a person or thing is of reduced status or size. English has several diminutive suffixes:

    -ie: laddie, lassie

    the slightly archaic -kin: bumpkin, manikin

    -let: booklet, hamlet

-ling: fledgling, seedling

-ock: hillock, paddock

-rel: mongrel, scoundrel

-y: mummy, daddy.

Some personal forenames have diminutive forms, usually to express affection or familiarity:

Betty, Liz and Lizzie for Elizabeth

Ted, Ed and Eddie for Edward.

Diminutives can be part of the language of childhood: *doggy*, *horsie*; they can also be part of the language of contempt: *princeling*, *wastrel*.

diphthong *(n.)*

A VOWEL that changes its sound within one syllable. Diphthongs can be represented by a single letter of the alphabet or by two. The /i/ in *high* and the /y/ in *sky* represent the diphthong /ai/; the same sound is represented by the /ie/ of *die* and the /ye/ of *dye*. The diphthong /au/ can be represented by /ou/ as in *house*, by /ow/ in *down* and by /au/ in words borrowed from German, for example, *Auslese* and *Frau*.

direct object and indirect object *see* OBJECT.

direct question *see* QUESTION.

direct speech and indirect speech

Direct speech consists of words actually uttered by a speaker. The speaker's words are normally punctuated by single or double inverted commas, also known as quotation marks, to indicate the difference between the quotation and the surrounding material:

A spokesman for the company said, 'We apologize for the pollution,' when he met reporters at the news conference.

Quotations from written texts can be punctuated in the same way.

Indirect speech, also known as **reported speech**, is a systematic, third-person account of what a speaker said. The process of editing direct speech into indirect speech is governed by a set of rules: (a) the account normally opens with, or includes, a reporting verb, that is, a verb that denotes speech:

said, stated, claimed;

(b) the speaker's words are usually expressed in a subordinate clause beginning with the word *that*; (c) the speaker's use of first and second person pronouns, *I*, *we* and *you*, is changed to third-person pronouns, *he*, *she* and *they*; (d) the tenses of verbs are back-shifted to show the time lapse between the actual speech and the later account:

present tense becomes past tense,

present continuous becomes past continuous

past tense and present perfect become past perfect

perfect continuous becomes past perfect continuous;

(e) words denoting immediacy of time or place:

here, now, today

are changed to words that denote distance:

there, then, that day.

This passage of direct speech is followed by a version in indirect speech:

The spokesman said, 'We apologize for the pollution of the river that occurred yesterday. As a company, we have always shown concern for the environment, and we have today taken action to clean up the river.'

The spokesman apologized for the pollution that had occurred the previous day. He said that, as a company, they had always shown concern for the environment, and he added that they had taken action that day to clean up the river.

Free indirect speech is a modified form of direct speech that is sometimes used in fiction and in feature articles in newspapers and magazines.

Free indirect speech, like indirect speech, applies back-shift to verbs, changes personal pronouns to third person and changes adverbials, demonstratives and other words denoting immediacy of time or place to words that denote distance. Free indirect speech differs from indirect speech by omitting the reporting verbs and the reporting clause *He said that* ... and by retaining the sentence structure of direct speech, including such features as questions, exclamations and vocative appeals.

This passage of direct speech is followed by a version in free indirect speech.

'This is one of my jogging nights. I go jogging three nights a week because I shall be taking part in the fun run next month. I may not be fully fit in time but I am determined to complete the course because my friends and colleagues have sponsored me, and the money will go to a local charity. Will you join me in the run?'

That was one of his jogging nights. He went jogging three nights a week because he would be taking part in the fun run in the following month. He might not be fully fit in time but he was determined to complete the course because his friends and colleagues had sponsored him, and the money would go to a local charity. Would they join him in the run?

The reporting verb and its subject, or the reporting verb and the noun phrases that identify the speaker and the occasion, are neither direct nor indirect speech; those words are the reporter's, not the speaker's:

Addressing the party conference at Blackpool, the Prime Minister said, ' ... '

A spokeswoman for the company said, ' ... '

See also INDIRECT QUESTION *under* QUESTION.

directive speech act *see* SPEECH ACT.

disambiguation *(n.)*
The removal of ambiguity from a clause or sentence; selecting the appropriate meaning from a clause or sentence that has two or more meanings.

The term is sometimes applied to the ambiguity that can arise from sentences containing -ING FORMS:

Racing pigeons are expensive

Racing pigeons is expensive.

Such ambiguities are said to be eliminated by TRANSFORMATIONS (2) between the DEEP STRUCTURE AND SURFACE STRUCTURE of language, and between the UNDERLYING STRUCTURE AND DERIVED STRUCTURE of a sentence.

discontinuity *(n.)*
1 Lack of cohesion or coherence in speech or writing. Discontinuity in speech can be caused by digressions, asides, and by long or frequent pauses. In writing, discontinuity can be the result of omissions, contradictions, digressions and obscurity.

2 More specifically, breaking a phrase by inserting one or more words, as in negative and interrogative constructions.

Do not go.

Will you help?

This type of discontinuity also appears in expletives like:

not bloody likely

too damned clever.

discourse *(n.)*

1 A formal discussion in speech or writing of a serious topic; a dissertation or treatise.

2 More recently, and in contrast to (1), a spoken statement or statements of two or more sentences in length.

See also DISCOURSE ANALYSIS.

discourse analysis

Identifying and interpreting the linguistic features of a speech or dialogue. Discourse analysis takes account of the structure as well as the content, and takes account of the meaning that is implicit in the manner in which the discourse is delivered as well as the meaning of the words used by the speakers. Analysis of a conversation would note the words used to initiate the conversation, the taking of turns by different speakers, expressions of agreement or disagreement, hesitations, digressions and the form of words used to bring the discourse to an end.

See also CONTENT ANALYSIS.

disjunct *(n.)*

An adverbial or ADJUNCT that is usually placed at the beginning of a sentence and whose SCOPE covers the entire clause or sentence in which it appears; an alternative term for **sentence adverbial**.

> *At the weekend*, he mowed the lawn, visited friends, wrote a report for his employer and read the Sunday newspapers.

Disjuncts are often used to indicate the attitude of the writer or speaker to the reader or listener, or the attitude to the topic being discussed.

> *In strict confidence*, I can tell you he has resigned.

> *Inevitably*, he arrived late.

disjunctive *(adj./n.)*

1 A phrase, clause, sentence or sentences that express alternative or opposing ideas, usually by means of the conjunctions *or* and *either … or*.

> We can go by car or by train.

The disjunction is the contrast between the two phrases *by car* and *by train*. In this second example:

> Either we get out and walk or we just sit here in the car

the disjunction is the contrast between the first two clauses *Either we get out and [we] walk* and the third clause *or we just sit here in the car*.

2 A sentence that conveys two types, or levels, of information, one of which is a contrasting or adverse comment on the other. The contrast is normally made by using an adverb, adverbial phrase or adverbial clause:

> *As you well know*, I've a feverish cold.

> *Even so*, we must decide.

> *Alternatively*, I'll go for help while you wait here.

The adverbial element, which is usually placed at the beginning of the disjunctive, is sometimes known as a **sentence adverbial** because it comments on the whole sentence.

3 Some linguists state that all sentence adverbials have a disjunctive function, even when they do not express opposition.

> *All things considered*, that's the best option.

> *Actually*, I agree.

displacement *(n.)*

The property of language that frees it from its immediate context in place or time. Language can refer to places and times that are remote from those in which the language user speaks or writes the words. Displacement occurs more often in writing than in speech. At this moment, for example, students of English throughout the world are writing about Shakespeare's *Hamlet*.

dissonance *(n.)*

The use of jarring, harsh-sounding words or syllables in a sequence of writing or speech, either to echo actual sounds or to express disturbing incidents or ideas.

> He gashed his right arm and shattered the bone when he plunged over the edge onto the jagged rock.

See also CACOPHONY; ONOMATOPOEIA.

distal *(adj.)*

An alternative term for remote. *See* PROXIMATE AND REMOTE.

distinctive feature

A particular phonological quality that distinguishes one speech sound from another.

> What distinguishes the plosive consonants /g/ and /k/, as in *goal* and *koala*, is that /g/ is voiced and /k/ is unvoiced, that is, /g/ is pronounced by a vibration of the vocal cords but /k/ is not.

distribution *(n.)*

The set of linguistic contexts in which a particular linguistic unit can occur. The frequency of occurrence of a particular unit, for example, a PHONEME in a word or a phrase, or a word in a sentence or paragraph, can be noted by counting the number of occurrences, a process known as **distribution analysis**.

There are limits to the distribution of linguistic units. For example, English words can begin with the consonantal clusters /gh/ (ghastly), /gl/ (glass) and /gn/ (gnat) but not */gm/. MODAL AUXILIARY VERBS cannot function alone but must be followed by main verbs, except in elliptical constructions. *See also* COLLOCATION (2); LEAST EFFORT PRINCIPLE; SEMANTIC RESTRICTION.

distribution analysis *see* DISTRIBUTION.

distributive *(adj./n.)*

A word or phrase that refers to each member of a group or class individually rather than collectively. The distributive:

Each of you/Every one of you should have a ticket

contrasts with the collective:

Everyone should have a ticket.

distributive adjective

The adjectives *each*, *all*, *any* and *every*, and the words *either* and *neither* when used as adjectives.

Each applicant was interviewed.

You can have *any* item; *all* goods are for sale.

disyllable *see* MONOSYLLABLE AND POLYSYLLABLE.

ditransitive *see* TRANSITIVE VERB AND INTRANSITIVE VERB.

divergence *(n.)*

A process in which a language or a dialect evolves in two or more forms; sometimes contrasted with CONVERGENCE. French, Italian, Spanish, Portuguese and Romanian, for example, have diverged from the same parent language, LATIN. Some spellings in American English have diverged from British English spellings, and the pronunciation of American English, and Australian and Indian English, diverges from British English pronunciation.

Divergence occurs when speech communities develop separately. The process may also be the result of LANGUAGE PLANNING, that is, a deliberate cultural or political decision. When Norway gained independence in 1905, the country deliberately promoted divergence between Norwegian and the languages of its former rulers, Denmark and Sweden. Afro-Caribbean English in London is part of the divergent cultural identity of its speakers.

domain *(n.)*
The context in which a particular topic, or a particular word or phrase, is dominant.

An impassioned political speech at an annual party conference could be the domain of EMOTIVE LANGUAGE. The domain of voice of verbs would be a discussion, with examples, of the ACTIVE VOICE AND PASSIVE VOICE of verbs. The domain of DIFFUSION would be a discussion, again with examples, of the spread of a language or features of a language.

The range of key words in a given domain is known as REGISTER (2) or diction. In the emotive diction of the political speech, key words could be *freedom*, *loyalty*, *patriotism*, *progress* and *prosperity*.

dominance *see* LANGUAGE DOMINANCE.

double articulation *see* DUALITY OF STRUCTURE.

double comparative
The use of the comparative inflection *-er* and the comparative quantifier *more* with the same adjective or adverb.

> more easier, more happier, more noisier

Double comparison is acceptable in the folk grammar of some dialects but not in standard English. *See also* DOUBLE SUPERLATIVE.

double genitive
The use of an of-genitive, or POSSESSIVE, and a possessive noun or pronoun in the same construction.

> a painting of Turner's, one of his landscapes

double negative
A phrase or clause in which negation is expressed twice.

> They did not give him nothing.

Standard English expresses negation only once:

They did not give him anything

or

They gave him nothing.

The double negative was a standard construction in English from Anglo-Saxon to Shakespearean times, and the entry on CHANGE in English language in this Dictionary shows that Old English used multiple negatives. Double negation is still acceptable in folk grammar but is not regarded as being acceptable in current standard English. *See also* USAGE.

double passive

A clause or sentence that uses two verbs in the passive voice to denote one extended action or two linked actions.

She was advised to be inoculated before going to Africa.

The building was expected to have been completed last month.

See also ACTIVE VOICE AND PASSIVE VOICE.

double superlative

The use of the superlative inflection -*est* and the superlative quantifier *most* with the same adjective or adverb.

most loveliest, most ugliest.

Double superlatives, like DOUBLE COMPARATIVES and DOUBLE NEGA-TIVES, are acceptable in the folk grammar of some dialects.

doublet *(n.)*

Two words that have a common origin and a similarity of form and meaning. Doublets occur mainly because of the borrowing of foreign words. Sometimes an existing English word was duplicated:

ward (English), guard (French);

wise (English, as in *likewise*), guise (French).

Sometimes two or more versions of a foreign word entered English, for example, the French borrowings:

hotel, hostel, hostelry

penance, penitence

and *receipt* from French and *recipe* from Latin. *See also* PARONYM.

dual (*n./adj.*)

A linguistic form that denotes two, as distinct from singular or plural number. Some languages are inflected to show duality. In English duality is expressed by several words:

> dual, duality, duo, duplex, double, doublet, deuce, couple, couplet, pair, brace, twin, two

and by the prefixes:

> *ambi*lingual, *bi*lingual, *di*phthong.

duality of structure

The organization, or structuring, of language at two levels simultaneously. At the phonological level speech is a sequence of sounds; at the semantic level the same sequence of sounds expresses meaning. Although duality of structure is usually considered to be a feature of spoken language, the term can also be applied to writing, where words are simultaneously sequences of morphological forms and of meanings.

dummy (*n.*)

The colloquial term for a word that adds little or no meaning to a sentence and performs a minimal grammatical function. The words *It* and *There* are dummy subjects in sentences such as:

> *It* is time to go.

> *There* is a telephone call for you.

It and *There* are the grammatical subjects but they offer no real information. *See also* PROP.

dummy operator

The verb *do* when it is used as an auxiliary verb.

> *Does* he have a ticket?

> He *didn't* know he needed one.

Although the term 'dummy' is applied to the verb *do* in constructions like these, the verb has a significant grammatical function: *Does* indicates interrogation, and *didn't* indicates negation. *See also* OPERATOR.

durative verb and punctual verb

A **durative verb** form is one that expresses duration, that is, action over a period of time.

> Jake *was reading* a magazine while Anna *was listening* to music.

A **punctual verb** is one that expresses instantaneous or brief action.

> He *stopped* the car and *switched off* the engine.

See also ASPECT; DYNAMIC VERB AND STATIVE VERB; INSTANTANEOUS VERB.

dyad *(n.)*

Two people engaged in face-to-face communication. The term implies the reciprocal nature of such an encounter and assumes that the dyad will use NON-VERBAL COMMUNICATION as well as speech. A dyad could be a consultant and a client, a lecturer and a student, or domestic partners. *See also* DISCOURSE ANALYSIS.

dynamic verb and stative verb

A **dynamic verb** is one that denotes action, change or sensation.

> The gardeners *perspired* as they *mowed* the lawns and *trimmed* the hedges.

A **stative verb**, also known as a state or static verb, is one that denotes a state or condition.

> The head gardener, who *has held* the post for ten years, *knows* the job thoroughly and *has* pride in his craft.

dyslexia *(n.)*

An inability to read, usually because the person has failed to learn to read. The condition is regarded as a learning disability that can be overcome by special tuition. Dyslexia in children or in adults is sometimes known as specific developmental dyslexia in order to distinguish it from ALEXIA.

dysphemism *(n.)*

The use of an offensive term instead of a neutral or favourable one.

> brats/children, cow/woman, pig/policeman.

See also BAHUVRIHI; EUPHEMISM.

e

echo *(n.)*

1 The repetition of two or more letters of the alphabet in order to create an echoic effect.

In this general sense, the word 'echo' can be applied to the phonological devices of ALLITERATION, ASSONANCE, CACOPHONY, CONSONANCE, DISSONANCE, ONOMATOPOEIA and PHONAESTHESIA.

2 More precisely, a word whose sound reproduces, or partly reproduces, the sound that the word denotes; also known as an **echoic word**, which is another term for ONOMATOPOEIA.

echo question

A QUESTION that repeats all or part of a statement. The statement:

> I've just seen a traffic warden talking to a parking meter

could prompt the full echo question:

> You've just seen a traffic warden talking to a parking meter?

or a partial echo:

> You've just seen a traffic warden do what?

An echo question is seldom a request for information; it is more likely to be an expression of incredulity or PHATIC COMMUNICATION that sustains the conversation and the relationship between the speakers.

echoic word

An alternative term for ECHO (2).

-ed form

The colloquial, widely used term for the simple past tense form and the **past participle** form of a regular verb.

All regular verbs have the *-ed* form for the simple past and the past participle:

> arrived, has arrived; listened, has listened.

The occasional application of the term to irregular verbs, for example:

> gave, has given; swam, has swum,

can be misleading.

egocentric speech

Speech that is not intended for a listener; speech in which the speaker communicates with himself or herself.

Although the term is usually applied to the speech of young children, egocentric speech is also normal, but usually socially unacceptable, behaviour in adults. *See also* APOSTROPHE (3); INNER SPEECH.

eidetic imagery
A particularly vivid form of visual IMAGERY.

elaborated code and restricted code
Formal and informal uses of language. The terms were coined by the British sociologist Basil Bernstein (b.1924), who argued that modes of communication can be affected by family and social background.

Features of the **elaborated code** are that is not bound by immediate circumstances but makes some use of displacement; it includes third person or impersonal narrative standpoints as well as first and second person; it has a wider range of references and is more explicit and complex than the restricted code.

The **restricted code** assumes a common body of experience and a common set of expectations; it is more context-bound, less complex and less firmly structured that the elaborated code.

Bernstein argues that, in general, middle-class children can use both codes but working-class children tend to use only the restricted code. Neither code is a measure of intelligence. *See also* DEFICIT THEORY AND DIFFERENCE THEORY.

elision *(n.)*
The omission of sounds in the pronunciation of words. Even in formal speech it is normal to say:

> He as't a diff'rent, more int'resting, question on We'n'sday

for

> He asked a different, more interesting, question on Wednesday.

Many elisions are acceptable and understandable, partly because the linguistic unit in spoken English is not the single word but the word cluster, in which words are fused together.

ellipsis *(n.)*
1 Omitting one or more words from a sentence, mainly in spoken English, and usually without obscuring the meaning of the sentence. For example, in reply to the question:

> What will you have? Tea or coffee?

the elliptic, one-word answer *Tea* or *Coffee* is a normal response.

2 The omission of one or more sentences or paragraphs from a written text. Such an omission, or abridgement, can be indicated by the punctuation mark of three full stops, [...], which is also known as an ellipsis.

3 A literary device in poetry and prose that highlights imagery and incident by simplifying syntax:

> The roar of the engines. The whine, the high-pitched whine. The feeling of being pushed back into the seat. Below ... like matchboxes and matchstick people.

embedding *(n./v.)*

The inclusion of one linguistic unit, normally a phrase or a clause, within another unit.

> He worked, despite his illness, until midnight.

The phrase *despite his illness* is embedded in the sentence. In this example:

> Cradle Bay, which was once a busy fishing port, now depends on tourism

the subordinate relative clause *which was once a busy fishing port* is embedded in the main clause *Cradle Bay now depends on tourism*.

A sentence containing an embedded clause is sometimes known as a **matrix sentence**, from Latin *matrix*, meaning womb or the breeding stem of plants.

emotive language

Speech or writing that arouses emotion in the listener or reader. Emotive language is often an expression of opinion rather than fact, and the key words are used for their connotations rather than denotations. Various forms of emotive language are used deliberately in tabloid newspaper headlines, political speeches, advertising copywriting and in poetry, fiction and drama.

The term 'emotive language' is sometimes used as an alternative for **affective language** or **expressive language**, but distinctions can be drawn. Affective language, which indicates a writer's or speaker's emotion or mood, and expressive language, which indicates attitude or emotion, can be used without trying to arouse the emotions or attitudes in the reader or listener. The use of emotive language, by contrast, is usually a deliberate attempt to arouse emotion.

References to emotion are not necessarily emotive. The two statements:

> I know that he is jealous
>
> He suffers from acute anxiety

are denotative, referring to the emotions rather than arousing them. These following two statements, by contrast, are emotive:

He is childishly, pathetically, jealous, the fool

That cowardly, quivering idiot says he suffers from acute anxiety.

emphasis *(n.)*

Additional stress that indicates an important point in speech or writing.

Emphasis in speech is achieved by increased loudness and deliberate enunciation. Equivalent emphasis in writing can be achieved by increasing the size and density of the type face. There are also several grammatical constructions for creating emphasis in writing:

the cleft sentence: *It was Bill* who did the driving

the cleft sentence and a negative: It was Bill, *not Wendy*, who did the driving

the cleft sentence with a reflexive pronoun: It was Bill *himself* who did the driving.

Other constructions are the use of the IMPERATIVE mood of a verb rather than the INDICATIVE mood:

Sit down

rather than:

I'd like you to sit down.

The use of *do* as an auxiliary verb can add emphasis:

She *does* talk a great deal.

Emphasis can be achieved by front focus, that is, focusing attention on a word, phrase or clause at the beginning of a sentence:

Talkative is how I should describe her.

Emphasis can also be achieved by end focus, that is, creating a deliberate delay by placing a key word or a key phrase at the end of a sentence:

Eventually, after driving around for an hour, *we found the house*.

See also END FOCUS AND FRONT FOCUS.

emphatic pronoun

A pronoun compounded with the word *self* or *selves*. The emphatic reflexive pronouns are:

myself, yourself, himself, herself, itself, ourselves, yourselves, themselves.

enclitic and proclitic *(adj./n.)*

An **enclitic** word or syllable is one that is so unaccented that it is pronounced as if it were part of the preceding word. The word *at* in *not at all*, *of* in *a stroke of luck* and *and* in *over and out* are enclitic.

A **proclitic** word or syllable is one that is so unaccented that it is pronounced as if it were part of the following word. The article *an* in *an average score*, the *in* of *in America* and the prefix *un-* in *unimaginable* are proclitic. *See also* ASSIMILATION; ELISION.

encode *see* CODE.

end focus and front focus

End focus is the placing of new information at the end of a sentence in order to focus the reader's attention on that information.

> The department offered the scholarship *to Harriet Stark.*

> When Harriet heard the news *she telephoned her parents.*

End focus, also known as **end weight**, is the usual way of structuring information in a sentence.

Front focus gives prominence to material at or near the beginning of a sentence. Because the normal sentence-order is subject + verb + object + complement + adverbial, any sentence that begins with a component other than the subject will achieve front focus. For example, the subject + verb + object order of:

> He stacked the shelves quickly

can be changed to a front focus sentence:

> Quickly, he stacked the shelves (adverbial)

or

> The shelves he stacked quickly (object)

See also EMPHASIS.

end weight

An alternative term for end focus. *See* END FOCUS AND FRONT FOCUS.

endocentric and exocentric *(adj./n.)*

An **endocentric** phrase or clause is based, or centred, on a headword in such a way that the phrase has the same function as the headword.

> The overworked, underpaid security officer resigned last week.

The subject is the noun phrase *The overworked, underpaid security officer,* and the headword in the phrase is *officer.* If the phrase were reduced to the headword and the definite article *The officer,* that, too, would function as the subject of the sentence.

An **exocentric** construction is one that is not centred on a headword. In this example:

Harriet Stark telephoned her parents

each part of the sentence – the subject, *Harriet Stark*, the verb, *tele-phoned*, and the object, *her parents* – is of equal importance. The noun *parents* is the headword in the noun phrase *her parents*, but, because there is no single centre to the sentence, the construction is exocentric.

endoglossic and exoglossic *(adj./n.)*

A language is **endoglossic** when it is the NATIVE LANGUAGE of a country or region in which it is used. French, for example, is endoglossic in Quebec.

A language is **exoglossic** when it is not the native, or indigenous, language of the country or region in which it is used. Urdu and Hindi are exoglossic in Britain. *See also* NATIONAL LANGUAGE.

endophasia *(n.)*

An alternative term for INNER SPEECH.

endophora and exophora *(n.)*

An **endophora**, or endophoric reference, is a reference within a text that gives the text cohesion and continuity. An endophoric reference can be an ANAPHORA, that is, a reference to a person or thing appearing earlier in a text, or it can be a CATAPHORA, a reference to a person or thing appearing later in the text.

An **exophora**, or exophoric reference, depends for part of its meaning on an extralinguistic factor. For example, an article in a specialist journal on cricket might name some players without identifying them as batsmen or bowlers, leaving the reader to supply the extraneous information, or exophoric reference.

-en form

A term sometimes used for the past participle form of some irregular verbs.

broken, chosen, forgotten, frozen.

The term can also be applied to participial adjectives and to nouns that have the same form as the verbs:

forbidden fruit, *stolen* goods (adjectives)

the *chosen*, the *fallen* (nouns).

English language

English, the most widely spoken language in the world, began as the West Germanic dialects of the Angles, Saxons and Jutes who settled in England and southern Scotland from around the year 450. The Old English language of the Anglo-Saxons survived the impact of the invading Scandinavians, whose language, Old Norse, was largely displaced by English. The Old English period of the English language, from around the year 750 to around 1100, ended when French, the language of the Norman invaders in 1066, became the official language of England. But English remained the majority language, and this fact, along with the Normans' increasing isolation from mainland France, gradually undermined French until, in 1362, Edward III opened the English parliament with a speech in English.

The English of Edward III had been so greatly influenced by French that it was a Franco-Germanic language rather than a purely Germanic one. Latin, too, exerted an influence. It was the language of the church until the Reformation, and in post-Reformation England and Scotland, Latin was for a time as important as English in most fields of scholarship. By the end of the Middle English period, around 1450, almost all the inflections had disappeared from nouns, adjectives and verbs, and some inflections had disappeared from pronouns. Relationships between nouns, pronouns, verbs and prepositions were expressed not by inflections but by a word order that began to resemble the syntax of Modern English.

In the modern period, some of the main developments have been the steady growth in the size of the lexicon accompanied by an increasing precision in etymology; the standardization of spelling; the partial standardization of syntax and punctuation; and the emergence of English as an international language.

English became a world language because imperial Britain took the language to all parts of the British Empire. And when the Empire was at an end, effectively in 1945, English was the first language of North America, Australia and New Zealand, and the second language or LINGUA FRANCA of the Indian subcontinent and several countries in Africa. The continuing diffusion of English since 1945 has been a result of United States' supremacy as a military and economic power, and in the communications and entertainment industries. *See also* CHANGE.

engram *see* LOGOGEN.

entailment *(n.)*

A semantic relationship between two PROPOSITIONS such that, if the first proposition is true, then the second proposition must also be true; a fact that is a necessary consequence of another.

The statement:

> He has a wife and children

entails

> He is married and is a father.

See also CONTINGENCY AND NECESSITY.

epicene *(adj./n.)*

A noun that can refer to either sex.

> dentist, professor, victim

Originally, in Greek and Latin grammar, a noun that could refer to either sex without changing its grammatical gender.

epistemic and deontic *(adj./n.)*

An **epistemic** construction is a phrase, clause or sentence containing a MODAL AUXILIARY VERB and expressing inferred knowledge or assumption, in contrast to a **deontic** construction, which expresses duty or obligation. The sentence:

> He ought to arrive on time

can be epistemic, with the meaning:

> I assume he will arrive on time

or

> It is likely that he will arrive on time.

But the same sentence can be deontic, meaning:

> He is morally obliged to arrive on time

or

> It is his duty to arrive on time.

epithet *(n.)*

1 A word or a phrase, usually an ADJECTIVE or adjective phrase, that expresses a quality or attribute of a noun.

> free-range eggs, organic farming.

2 The recurring use of a particular word or phrase to describe a person or thing.

> Alfred the Great, a desirable residence, a gripping thriller.

eponym *(n.)*

A type of WORD FORMATION by which a place or thing is named after a person.

> Mackenzie Mountain, Kalashnikov rifle, Victorian furniture.

Some eponyms are assimilated into the language as common nouns:

> becquerel, magnolia, watt

or as common adjectives:

> diesel fuel, geiger counter.

Other eponyms remain proper nouns and adjectives:

> Beaufort scale, Richter scale.

equivalence *(n.)*

The relationship between two linguistic units with the same or a similar meaning. Equivalence exists between a pronoun and its antecedent noun, between noun phrases in apposition to each other, between synonyms, between the coordinates in similes, and in some forms of comparison:

> She is as intelligent as I am.

ergative *(adj./n.)*

A verb that can be used transitively, that is, with a direct object, or intransitively, that is, without an object, particularly when the object of the verb in its transitive function becomes the subject of the verb in its intransitive function. In the sentence:

> Gunfire scattered the crowd

the crowd is the direct object of the TRANSITIVE VERB *scattered*. But in the sentence:

> The crowd scattered

The crowd is the subject and *scattered* is intransitive.

error *(n.)*

A fault in speech or writing, especially by someone who is learning a language.

In linguistics a distinction is made between the patterned nature of errors and the more random aberration of mistakes. Errors are regarded as features of the language user's competence and suggest that the speaker or writer misunderstands the rules of the language. For example, speakers whose second language is English sometimes say:

> I would to go with you

for

> I would go with you.

Such an error is a grammatical error; an error in pronunciation can be defined as a phonological error.

The study of a person's errors, sometimes known as error analysis, can help the person to understand the rules and may also help the linguist to understand the processes involved in learning a second language. *See also* COMPETENCE AND PERFORMANCE.

etymology *(n.)*
The study of the formation and development of words and their meanings; the history of words and their meanings.

The etymological fallacy is the mistaken belief that an earlier meaning of a word is more valid, more 'correct', than a later meaning; for example, that the original Latin meaning of *sinister* (left hand, left side) is somehow better than the current meanings of *sinister* (adverse, corrupt, inauspicious). The belief is mistaken because, as a living language evolves, so the meanings of words inevitably change; mistaken, too, because the origin of language, and thus the original meanings of words, is not known.

euphemism *(n.)*
A form of words that is milder or more pleasant, but less precise, than what is thought to be a harsher expression. The word *died* has many euphemisms, including *departed, passed away, passed to the other side, gone to meet one's maker.*

Euphemism is a way of avoiding taboo subjects and taboo words, or subjects that were once taboo, like sexual activity, excretion, some forms of illness and death. Euphemism is sometimes contrasted with SLANG.

exclamation *(n.)*
1 A word or phrase, usually punctuated with an exclamation mark, that expresses sudden or intense feeling.

> How stupid! What a farce!

2 A phatic, or social, utterance, with or without an exclamation mark.

> How wonderful to see you!
>
> What a pity.

exclamation mark *see* PUNCTUATION.

exclamatory question *see* QUESTION.

exclamatory sentence

A sentence, often beginning with the word *How* or *What*, that expresses sudden or intense feeling.

> How disgusting you are!

> What fools we were to trust you.

An exclamatory sentence can take the form of a question that can be punctuated with a question mark or an exclamation mark:

> Isn't this an outrage?

> Who asked your opinion!

exclusive *see* INCLUSIVE AND EXCLUSIVE.

existential *(adj./n.)*

A statement that implies or questions the existence of a set of circumstances. One type of existential sentence uses the word *there* and the verb *be*:

> There was an accident here last week.

> Were there many casualties?

In another type of existential sentence the subject precedes the verb *have*:

> A driver had his arm broken.

> He still has his arm in plaster.

exocentric *see* ENDOCENTRIC AND EXOCENTRIC.

exoglossic *see* ENDOGLOSSIC AND EXOGLOSSIC.

exophora *see* ENDOPHORA AND EXOPHORA.

expansion *(n.)*

1 Increasing the length of an expression, for example, from a word to a phrase, while keeping the same grammatical function.

> Demonstrators assembled in the park.

The noun *Demonstrators* is the subject of the sentence above. When the noun is expanded to a noun phrase:

> *Noisy but good-humoured demonstrators* assembled in the park

the expansion remains the subject of the sentence. *See also* RECURSION.

2 A term used for parents' attempts to extend or correct a young child's vocabulary or grammar. In response to a child's statement *I goed shop* a parent might offer the expansion *We went to the shops*. Such attempts at expansion and correction are seldom effective because young children acquire language at a pace determined by the size and structure of their brains.

expressive language
Language that reveals a writer's or speaker's attitude or emotion; also known as **affective language**. The term 'expressive language' is sometimes used as an alternative for EMOTIVE LANGUAGE, but the two are not always interchangeable; emotive language often means the arousal of emotion in the listener or reader.

expressive meaning
An alternative term for affective meaning. *See* MEANING.

expressive speech act *see* SPEECH ACT.

extension *(n.)*
1 An increase in the scope, or extent, of a word's meaning.
   Words for parts of the body – arm, foot, hand, head, neck, nose, spine – have gained many additional, mainly metaphorical, meanings over the centuries.

2 The range of things or persons to which a word can refer. Tree, for example, covers a range from alder, ash and aspen to whitebeam, willow and yew.

extensive *see* INTENSIVE AND EXTENSIVE.

external evidence *see* INTERNAL EVIDENCE AND EXTERNAL EVIDENCE.

extralinguistic *(adj.)*
1 Generally, things that are not linguistic; everything but language itself.

2 More precisely, the NON-VERBAL COMMUNICATION that accompanies speech, for example, facial expressions and gestures.

extraposition *(n.)*

A form of POSTPONEMENT in which the subject is said to be placed out of position, or extraposed, at the end of the sentence and a substitute subject placed at the beginning of the sentence; a form of postponement in which the subject of the sentence appears after a substitute subject.

> It would appear that you have won the contest.

It is the substitute, or anticipatory, subject and *you have won the contest* the extraposed subject. In fact, this form of extraposition is the norm in such sentences, although the sentence above could be written as:

> You have won the contest, it would appear.

The objects of sentences can also be extraposed:

> Don't you find it too quiet living here?

It is the substitute object and *living here* is the extraposed object. The sentence is still acceptable when it is written as:

> Don't you find living here too quiet?

extrinsic *see* INHERENT.

f

factitive *(adj./n.)*

A transitive verb that expresses the idea of creating a new quality in its direct object; a transitive verb that acts on its direct object in such a way that the object is transformed.

> He composed two melodies and arranged them for string orchestra.

In the sentence above, the factitive verbs are *composed* and *arranged*; the direct objects of the verbs are *two melodies* and *them*. Some linguists apply the term 'factitive case' to the noun phrases that are the objects of factitive verbs, that is, things that are created or transformed.

factive *(adj./n.)*

A verb that has as its object some form of knowledge, assumption or supposition.

> We *know* you took the car, and we *understand* why you did it.

factual knowledge *see* KNOWLEDGE.

factual meaning
An alternative term for denotative, referential meaning. *See* MEANING.

fall/falling *see* INTONATION; PITCH (1); TONE.

false cognate
A word that is identical or similar in form to a word in another language but is different in meaning; also known as a false friend.

> French: *singe* (monkey, ape), *trouble* (cloudy, confused)
>
> Gaelic: *beach* (bee), *canal* (cinnamon)
>
> Italian: *concussione* (extortion), *delusione* (disappointment)

See also COGNATE (2).

family of languages
A group of languages that have evolved from the same parent language. European languages and the languages of the Indian subcontinent and Iran are descended from INDO-EUROPEAN. These languages can be subdivided into families; for example, English, German, Dutch, Flemish, Swedish, Danish, Norwegian and Icelandic are all members of the Germanic family of languages. Gaelic, Irish, Welsh and Breton are members of the Celtic family. *See also* COGNATE (1).

feminine *see* GENDER.

figurative language
Language that contains figures of speech, that is, linguistic devices that are designed to make the spoken or written word more vivid or succinct and thus more memorable.

Some figures of speech compare two or more factors: METAPHOR, PERSONIFICATION, SIMILE; some suggest opposition: ANTICLIMAX, ANTITHESIS, CHIASMUS; some create tension or pace: ANACOLUTHON, APOSIOPESIS, ASYNDETON; and some figures of speech create sound effects: ALLITERATION, ASSONANCE, CONSONANCE, ONOMATOPOEIA.

figurative meaning *see* LINGUISTIC MEANING *under* MEANING.

filled pause *see* PAUSE.

final *see* INITIAL, MEDIAL AND FINAL.

final cluster *see* CONSONANT CLUSTER.

finite and non-finite forms of verbs

A **finite** VERB is one that expresses tense, mood and number, and is usually preceded by a subject.

In *She loves*, *She* is the subject; the form of the verb *loves* is present tense, indicative, or declarative, in mood, and singular in number. The term 'finite' can be applied to the CLAUSE in which the finite verb appears.

Non-finite forms of verbs do not express tense, mood or number, and need not be preceded by a subject. The four non-finite verb forms are:

the *to* infinitive: to love

the bare infinitive: love

the participial -ING FORM: loving

the participial -ED FORM: loved.

The term 'non-finite' can also be applied to the clause in which the non-finite verb appears.

first language

The earliest, or first, language a speaker acquires; a person's NATIVE LANGUAGE or mother tongue.

first person *see* PERSON.

fixed expression

An invariable form of words. Fixed expressions, which are also known as **fixed phrases** and **set expressions**, include collocations, clichés, maxims, quotations and proverbs.

Bag and baggage.

Like a bolt from the blue.

We'll cross that bridge when we come to it.

fixed phrase

An alternative term for FIXED EXPRESSION.

focus *(n./v.)*

1 The part of a sentence that offers new information; the focal point of a sentence in terms of its information content. By this definition, focus is

similar to new in GIVEN INFORMATION AND NEW INFORMATION, to rheme in THEME AND RHEME, and to comment in TOPIC AND COMMENT.

2 Words to which a speaker or writer particularly wishes to direct the attention of the reader. By this definition, focus is similar to EMPHASIS. *See also* END FOCUS AND FRONT FOCUS.

foreign plurals

Words that keep the plural forms of the languages from which they are borrowed or derived. The spellings of some foreign plurals are fixed. For example, the Greek *-is* singular ending takes the plural form, *-es*:

analysis/analyses, basis/bases.

The French *-eau* singular ending usually takes the plural form *-eaux:*

bureau/bureaux, gateau/gateaux.

Some plurals can appear either in the foreign form or an anglicized form:

maximum/maximums/maxima, appendix/appendixes/appendices.

A few foreign plurals have come to be used as collective nouns and are mistakenly thought to be singular forms:

data, media (plural); datum, medium (singular) criteria, phenomena (plural); criterion, phenomenon (singular).

form *(n.)*

1 The shape, spelling or inflection of a word. Regular verbs, for example, have four forms, the base form and three inflected forms:

walk, walks, walking, walked.

Some spellings have two forms:

dreamed/dreamt, spelled/spelt.

2 The shape and structure of a linguistic unit as distinct from its meaning. A sentence can be analysed as a syntactic structure without reference to the meanings of the words in the sentence.

3 The physical expression of a language as a writing system, its written form, or as a phonetic system, its spoken form.

form word

An alternative term for function word. *See* CONTENT WORD AND FUNCTION WORD.

formal grammar *see* FORMALIZE; GRAMMAR.

formal language and informal language

Formal language is speech or writing that observes agreed standards of linguistic and social acceptability and CORRECTNESS. In formal written English, sentences and paragraphs are firmly structured, sentences observe the norms of word order and grammar, vocabulary consists of standard rather than non-standard words, and all spellings used are standard.

Formal spoken English observes some of the norms of formal written English; in addition, enunciation is precise, and an attempt may be made at RECEIVED PRONUNCIATION (RP) or a regional version of RP. The tone of the language will sometimes be impersonal and will usually be conventionally courteous.

Informal language is less regulated and more casual than formal language. Informal speech and writing are frequently loosely structured and sometimes ignore the norms of grammar. Unlike formal language, informal language can include colloquial, slang and regional expressions, and it can be expressed in a variety of tones: jocular, bawdy or intimate.

The word 'formal' can also be applied to a system of grammar that has been FORMALIZED. *See also* NORMATIVE; STANDARD AND NON-STANDARD ENGLISH.

formalize *(v.)*

Systematically and precisely to formulate the RULES of GRAMMAR and to specify the modes of operation of the rules.

A fully formalized system, or theory, of grammar can offer a logical, sometimes a formulaic, account of the rules of syntax of a language, and some account of the morphological and phonological rules. Formalized grammar is sometimes contrasted with notional grammar.

formula *(n.)*

1 A conventional form of words, especially to express social contact or a specific social occasion.

> Get well soon.

> Please call again.

> I name this ship *Ajax*.

2 An alternative term for RULE. For example, the rewrite rule

> a sentence consists of a noun phrase and a verb phrase

can be written as the formula

$$S \rightarrow NP\ VP.$$

fossil *(n.)*
An unproductive and archaismic form of words, that is, a form of words that cannot be used to produce new expressions of the same type, and is archaic in style although still in use.

> This bodes ill/well.
>
> The gale wreaked havoc.
>
> Please charge your glasses and be upstanding.

Fossils are also known as fossilized expressions.

free form
The smallest grammatical or linguistic unit that can function as a word; an irreducible lexical item. The word *small*, for example, is a free form but *smallest* is not because it can be reduced to *small* and *-est*. Similarly, *grammar* is a free form but *grammatical* is not because it can be reduced to *gramma[r] + -ic + -al*. Free forms are also known as free MORPHEMES.

free indirect speech *see* DIRECT SPEECH AND INDIRECT SPEECH.

free morpheme *see* MORPHEME.

free variation
The substitution of one PHONEME for another without changing the meaning or spelling of the word in which the substitution is possible. When a word has two acceptable pronunciations, the optional phoneme is the free variation. The word *ate*, for example, can be pronounced *et* as in *met* or *eit* as in *mate*; the free variation is /e/ or /ei/.

French *(n./adj.)*
French was the official language of England for almost three centuries, from the year of the Conquest until 1362, when Edward III opened Parliament with a speech in English. French was never the majority language in England, but it changed English SPELLING and pronunciation and had a major influence on vocabulary, especially in the period between 1250 and 1400.

The influence lies not only in the total number of French words that were borrowed but also in those aspects of life denoted by the words.

French, or rather, the language that once was French but has long been anglicized, is the language of government:

> parliament, member, election, chancellor, exchequer, minister, nation, country, act, bill, tax, council, councillor.

It is the language of social class:

> common, people, popular, monarch, sovereign, majesty, prince, princess, baron, duke, duchess

but *king, queen, lord* and *lady* are from Old English.

French is part of the language of civic and domestic organization, including cookery:

> boil, fry, grill, roast, toast, dinner, supper, apartment, chamber, domicile, residence, city, village, county, mansion, palace

but *hall, hamlet, home, house, town* and *shire* are English.

The language of law is partly French:

> judge, jury, just, justice, attorney, court, jail, prison, guard

as is the language of the church:

> religion, service, saviour, virgin, clergy, parish, pray, preach, sermon

but the word *church* itself and *priest* are English. French is part of the language of military affairs:

> arms, armour, soldier, troop, sergeant, officer, lieutenant, colonel, general, cavalry, infantry.

And, as the entries in this dictionary show, French, along with Latin and Greek, is one of the METALANGUAGES, the language used to discuss language itself, of English grammar.

Other changes accompanied these borrowings. The loss of inflections of nouns, verbs and adjectives, a process that began in the Old English period, continued in the Middle English period, from around 1150 to around 1450, which overlaps with the Old French period, from around 1066 to around 1300. Changes in spelling and pronunciation were the result of French influence; indeed, the sound changes that began around 1400 and are known as the Great Vowel Shift were partly the result of the collision and then the fusion of Old English and Old French sound systems. *See also* CHANGE; ENGLISH LANGUAGE.

frequency *(n.)*

1 The number of times a linguistic unit appears in a given context; the rate of occurrence of a word in a language; also known as frequency of occurrence. In a given context, the frequency of a word, a phrase or an

AFFIX can be counted by computer; in a language generally, frequency can be assessed by representative samples from language surveys. Frequency can be high – *the*, *it*, *of*, *is* – or low – *zygapophysis*. *See also* DISTRIBUTION; LEAST EFFORT PRINCIPLE.

2 An adverbial that denotes the rate of occurrence of the action denoted by a verb.

> always, frequently, often, repeatedly, sometimes, now and again, seldom, never.

See also TIME ADVERBIAL.

3 In acoustic PHONETICS, the rate of repetition of the vibration of speech sounds. The rate is measured in hertz (Hz, after Heinrich Hertz); one Hz is one cycle per second.

frequentative *(adj./n.)*
A verb that denotes frequency, repetition or intensity of action:

> bicker, glitter, gossip, twitter.

fricative *(adj./n.)*
A consonant sound produced by the friction of breath. The fricatives are: /f/, /v/, /th/, /s/, /z/ and /sh/, and /ch/ as in Scots *loch*.

front focus *see* END FOCUS AND FRONT FOCUS.

full sentence
An alternative term for major sentence. *See* SENTENCE.

full stop *see* PUNCTUATION.

full verb
Any VERB other than a MODAL AUXILIARY VERB or a PRIMARY VERB; an alternative term for **lexical verb**. Most full verbs are also main verbs. The exceptions are the primary verbs *be*, *do* and *have*, which can function as main verbs or as auxiliaries but are not classified as full or lexical verbs.

full word
An alternative term for CONTENT WORD.

function *(n.)*

1 The syntactical purpose or effect of a linguistic unit within a larger unit; the nature of the interrelationship between two or more linguistic units in a clause or sentence.

In the noun phrase *the last word* the linguistic units are *the*, which functions as a DETERMINER, and *last*, which functions as an adjective modifying *word*, which functions as a noun and as the headword in the noun phrase. The phrase could function as a unit in a clause:

> He uttered the last word.

The clause in turn could function as a unit in a sentence:

> The last word he uttered was 'mercy'.

2 The semantic purpose of a sentence or phrase. Function in this sense can be classified as a statement, a question, a command or an exclamation.

3 The wider social and communicative purpose of language, for example, to convey information, to issue commands or to establish and maintain relationships.

function word *see* CONTENT WORD AND FUNCTION WORD.

functional atrophy *see* CRITICAL PERIOD.

functional change/shift

Alternative terms for CONVERSION.

functional knowledge *see* KNOWLEDGE.

functional load

1 The significance of a linguistic unit within a system when contrasted with another unit in the same system.

2 More specifically, the significance of a PHONEME when contrasted with another, similar phoneme. In the English sound system, the similarity of the phonemes /b/ and /p/, as in *butter* and *putter*, or the phonemes /d/ and /t/, as in *down* and *town*, imposes a greater functional load on these phonemes than on, say, /k/ and /l/.

functionalism *(n.)*

The belief that the grammatical, semantic and phonological structures of a language are determined by the ways these structures function in societies. Functionalism takes the pragmatic view that language is primarily an instrument of communication and a medium of social interaction rather than a set of abstract systems.

future continuous *see* FUTURE TENSE.

future in the past *see* FUTURE TENSE; PAST TENSE.

future perfect *see* FUTURE TENSE; PAST TENSE.

future perfect continuous *see* FUTURE TENSE; PAST TENSE.

future tense

A form of a VERB that refers to future time; a form of a verb that refers to actions that have not yet occurred or conditions or states that do not yet exist.

We think, speak and write about the future, and about the past and the present, in so many different ways that it is clear that our concept of the future is not a single time-state but several. It is clear, too, that each dimension of time – past, present or future – includes features of the others.

Some linguists state that the English language does not have a future TENSE because English verbs do not have a one-word form that expresses futurity. But a grammatical category need not be expressed in a single morphological form. A grammatical category is an abstraction, a concept; as a concept, the future is no more and no less abstract than the past or the present. English verbs have agreed forms that refer to future time, and it not unreasonable to say that these forms express a future tense.

The forms that are employed are: the simple future, the future continuous, the future perfect, the future perfect continuous and the future in the past.

The **simple future** is expressed by a two-word verb, the modal auxiliary *shall* or *will*, and the base form of the main verb. (In traditional grammar *shall* was used with the personal pronouns *I* and *we*, and *will* was used with the other personal pronouns.)

> I shall meet you next week.

> They will arrive tomorrow.

The **future continuous**, which is also known as the **future progressive**, takes the form of a three-word verb, the modal auxiliary *shall* or *will*, the bare infinitive *be*, and the -ING FORM of the main verb:

I shall be waiting for you.

They will be leaving soon.

The **future perfect** is also known as the **past in the future** because it looks forward to a time in the future when an action or state will have been completed. The future perfect is a three-word verb consisting of *shall* or *will*, the base form, *have*, and the -ED FORM of a main verb:

We *shall have decorated* the rooms by the end of the week.

The **future perfect continuous**, which is also known as the **future perfect progressive**, is a four-word verb consisting of *shall* or *will*, *have*, the past participle of *be* (*been*), and the -ING FORM of the main verb:

By the time you arrive they *will have been waiting* for hours.

The **future in the past** is a form of hindsight. It assumes a viewpoint in past time and then looks forward to the future. The future in the past usually requires a construction such as *would be*, *was to* or *were to*:

At that first encounter he had no idea that they *would become* close friends.

He *was to* pay a heavy penalty for his moment of folly.

Future time can be expressed in four more ways: the simple present, the present continuous, the construction *be going to*, which can be followed either by a verb or a noun, and the construction *be about to*, which is followed by a verb.

They *fly* to Italy tomorrow. (simple present)

He *is retiring* from work next year. (present continuous)

She *is going to* a party.

They *are about to* close the shop.

See also MODAL AUXILIARY VERB.

fuzziness *(n.)*

A colloquial term for GRADIENCE.

g

gap *(n.)*

A form of ellipsis in which the second linguistic unit in a coordinated pair of units is omitted; also known as gapping.

You prefer red wine and I white.

for

You prefer red wine and I prefer white wine.

gender *(n.)*

The classification of nouns and personal pronouns as masculine, feminine, common, that is, either masculine or feminine, and NEUTER, that is, neither masculine nor feminine.

masculine: man, waiter, he

feminine: woman, waitress, she

common: doctor, guest, it, them

neuter: telephone, it, them.

The thing referred to, for example, an animal or even a plant, may have biological gender, but the thing is grammatically neuter when referred to as *it*.

The English language observes only biological, or natural, gender. Other languages, French, for example, have grammatical gender as well as biological in nouns, pronouns, adjectives and determiners. The French word, *porte* (door) is feminine, and *the green door* in French is *la porte verte*. The French word *plafond* (ceiling) is masculine, and *the green ceiling* is *le plafond vert*.

Social awareness of matters of gender has been changed by equal opportunities legislation and campaigns by women's movements, and this change in awareness has brought about changes in the language of gender. *Firemen, policemen* and *postmen* are now often referred to as *fire-fighters, police officers* and *postal workers*. The masculine suffix *-man* alternates with the suffix *-woman* in *countrywoman, horsewoman* and *sportswoman*, but the words, *craftsman, statesman* and *chairman* are not so easily replaced; chairman is sometimes reduced to *chair*. The feminine suffix *-ess* remains in *duchess, lioness* and *waitress*, but the feminine nouns *authoress, instructress, manageress, poetess* and others, are seldom used; instead, the masculine nouns *author, instructor, manager* and *poet* are used as common, masculine and feminine, nouns. Similarly, the feminine *-ix* suffix and *-ix* words such as *administrix, curatrix* and *proprietrix*, have been replaced by *administrator, curator* and *proprietor*, which now function as common nouns. *Housewife* has long had the common gender alternative, *housekeeper. See also* COMMON NOUN AND PROPER NOUN.

generative grammar

A GRAMMAR that is based on a finite set of formal rules and can account for a theoretically infinite number of sentences in the language in which the grammar is based. In this system of grammar, which began to be formulated by Noam Chomsky in the 1950s, generative means imposed, projected or predictive rather than productive or creative.

generic and specific *(adj./n.)*

A **generic** word or phrase is one that is applicable to a whole class of persons or things.

> Those most at risk are the elderly, the homeless and the unemployed.

The words, *elderly, homeless* and *unemployed*, function as generic nouns in the sentence above. The generic property can be expressed by using the definite article and a singular noun:

> The snow leopard is an endangered species

and by using a plural noun without a preceding article:

> Owls are nocturnal.

The sentences refer to all members of the classes *snow leopard* and *owl*.

A **specific** linguistic unit is one that refers to, or specifies, a particular example. Specificity can be expressed by the demonstratives *this*, *these*, *that* and *those* or by a detailed form of words:

> The second door on the right

and by a proper noun when the specific referent is a particular person, place or thing:

> George Partridge, Cheltenham, the Gold Cup.

genitive *(adj./n.)*

An inflection in a noun to indicate the genitive case, that is, to indicate belonging or possession; an alternative term for POSSESSIVE case.

The possession may be indirect:

> a year's work (the work of a year)
>
> a hair's breadth (the breadth of a hair).

When possession refers to two or more persons or things, as in:

> Anna and Jake's café

it is known as the **group possessive** or **group genitive**. When possession is indicated not by an APOSTROPHE but by of:

> the cost of living
>
> the father of the bride

it is known as a **postmodifying possessive** or **postmodifying genitive** or simply as the **of-possessive** or **of-genitive**.

Germanic *(n./adj.)*

Germanic is a branch of the INDO-EUROPEAN family of languages and includes German, Dutch, Flemish, Frisian, Swedish, Danish, Norwegian and Icelandic. English is classified as a West Germanic language, but Modern English is so different from its Germanic origin that the classification is misleading.

In its evolution from Old English, the language has changed in morphology, syntax, phonology and vocabulary. The English writing system changed from runic to the Latin alphabet; its vocabulary and morphology were affected by OLD NORSE; vocabulary, spelling and pronunciation were strongly influenced by FRENCH, a Romance language; and there were then further influences of LATIN and GREEK.

What was once a synthetic, or inflecting, language is now an analytic, largely uninflected, language. Syntax in Modern English is more regular than other Germanic systems, partly because the loss of inflections, especially from nouns and verbs, gave added importance to the word order of sentences. Although the phonology of Old English is a matter of conjecture, it is certain that the great sound changes of the fifteenth century, which were partly the result of the fusion of French and Germanic sound systems, transformed the sound of English. Old English sounded different from Modern English, but it may have sounded like some of the dialects, still in use but gradually disappearing, of Scots language, because Scots was not affected by the Great Sound Shift.

The vocabulary of Old English was almost exclusively Germanic. In Modern English, the words of Germanic origin are outnumbered by the words borrowed or derived from French, Latin and Greek, and by the three-stage transmutational derivations from Greek to Latin to French and then to English. *See also* CHANGE; ENGLISH LANGUAGE.

gerund *(n.)*

The traditional term for the present participle of a verb, the -ING FORM, when it is used as a noun.

> When *dieting* proved too difficult, Harry tried *swimming* and *cycling*.

Gerunds, which are also known as **verbal nouns**, cannot normally take plural forms. If the *-ing* word can take a plural form – *blessings, spellings, writings* – and has no verb function in a given context, the word is not a gerund but a noun.

get passive *see* ACTIVE VOICE AND PASSIVE VOICE.

given information and new information

Terms that refer to the information content of speech or writing. **Given information** is that which has already been conveyed by a speaker or a writer and is already known to the listener or reader. **New information**, clearly, is that which has not already been conveyed. Most clauses, sentences and longer narrative sequences proceed from the given, or known, to the new:

> Anna and Jake parked their van *behind the café*. As they approached the building they saw that *the door had been forced open*.

In discussions of information content and structure, the words 'given' and 'new' are sometimes used as nouns – *the given, the new*; the terms are also used as alternatives for THEME AND RHEME and TOPIC AND COMMENT.

glossary *see* VOCABULARY (4).

glottal stop

A speech sound produced by rapid closure of the glottis, that is, the upper aperture between the vocal cords, followed by an abrupt release of breath when the glottis is re-opened. In some varieties of English, the sound, symbolized by /?/, replaces the sound /t/:

> kæ?l/cattle, ke?l/kettle

goal *(n.)*

The noun phrase that is affected by the action denoted by a verb. When the voice of a verb is active, the goal is usually the object of the verb:

> Bulldozers churned the soil.

When the voice of the verb is passive, the goal is normally the subject of the verb:

> The soil was churned by the bulldozers.

The concept of goal implies an ACTOR or agent who performs the action denoted by the verb. In the examples above, the actor is *bulldozers*. *See also* ACTIVE VOICE AND PASSIVE VOICE.

government *(n.)*

A grammatical relationship in which one word determines, or governs, the form or function of another. Verbs and prepositions are said to govern nouns and pronouns by requiring the nouns and pronouns to take the objective case. In English only the personal pronouns are inflected to show the objective case. In the sentence:

> They invited me
>
> *They invited I

the verb *invited* governs the pronoun *me*. In this example:

> He offered to go with them but they left without him

the preposition *with* governs the pronoun *them*, and the preposition *without* governs the pronoun *him*.

government-binding theory

A theoretical model of grammar proposed by Noam Chomsky. The traditional grammatical concept of the government of an object by a verb is extended to other linguistic units in a sentence. The term **binding** is applied to items, for example, pronouns and antecedent nouns, that integrate, or bind, linguistic units in a sentence.

gradability *(n.)*

Variation in degree or intensity of meaning; a grammatical property that allows ADJECTIVES and ADVERBS to be compared or intensified.

gradable *see* ADJECTIVE; ADVERB; ANTONYM.

gradation *(n.)*

An alternative term for ABLAUT.

gradience *(n.)*

1 The semantic condition of being continuously variable across three or more words; also known colloquially as **fuzziness**. In synonymy, for example, there is a gradual change in meaning across a synonymous set of words:

> chubby, rotund, stout, corpulent, fat, portly, tubby, podgy, obese.

2 The property of a word that crosses the boundary from one word class to another; also known as **fuzziness**. This second type of gradience is shown by the -ED FORM and -ING FORM, which can function as verbs, adjectives and nouns, and can function simultaneously as adjective and verb, and as noun and verb.

> We *defeated* the rival team. (verb)
>
> The *defeated* team left the field. (adjective)
>
> He is one of the *defeated*. (noun)

the *rising* tide, the *setting* sun (adjective and verb)

the *rising* of the tide, the *setting* of the sun (noun and verb)

grammar *(n.)*

1 The system of structural and semantic relationships of words and phrases in a language; the ways in which roots, AFFIXES, words and phrases combine to form clauses and sentences in writing and speech. This comprehensive definition includes SYNTAX, the order in which words appear in sentences; SEMANTICS, the meanings and inter-relationships of meaning of words; MORPHOLOGY, the forms that words take; and PHONOLOGY, the system of sounds in the spoken language.

2 The rules of morphology and syntax, and the ways in which words combine to form clauses and sentences. This traditional definition excludes semantics and phonology.

3 An account of one or more person's thoughts about the nature of some features and functions of language. This loose definition accepts that grammar does not include all features of language, and that concepts of grammar and the language of grammar have changed over the years, and are still changing.

English morphology has become simpler over the centuries; inflections have largely disappeared from nouns, adjectives and verbs, and comparatively few inflections remain in pronouns. Two areas of constant morphological change are the derivation of new words, mainly from Latin and Greek, and the formation of new words by hyphenating existing words and then, when the compound word is accepted as standard, dropping the hyphen so that the two words become one.

Syntax, too, has changed. Most sentences in written standard English are variations on the pattern, Subject (S) + Verb (V) + Object (O), but there is an infinite number of variations because there is an infinite number of possible word combinations in English sentences.

Semantics has been transformed since Johnson published his dictionary in 1755, partly because later lexicographers have shown in great detail the evolution of meanings of words, and partly because of the constant increase in the size of the English lexicon.

The phonology of the prestige form of spoken standard English, RECEIVED PRONUNCIATION (RP), is fairly constant, but RP also evolves, as one can hear from the soundtracks of British films from different periods. Only a small minority of English speakers use RP; most speakers have regional or national accents. The pronunciation of English is, in fact, infinitely variable.

An important development since the 1950s has been the increased attention given to the linguistics of speech. An even more important change is that, from around the year 1950, most studies of grammar have been **descriptive**, showing how language actually works, in contrast to the traditional PRESCRIPTIVE grammars, which asserted how language ought to work and sometimes imposed the rules of Latin grammar on English. The two approaches, descriptive and prescriptive, are not mutually exclusive; earlier generations of linguists were sometimes concerned with rules, not as prescriptions or prohibitions but as the principles and properties of language, and most of the old grammar books contained some descriptive material.

Of the various systems and theories of grammar – some of them contradictory – produced since 1950, the most influential have been Noam Chomsky's transformational grammar (*see* TRANSFORMATION) and GENERATIVE GRAMMAR. A transformational grammar is one that recognizes the simultaneous existence of a DEEP STRUCTURE AND SURFACE STRUCTURE in virtually every sentence that it generates. On the basis of this recognition, transformational grammars offer sets of rules that can change active sentences into passive sentences, and rules that change declarative statements to interrogatives and negatives. Chomsky has revised his theories several times since they were first published in 1957.

Other grammar systems are summarized here.

Case grammar is a system of analysis based on the semantic functions of nouns in relation to verbs and other nouns in sentences. The system uses six CASES of nouns: genitive, equivalent to an actor or agent; INSTRUMENTAL, an inanimate force operating as an agent; DATIVE, the person or animal affected; FACTITIVE, the result of the action; LOCATIVE, the location of the action or of the result; and objective, a neutral category.

Dependency grammar is a system in which verbs are regarded as superordinate units on which noun phrases are said to be dependent. The number of dependent noun phrases determines the VALENCY of the verb.

Formal grammar is one that is based on FORMALIZED sets of rules that take account of the syntactic structures and functions and the grammatical categories of linguistic units. Formal grammar is sometimes contrasted with notional grammar.

Functional grammar assumes a PRAGMATIC approach to grammar and examines the rules that underlie the use of language as a means of social exchange.

Notional grammar (Latin *notio*, conception, idea) is a term used by modern grammarians to refer to the extralinguistic, or notional, approaches of traditional grammar, which sometimes defined linguistic units in non-linguistic terms. A verb, for example, was sometimes referred to as *a doing word*. Modern grammar, by contrast, usually defines linguistic units in terms of their syntactic functions or grammatical categories. Notional grammar is sometimes contrasted with formal grammar.

Universal grammar is the attempt to identify grammatical features that are common to all natural languages. It can be discussed in terms of Chomsky's claim that a person's grammatical competence, that is, the person's knowledge of the principles of his or her native language, is in fact a universal competence that happens to operate in a particular language but could, theoretically, operate in any language. Such a theory is, in part, also a theory of the universal human faculty for language.

grammatical *(adj.)*
A use of language that observes the rules of morphology and syntax in a system of GRAMMAR.

grammatical collocation *see* COLLOCATION.

grammatical meaning *see* LINGUISTIC MEANING *under* MEANING; SEMANTICS.

grammatical relationship *see* RELATIONSHIP.

grammatical word
An alternative term for function word. *See* CONTENT WORD AND FUNCTION WORD.

graph *(n.)*
The smallest visual symbol in a writing system. Graphs include letters of the alphabet, punctuation marks and such symbols as £ and $. *See also* ALLOGRAPH; GRAPHEME.

grapheme *(n.)*
A visual symbol that represents a PHONEME, or sound; a minimal distinctive unit in a writing system. In an alphabetical language like English, graphemes are individual letters of the alphabet and combina-

tions of letters such as /ch/, /th/ and /wh/ that represent a sound. The word 'grapheme' was coined in the mid-twentieth century by analogy with the word 'phoneme'. *See also* ALLOGRAPH; GRAPH.

graphology *(n.)*

1 The study of the writing system of a language; the study of GRAPHEMES.

2 The study of handwriting in the belief that aspects of the writer's character can be deduced from the visual quality of the handwriting.

Great Vowel Shift

From around 1400 a change in the sounds of the long vowels, partly as a result of the influence of the French sound system on English. The change affected much of England but had limited effect in the northeast and did not affect the Scots language. By the end of the fifteenth century the pronunciation had changed to the modern:

> bane, eat, mine, so, do, brow

from pronunciations that would have sounded like:

> ban, ate, mean, saw, doe, brew.

Greek *(n./adj.)*

Greek has had a great influence on English vocabulary, but until the twentieth century the majority of Greek derivations entered English indirectly by way of LATIN or Latin and FRENCH. Greek influence was less direct than Latin for several reasons. With a writing system dating from around 1500 BC, Greek was an older, more remote language than Latin; Greek civilization, and to an extent Greek language, was overwhelmed by Roman and the Latin language in the second century BC; Latin was the language of the Church of Rome, although the New Testament was written in Greek. And Latin gained a form of continuity through its descendant Romance languages, Italian, French, Spanish, Portuguese and Romanian; Greek had no such offspring.

At a practical level, Greek had to be transliterated as well as translated from the Greek alphabet to the Roman alphabet of Latin and English. This, and its highly inflected nature, made Greek harder to learn than Latin.

With the development of the sciences, new words began to be derived more directly from Greek. The derivations in the glossary of later editions of Charles Darwin's *The Origin of Species*, first published in 1859, are mainly Latin but there are several Greek words, including

Cephalopod, Cetacea, Cheloniai, Teleostean, Trachea and *Trimorphic*. The growth of science in late nineteenth-century Britain coincided with a rapid growth in the number of universities and brought a need for new nomenclatures. Botany remained Latin-based, but other sciences, including medical science, derived their terminologies from Greek. Indeed, the history of modern medicine is also a history of Greek derivations:

> cardiography, cytochemistry, gastroscope, neurone, psychopharmacology, zygogenesis.

Grimm's Law

The conclusion reached by the German philologist and folklorist, Jacob Grimm (1785–1863), that the differences in the consonants of related words in different languages accounted for the separation of the Germanic languages from the other languages descended from INDO-EUROPEAN. The Latin plosive /p/, for example, is related to the Germanic /f/ – *pater, father* – and the Latin /d/ is related to the Germanic /t/ – *duo, two*.

group *(n.)*
An alternative term for PHRASE.

group genitive/possessive *see* GENITIVE.

h

---

habitual *(adj./n.)*
An adverb or a verb that denotes regular or repeated, and thus habitual, action.

The adverbs:

> always, constantly, continually, continuously, frequently, often, regularly, routinely

express a habitual quality.

Verbs in the present tense or the past tense may have a habitual quality, depending on the context. In the sentence:

> He watches television in the evening

the verb *watches* is habitual because the sentence clearly implies every evening or most evenings. In the sentence:

He has driven the same car for eleven years

the habitual quality of the verb *has driven* is reinforced by the adverbial *for eleven years*.

hanging participle *see* MISRELATED PARTICIPLE.

hapax legomenon

1 A word that occurs only once in a particular text, or only once in the works of a particular author.

2 A word or form of which only one recorded instance is known. *See also* NONCE-WORD.

haplology *(n.)*

1 Omitting one or more letters or syllables in the pronunciation of a word:

laborat'ry/laboratory, temp'rature/temperature.

See also APOCOPE AND SYNCOPE; ELISION.

2 Omitting one or more words in a phrase. The practice is common with the names of institutions. The British Foreign and Commonwealth Office is usually known as the Foreign Office; the Ministry of Agriculture, Fisheries and Food is known simply as the Ministry of Agriculture; a Rolls Royce car is sometimes referred to simply as a Rolls.

headline English

The particular use of English language in British newspaper headlines. A distinction can be made between headlines in broadsheet, or 'quality', newspapers, and tabloid, or 'popular', newspapers. In broadsheet newspapers, the headlines of most news stories take the form of elliptical sentences that indicate the nature of the story:

Government promises tax cuts

Eight drown as yacht sinks.

The headlines are in standard English, the diction is usually neutral and, in an attempt to gain topicality, verbs are in the present or in the *to* infinitive form of the future tense:

Building societies to merge.

Tabloid newspapers sometimes use sentence headlines but they more often use short phrases or single words; the diction is often emotive and, unlike broadsheet headlines, is sometimes punctuated by exclamation marks:

Me Tarzan!

Inferno!

Bastards!

(*Me Tarzan!* was the headline of a story on the politician, Michael Heseltine, nicknamed Tarzan.)

Some ambiguous headlines may be deliberate wordplay or sub-editorial errors:

Fish talks after skippers clash

Children hit as teachers strike

Medics lick salmonella outbreak

See also JOURNALESE; TABLOIDESE.

headword *(adj./n.)*

1 The key word in a PHRASE; the essential element that, if isolated from the phrase, would have the same function as the phrase. The headword in a noun phrase is usually a noun:

a long, relaxing *holiday*

and can also be an -ING FORM or -ED FORM functioning as a noun:

a good day's *fishing*

the dejected, the dispossessed.

The headword in an adjective phrases is an adjective:

not so *important*.

The headword in an adverbial phrase is usually an adverb:

She disappeared *quite suddenly*.

Although PREPOSITIONAL PHRASES can sometimes function as adverbials:

She disappeared *in an instant*

they are still classified as prepositional phrases.

2 The word, often in bold type, at the beginning, or head, of a dictionary entry.

hesitation pause *see* PAUSE.

heterograph *(n.)*

A word with the same sound as another but with a different meaning and a different spelling.

boy/buoy, right/rite/wright/write

See also HOMOPHONE.

heteronym *(n.)*

A word with the same spelling as another but with a different meaning and a different origin. For example, *bow*, from Old English *boga*, is an arch, curve or knot; *bow* from Low German *boog* is the front part of a ship; *bow* from Old English *bugan* is to bend forward. *See also* HOMONYM.

heterophone *(n.)*

A word with the same spelling as another but with a different sound and a different meaning. For example, *wind* the noun and *wind* the verb; *slough* the noun, meaning soft muddy ground, and *slough* the noun and verb, meaning a skin or membrane, and to cast a skin.

hiatus *(n.)*

1 A break in the pronunciation of two vowels that are immediately adjacent in two syllables or two words.

cinem*a a*udience, d*i a*bolic, hydr*oe*lectric.

2 A gap, usually a missing word or words, that makes a text ambiguous or unintelligible.

3 A break in a chain of reasoning that makes the sequence illogical or incomplete.

hierarchy *(n.)*

A number of linguistic units that can be classified at successive levels of size or importance; also known as **rank**. Each of these linguistic units is a stage in a hierarchy:

word, phrase, clause, sentence.

A hypernym and its associated hyponyms form a simple hierarchy, with the hypernym as the SUPERORDINATE word and the hyponyms as subordinates:

poem (hypernym)

ballad, elegy, epic, haiku, lyric, sonnet (hyponyms).

hieratic *see* DEMOTIC.

high variety and **low variety**

1 The **high variety** is the more formal and the **low variety** the less formal of two dialects.

2 The high variety of a language is the standard or prestige form; the low variety is the non-standard, DEMOTIC form.

See also BIDIALECTALISM; DIGLOSSIA; FORMAL LANGUAGE AND INFORMAL LANGUAGE; STANDARD AND NON-STANDARD ENGLISH.

historic present

The use of the simple PRESENT TENSE or the present continuous to add immediacy and drama to an account of past events. The practice is common in conversation:

> *I'm driving* home last night when I *see* this idiot *is overtaking* me in the inside lane.

The historic present is also used in newspaper headlines in order to give a sense of topicality to the past:

> Prime Minister *flies* to Paris
>
> Rebels *seize* victory.

A contrast to those uses of the historic present is its particular use in literary criticism, where long-dead authors are sometimes referred to in the present tense, and their audiences in the FUTURE TENSE:

> When Shakespeare *writes*, 'Let your indulgence set me free', he *knows* that some of the audience will be aware of the ambiguity.

holograph *(n.)*

A manuscript or document written by hand by the person identified as its author.

holophrase *see* HOLOPHRASIS (1).

holophrasis *(n.)*

1 The use of a single word to express a number of ideas; also known as **holophrase**. The word *lunch*, for example, could mean *Let's go for lunch now*; the word *fire* could mean *The building is on fire*.

2 The one-word, or holophrastic, stage in the acquisition of language by children, usually around the age of eighteen months. The single word *Teddy* could mean *I want my teddy bear* or *Where is my teddy bear?*

homograph *(n.)*

A word with the same spelling as another but with a different meaning. The noun *stalk*, meaning a stem, and the verb *stalk*, meaning to pursue stealthily, are homographs; so, too, are the noun *hawk*, the bird of prey, and the verb *hawk*, to travel around selling goods. *See also* HOMONYM.

homonym *(n.)*

A word with the same sound and spelling as another, but with a different meaning and a different origin. The noun *rush*, a reed-like plant, derives from Old English *rysc*; the verb *rush*, is from Old French *russer*. *See also* HETERONYM.

homophone *(n.)*

A word with the same sound as another but with a different spelling, meaning and origin.

> hoard/horde, lama/llama, ewe/yew/you

See also HETEROGRAPH.

honorific *(adj./n.)*

A form of words that expresses respect or honour. There are three main forms of honorific in English.

1 The general expression of respect through such forms of address as *Mr, sir, madam, lady*.

2 The honorific that accompanies an office and thus the office-holder: *Your Honour/My Lord*, a judge; *Maestro*, an orchestra conductor.

3 The institutionalized honorifics of an aristocratic social class.

hybrid *(adj./n.)*

A word formed from words or elements from different languages. *Contraflow*, for example, is formed from Latin *contra* (against) and Old English *flowan* (to flow). *Cyberspace* is formed from Greek *kubernetes* (steersman) and Old French *espace*, which in turn is from the Latin *spatium*. *Videotape* is from Latin *video* (I see) and Old English *tæppe* (tape).

hypallage *(n.)*

A figure of speech in which a quality or epithet is transferred from an appropriate noun and attributed to another noun.

> The term is usually applied to rhetorical expressions such as:

> an anxious time

such cruel weather

but it can also be applied to colloquial expressions:

a pig of a day

a brute of a job.

hyperbole *(n.)*

1 A figure of speech consisting of an extravagant claim that is meant to impress a reader or listener. A literary example of hyperbole appears in Robert Burns's song 'My Love Is Like A Red Red Rose':

And I will love thee still, my dear,
Till a' the seas gang dry.

2 Generally, an exaggerated claim or statement.

I've told you a thousand times.

The telephone hasn't stopped ringing all morning.

The colloquial form of the word 'hyperbole' is the clipping *hype*, which means to publicize by making excessive claims.

hypercorrection *(n.)*

The use of what is mistakenly thought to be the standard or prestige form of a word in speech or writing; also known as hyperurbanism and overcorrection.

A common hypercorrection is *between you and I*, which some people believe to be more polite than the grammatically correct *between you and me*. The place-name Badminton and the game of badminton are sometimes pronounced as *badmington* by people who think the letter /g/ has been dropped from the word.

hyperlect *(n.)*

A marked, or extreme, form of current RECEIVED PRONUNCIATION and some older forms of RP that sound marked by present standards. *See also* ACCENT.

hypernym and hyponym *(n.)*

A **hypernym** is a word or phrase for a general class of things, in contrast to a **hyponym**, which is a word for a member of the class.

Bird is a hypernym that includes the hyponyms *thrush*, *blackbird* and *wren*; *bird of prey* is a hypernym that includes the hyponyms *eagle*, *osprey* and *sparrowhawk*.

The hypernym encompasses the hyponyms. A hypernym is an example of a SUPERORDINATE word, and a hyponym an example of a subordinate word. *See also* HIERARCHY; SUBORDINATION.

hyperurbanism *see* HYPERCORRECTION.

hyphen *see* PUNCTUATION.

hyphenation *(n.)*
A type of WORD FORMATION in which two or more words or elements are compounded by a hyphen, which is the only punctuation mark that links rather separates words.

Words that are always hyphenated include:

Anglo-Saxon, fox-hunting, mother-in-law.

Words beginning with certain prefixes are hyphenated:

anti-hero, ex-president, pre-election.

Hyphenation also takes the form of ready-made, slightly colloquial expressions that usually function as adjectives:

a blow-by-blow account, a down-to-earth manner.

Hyphenated adjectives can be formed for specific occasions:

a two-goal lead, his blood-spattered shirt.

The other word classes mainly affected are nouns:

child-minder, road-map, ski-lift, time-switch

and verbs:

cross-examine, dive-bomb, freeze-dry, kick-start.

When the hyphenated word is regarded as standard the hyphen is sometimes dropped and the two words are written as one. The process is not uniform; the words *word class* and *word formation* are also written as *wordclass* and *wordformation* and as *word-class* and *word-formation*.

hypocoristic *(adj./n.)*
A pet name; a term of endearment or intimacy:

sweetie, luv, nanna (for grandmother).

See also DIMINUTIVE.

hyponym *see* HYPERNYM AND HYPONYM.

hypotaxis *see* PARATAXIS AND HYPOTAXIS.

hypothetical past

The use of the PAST TENSE to refer to a supposition, a possibility or an imagined circumstance.

> If I *had known* you were in town last week I *could have met* you.

See also TENSE.

i

iconicity *(n.)*

A similarity between an image or symbol and what it symbolizes; the quality of being an icon; a likeness. There is linguistic iconicity in those nicknames (from *eke-name*, an extra name), or BAHUVRIHI terms, that are physical or visual epithets:

> Spotty Williams, Hippo Brown, Shorty Smith.

A different form of iconicity, aural rather than visual, is present in the phonological devices of onomatopoeia, assonance, consonance, dissonance, cacophony and phonaesthesia. But an icon is essentially a visual image, and iconicity is most obvious in the kind of similarity that exists between, say, a portrait and the sitter, or between an architect's plan and the actual building.

Iconicity can be contrasted with ARBITRARINESS.

ideation *(n.)*

The forming of ideas and concepts; mental representation of experience; the conscious processing of information; cognition.

The process of ideation can be linguistic, that is, the ideas can be formulated in words, or it can be mental activity of a non-linguistic or pre-linguistic nature. An example of non-linguistic ideation is musical composition and the use of musical notation.

identifier *(n.)*

A DETERMINER that specifies, or identifies, a person or thing. The most common identifiers are the articles:

> a, an, the

the demonstratives:

> this, that, these, those

and the possessives:

> mine, yours, his, hers, ours, theirs.

Identifiers are sometimes contrasted with QUANTIFIERS.

ideogram *(n.)*

A symbol that expresses a word, a phrase or an idea but does not represent the sound of speech. Ideograms are also known as **ideographs**. An ideogrammic, or ideographic, writing system differs from pictorial systems because it expresses ideas as well as things; ideogrammic systems differ from alphabetical systems because they do not represent the sounds of a spoken language.

ideograph *see* IDEOGRAM.

idiolect *(n.)*

A person's uniquely distinctive and personal use of spoken or written language, notably vocabulary and pronunciation but also including grammar.

Everyone's command of language is different because each person's experience of language – in education, listening, speaking, reading, writing and thinking – differs to some extent from that of all other users of the language. A second reason, closely related to experience, is that each person's cerebral network, and thus each person's memory, imagination and intelligence, is also unique.

idiom *(n.)*

1 A form of words, often a fixed expression, the meaning of which is partly exophoric (that is, shaped by an extralinguistic factor) and a result of popular metaphorical usage rather than the lexical meanings of the words in the expression. The British idiom *to miss the bus* or *miss the boat* is not a question of transport but of lost opportunity. The Scottish idiom *to go the messages* means to go shopping for food and essential items.

2 The use of language in a particular region by a particular speech community.

3 The particular nature of a language or dialect.

idiomatic *(adj.)*

1 A use of language that includes idioms and thus is likely to be informal or colloquial rather than formal.

2 Descriptive of speech, and sometimes writing, that conforms to the idioms of a language.

illiterate *(adj./n.)*

Unable to read or write; uneducated. The word is used of a person in a literate society. *See also* ALITERATE; NON-LITERATE.

illocution, locution and perlocution *(n.)*

Illocution is a SPEECH ACT in which the speaker performs an act simply by uttering certain words. The utterance 'May God bless you' is a blessing, and 'I promise not to tell the police' is a promise. Illocutionary acts also include commands, invitations, prohibitions, warnings, appeals and apologies.

Locution is a speech act that is considered only as a linguistic unit and without reference to the speaker's intention or the effect on the listener.

Perlocution is speech or writing that attempts to influence the listener or reader but that does not constitute an act in itself. A perlocutionary effect can be the result of an illocutionary act.

imagery *(n.)*

A mental representation of sensory impressions; a representation in words of sensory mental activity. Language can represent the impressions of any of the five senses: sight (visual imagery), hearing (auditory imagery), touch (tactile), smell (olfactory) and taste (gustatory); it can also represent movement (**kinetic imagery**). Particularly vivid forms of visual imagery are sometimes known as eidetic images (from Greek, *eidos*, form).

Imagery is a feature not only of literary language but of everyday, idiomatic speech. Images occur more frequently in concrete, idiomatic or metaphorical language than in abstract or denotative language.

immediate constituent *see* CONSTITUENT ANALYSIS.

imperative *(adj./n.)*

The grammatical MOOD of a VERB that expresses an order or command. The base form of the verb is used, with or without an exclamation mark:

Stop! Wait for me.

The base form of the verb can be preceded by the verb *do*:

Do behave yourself! Don't act like a fool.

The term 'imperative' can be applied to a clause or a sentence that contains a verb in the imperative mood. An imperative sentence usually has a ZERO SUBJECT or an implied subject, *you*.

The imperative mood contrasts with the INDICATIVE and SUBJUNC-TIVE MOOD.

imperfect *(adj./n.)*

In traditional grammar the PAST TENSE of a verb expressed by the verb *was* or *were*, used as an auxiliary, followed by the present participle, the -ING FORM, of the main verb:

> was following, were following.

The construction is now known as the past continuous or past progressive form, and is discussed in terms of ASPECT as well as TENSE.

imperfective *(adj./n.)*

A term sometimes used to emphasize the continuous, or progressive, ASPECT of a verb; in some grammars, an alternative term for progressive or CONTINUOUS FORM.

impersonal *(adj./n.)*

A construction with an indefinite subject, usually expressed as *It*. *It* constructions are commonly used to refer to weather and time of day:

> It's late, it's getting dark and it's beginning to rain.

Another common impersonal construction uses the word *things* as the subject:

> As things stand, we must pay up.

> Things being as they are, you are not eligible.

implication *(n.)*

A meaning that is expressed implicitly or indirectly rather than explicitly. If one colleague said to another:

> I shall, of course, continue to support your view

the implication of *of course* would be that the support would be certain, and the implication of *continue* would be that support had been given in the past.

Implication by a speaker often requires inference by the listener. Although there is usually a similarity between what is implied and what is inferred, there can be ambiguities, some of them deliberate.

> I shall, of course, give you all the support you deserve

could imply that no support would be given.

See also ENTAILMENT; IMPLICATURE.

implicature *(n.)*

The implicit meaning of an utterance; the meaning that is implied rather than explicitly stated by a speaker, and inferred by a listener. The implicature of:

I've got two tickets for the concert tonight

is that the speaker is seeking the listener's company at the concert. The implicature of the reply:

I have to finish that report for tomorrow

is that the second speaker cannot, or will not, accompany the first speaker. An invitation has been offered, and refused, by implicature. Implicatures of that type are known as **conversational implicatures**. A second type, known as a **conventional implicature**, is usually a fixed expression uttered in a specific circumstance:

You're looking well.

I'll see you on Monday. Have a good weekend.

Conventional implicatures have the same kind of social function as PHATIC COMMUNION. *See also* IMPLICATION.

inalienable possession *see* ALIENABLE POSSESSION AND INALIENABLE POSSESSION.

inanimate *see* ANIMATE AND INANIMATE.

inceptive verb

A verb that denotes the beginning, or inception, of an action or a condition.

You *are beginning to show* the benefit of the training. Tomorrow, when we *move on* to the next stage, we *shall try* some new exercises.

inchoative verb

A verb that denotes a change of condition.

The training has *toughened* your mind as well as your body.

Some linguists state that inchoative is an alternative term for inceptive, but a distinction can be made between the two. INCEPTIVE VERBS denote commencement:

The problem *arose* when the management *introduced* new timetables.

Inchoatives denote transformation:

> The river *dried up*. Plants *wilted* in the heat.

inclusive and exclusive *(adj.)*

The term **inclusive** is applied to the pronoun *we* when it refers to the speaker and the person being addressed.

> We [you and I] can travel together.

The term **exclusive** refers to *we* when it does not include the person being addressed.

> Because you are not ready we shall leave [without you].

incompatibility *(n.)*

A condition of inconsistency or opposition between two or more linguistic units. Incompatibility is not simply antonymy; *crooked* and *straight* are obviously incompatible. The term is applied to one or more words that break the continuity of a gradient set, for example, of hyponyms, or applied to words at such different points in a gradience of synonyms that two or more words are incompatible with the others. In the hyponymous set:

> bench, chesterfield, couch, settee, sofa

bench is clearly incompatible with the other words. In the synonymous set:

> lean, slim, slender, thin, skinny, emaciated, skeletal

the first three words are clearly incompatible with the last two.

Words from different sets are often compatible with each other:

> blue chair, green sofa;
>
> tall and slender, short and thin.

incomplete predication

In traditional grammar the copular verbs *be*, *become*, *seem*, *appear*, and others that require a COMPLEMENT in order to complete the predication of the verb.

indefinite article *see* ARTICLE.

indefinite determiner *see* DETERMINER.

indefinite pronoun

A PRONOUN that refers to one or more persons, things or conditions without specifying who or what they are, usually because they have already been identified. Indefinite pronouns referring to people are:

one, anyone, someone, everyone, somebody, everybody, no one, nobody.

Indefinite pronouns referring to people or things are:

all, many, more, most, few, several, enough, others.

An indefinite **determiner** usually appears in front of the noun it modifies, while an indefinite pronoun appears instead of a noun:

All the software designers were university graduates. (indefinite determiner)

Most had joined the company straight from university. (indefinite pronoun)

independent *see* DEPENDENT AND INDEPENDENT.

independent clause

An alternative term for main clause. *See* CLAUSE.

indeterminacy *(n.)*

A lack of definition, or determinacy; the condition of having no fixed value. There are a few indeterminacies in English spelling:

acknowledgement/acknowledgment; jewellery/jewelry

and a few indeterminate pronunciations:

'controversy/con'troversy, 'kilometre/kil'ometre

but the main areas of indeterminacy in English are grammar and the joint area of vocabulary and MEANING. The sentence:

Your car has been stolen

can be declarative, interrogative or exclamatory and can be punctuated by a full stop, a question mark or an exclamation mark.

Notional AGREEMENT is a form of indeterminacy that allows a collective noun to be followed by a verb that is singular or plural in number.

Gender suffixes became increasingly indeterminate in the late twentieth century. The *-ix* feminine suffix disappeared; the *-ess* suffix disappeared from some words – *poet[ess]*, *author[ess]*, partly disappeared from *actress* and *manageress* but remains in *waitress*.

Word class, too, can be indeterminate:

a *howling* wind (adjective and verb)

the *howling* of the wind (noun and verb)

Insulted, he left the room (adjective and verb)

There is indeterminacy, too, in the meanings of words. The boundary between sense and reference, that is, between meaning determined by context and meaning determined by extralinguistic reality, is sometimes blurred. Human emotions and mental states – anger, fear, love – are usually treated as abstractions and their meanings as matters of sense, but they also have referential, physiological, reality in the brain.

Social exchanges such as:

How do you do? How are you?

We must meet again soon

are indeterminate in that they are used for their social content rather than their information content.

indexical feature

Personal information about a language user that emerges unintentionally or indirectly from speech or occasionally from writing; also known as a **speech marker**.

Accent, dialect and voice quality may indicate a speaker's social status, regional or national origin, sex and age. In writing, the particular treatment of the topic, along with the writer's use of standard or non-standard, formal or informal, language may give some indication of a writer's education, pattern of thought or state of mind.

indicative *(adj./n.)*

The grammatical MOOD of a VERB that expresses a statement or a question; usually contrasted with the IMPERATIVE and SUBJUNCTIVE MOOD.

We *have* white wine and red. Which *would* you *like*?

The word 'indicative' includes declarative and interrogative verbs. The term can also be applied to a clause or sentence that contains a verb in the indicative mood.

indirect object *see* OBJECT.

indirect question *see* QUESTION.

indirect speech *see* DIRECT SPEECH AND INDIRECT SPEECH.

Indo-European *(adj./n.)*

The large and varied FAMILY OF LANGUAGES that includes most European languages: the Germanic, Romance, Slavonic and Celtic groups, along with Sanskrit and modern Bengali and Hindi, Iranian and modern Persian.

The original language, which is known only through conjectural reconstruction, is called Proto-Indo-European (*proto* from Greek *protos*, first). The language's place of origin is disputed; it could have been Anatolia, which is the Asian part of modern Turkey, or an area of the Ukraine north of the Black Sea.

inference *(n.)*

1 A meaning that is deduced, or inferred, from an utterance or a piece of writing. By this definition, inference is the converse of IMPLICATION; the meaning of what is implied by the speaker or writer must usually be the same as, or similar to, the meaning inferred by the listener or reader.

2 A conclusion that is reached by reference to facts, or by reasoning, or by facts and reasoning. This second definition raises the theory of the deep structure of language and the TRANSFORMATION between DEEP STRUCTURE AND SURFACE STRUCTURE. If a listener or reader infers the meaning of an ambiguous sentence by reference to extralinguistic reality, for example, the relationship between two or more persons, or the person responsible for an action, it is possible that the ambiguity has been eliminated without reference to a deep structure of language. If the inference is reached by reasoning, it is possible that the reasoning process consists of non-linguistic ideation or imagery or other forms of non-linguistic mental activity. *See also* UNDERLYING STRUCTURE AND DERIVED STRUCTURE.

infinitive *(adj./n.)*

The non-finite base form of a verb. The form can be the bare infinitive:

> run, stand, walk

or it can be preceded by the particle *to*:

> to run, to stand, to walk.

Infinitive constructions include:

> He asked them not *to run*. (*to* infinitive)

> He watched them *walk*. (bare infinitive)

> *To have walked* along the crumbling cliff path was foolish. (perfect infinitive)

The dog waited *to be walked*. (passive infinitive)

See also FINITE AND NON-FINITE FORMS OF VERBS.

inflected/inflecting/inflectional language *see* ANALYTIC, SYNTHETIC AND AGGLUTINATIVE LANGUAGES.

inflection *(n.)*
A change in the form of a word to indicate a grammatical property such as CASE, NUMBER, PERSON, GENDER or TENSE. The most common inflections in English are -*ed* to mark the past tense of regular verbs, and -*s* to mark the plural forms of regular nouns. Also known as **accidence**.

English verbs are inflected to show tense:

walks, walked

and partly inflected to show person and number:

I walk (first person singular)

he walks (third person singular)

they walk (third person plural).

Nouns are inflected to show number:

student (singular), students (plural)

possessive case:

student's computer, students' computers

and sometimes gender:

waiter/waitress, widow/widower.

Personal pronouns are inflected to show person, number, case and gender:

first person: I/we

second person: you

third person: he/she/they

singular: I, you, he, she

plural: we, you, they

subjective case: I, you, he, she, we, they

objective case: me, you, him, her, us, them

possessive case: mine, yours, his, hers, ours, theirs

masculine gender: he

feminine gender: she

Adjectives and adverbs can be inflected to show comparison:

hot, hotter, hottest.

Most inflections are suffixes, but some inflections are vowel changes within words, for example, the verbs:

drive, drove, driven; sing, sang, sung

the nouns:

goose/geese, mouse/mice, woman/women

and the demonstratives, which are inflected to show number:

this (singular), these (plural), that (singular), those (plural).

See also MARKED AND UNMARKED.

informal language *see* FORMAL LANGUAGE AND INFORMAL LANGUAGE.

information *(n.)*
The COMMUNICATION of KNOWLEDGE or facts about a particular topic or occurrence. By this definition, information is not the same as knowledge; only when knowledge is communicated does it become information.

information content
The amount of information carried in a particular message. The information content of a message is related to the predictability of the message or the medium, for example, speech or writing, in which the message is expressed. The greater the predictability, the lower the information content. *See also* REDUNDANCY (2).

information processing
1 The adaptation of existing information to produce new information. A computerized information processing system, also known as a data processing system, can have a variety of clerical, logical and arithmetical functions. In distribution analysis, for example, the system can count the number of times a particular word appears in a text, and can do so more rapidly and accurately than an eye-count.

2 The coding, input, storage, retrieval and decoding of information. This comprehensive definition encompasses the complete cycle of communication and is sometimes used as an analogue for the human mental processes of perception, cognition, memory, recall and interpretation of information, and for problem-solving and decision-making.

information retrieval

Recovering particular information from a larger body of information. Information retrieval is made easier if the information is coded or indexed when it is first gathered or when it is stored. The index of a book and the card-index catalogue of a library are examples of traditional information retrieval systems. The advantages of computerized systems are that they are usually faster than manual systems and can access larger volumes of information stored in a much smaller space.

The earliest information retrieval system was human memory. *See also* INFORMATION PROCESSING.

information structure

A general term for the arrangement, or structure, of information in a message. *See also* END FOCUS AND FRONT FOCUS; GIVEN INFORMATION AND NEW INFORMATION; THEME AND RHEME.

-ing form

1 The form of the verb ending in *-ing* and used in the continuous, or progressive, tenses and aspects of verbs.

> I am waiting.

The *-ing* form was traditionally known as the **present participle** of a verb, but the simpler term, *-ing form*, is now preferred because *-ing* forms can be used in past and future tenses as well as the present:

> I was waiting.
>
> We have been waiting.
>
> They will be waiting.

2 The form can also function as a noun and as an adjective. In the sentence:

> Waiting can be a boring experience

Waiting functions as a noun, the subject of the verb, *can be*; *boring* functions as an adjective modifying the noun *experience*. Similarly, in:

> Mountaineering is a daring sport

Mountaineering functions as a noun, and *daring* as an adjective.

In traditional grammar, *-ing* nouns are known as GERUNDS and *-ing* adjectives as gerundives.

3 Some *-ing* forms cannot be assigned to a single word class. In the expression:

> the setting of the sun and the cooling of the land

setting and *cooling* function both as nouns and as verbs. In the expression:

the rising tide and the lapping waves

rising and *lapping* function both as adjectives and verbs.

inherent *(adj.)*

An adjective that denotes an essential, or inherent, quality in a noun; also known as **intrinsic**.

black paint, *heavy* metal, *priceless* masterpiece

in contrast to the non-inherent, also known as **extrinsic**, adjectives:

black humour, *heavy* heart, *priceless* idiot.

initial cluster *see* CONSONANT CLUSTER.

initial, medial and final *(adj./n.)*

The terms 'initial position', 'medial position' and 'final position' can be applied to two or more letters in a word, to a syllable in a word, a word in a phrase, a phrase in a clause or sentence and a clause in a sentence.

An **initial** linguistic unit is one that appears at or near the beginning of a larger unit. The letters *scr*, for example, form an initial CONSONANT CLUSTER in *scratch*. The noun *cloud* takes the initial position in the phrase *a cloud, black and ominous*. The adverbial component is in the initial position in:

Quite suddenly, a bolt of lightning struck the tree.

The subordinate clause is in the initial position in:

When we return, we'll tell you the whole story.

A **medial** linguistic unit is one that occurs at or near the middle of a larger unit. The vowel /a/ is in the medial position in *scratch*; the noun *cloud* is medial in the irregular but acceptable construction *a black cloud, and ominous*. The adverbial component is medial in:

A bolt of lightning *quite suddenly* struck the tree.

The main clause is in the medial position in:

When we return *we'll tell you the whole story* in order to satisfy your curiosity.

A **final** linguistic unit is one that appears at or near the end of a longer unit. The letters *tch* form a final consonant cluster in *scratch*; the noun *cloud* is in its usual, final, position in the phrase *a black and ominous cloud*. The adverbial is in the final position in:

A bolt of lightning struck the tree *quite suddenly*.

The subordinate clause is in its usual, final, position in:

We'll tell you the whole story *when we return*.

innateness *(n.)*

The theory that the ability to speak and a knowledge of the principles of language are innate; that is, that humans are biologically programmed for SPEECH and for some understanding of how language works.

There is now general acceptance by linguists that part of the human brain is designed for speech, that the vocal tract is designed for speaking as well as for breathing, and that the human mouth is designed for speaking as well as for biting and chewing. Current debate centres on whether speech is instinctive.

Some vocalizations – gasps, groans and grunts, shrieks, sighs and snorts – are clearly instinctive in the sense that they are uttered involuntarily and sometimes unconsciously. Similar vocalizations form the small class of words known as INTERJECTIONS – *hey, wow, ooh* – but interjections are partly determined by culture, for example, *och* and *ach* in Scotland as distinct from *oh* and *ah* in England. As children acquire language in the informal learning process of their first few years, they also acquire a sense of which words, including interjections, are appropriate, and how and when they should be used.

Without the ACQUISITION OF LANGUAGE there can be no speech. Studies of children who grew up without human company, or without being spoken to by humans – such children were once known as wolf children, then wild children, and now feral children – studies show that these children were unable to speak. And if children continue without speech until after the CRITICAL PERIOD of language development, which usually ends in adolescence, they may lose the ability to learn to speak, a condition that has been called functional atrophy. It would seem that, if the language areas of the left hemisphere of the brain are not activated, these areas may become inert. The child is programmed for speech, but the programme will be realized only if people speak to the child.

WRITING is a different activity. Speech, once acquired, can become part of one's unconscious or semi-conscious behaviour. Writing has to be learned as a separate, secondary code, a formal process the after-effect of which is to make writing a conscious, sometimes a self-conscious, activity. *See also* LANGUAGE ACQUISITION DEVICE.

inner speech

Thought processes that take the form of words; formulating knowledge, ideas and images into words without uttering the words; also known as **endophasia** and **sub-vocalization**.

The term is associated with the Russian psychologist Lev Semenovitch Vygotsky (1896–1934), but the process of inner speech is probably as old as language and consciousness. The argument that inner speech is a necessary prerequisite for thought is no longer accepted; there are complex and subtle forms of thought that do not require language: musical notation, painting, mathematical formulae, a game of chess.

Endophasia also includes 'silent speech'; that is, making the appropriate lip and tongue movements without sounding the words. *See also* EGOCENTRIC SPEECH.

instantaneous verb

A verb that denotes an action that is completed in an instant, or action that is simultaneous with the moment of utterance or the moment of thought.

> The glass *cracked*.

> The traffic lights *changed* to green.

The function of instantaneous verbs is similar to that of punctual verbs. *See also* DURATIVE VERB AND PUNCTUAL VERB; PRESENT TENSE.

instrumental *(adj./n.)*

The grammatical property of a noun or noun phrase that denotes the means, or instrument, by which the action of the verb is expressed.

Some languages have inflections to indicate the instrumental case of nouns; in English, instrumentality is expressed by a preposition with a noun:

> Foresters felled the trees *with chain saws*.

> She won her case *by intelligent argument*.

intensifier *(n.)*

An ADVERB that modifies a verb, adjective or another adverb in a sentence by indicating the degree, extent or intensity of a quality or an action.

> He was so completely bored that he could hardly stay awake.

The intensifying adverb *completely* modifies the adjective *bored*, and the reductive intensifying adverb *hardly* modifies the verb *stay*.

intensive and extensive *(adj./n.)*

The meanings of the terms 'intensive' and 'intension', and 'extensive' and 'extension', are disputed, but there is agreement on some applications of the terms.

An **intensive** construction is one in which two or more linguistic units are semantically related. A pro-form and its antecedent express this kind of intension:

> *Geoffrey Pendleton* is the *man who* edits the Bulletin

as do phrases in apposition:

> Geoffrey Pendleton, editor of the Bulletin

and some of the words in synonymous and hyponymous sets.

The term 'intensive verb' is an alternative for linking, or copular, verb.

An **extensive** construction, typically a sentence consisting of at least a subject, verb and direct object, is one in which the components are not related semantically:

> Geoffrey Pendleton mowed his lawn.

An extensive verb is usually transitive.

interchangeability *(n.)*

The substitution of one linguistic item for another without changing the meaning of the unit in which the item appears. Interchangeability is sometimes discussed in terms of SYNONYMS and the extent to which a replacement synonym affects the meaning of the larger linguistic unit. Almost all synonym substitutes will have some effect on meaning; indeed, this changeability of meaning or connotation is the usual function of synonyms.

An alternative criterion for interchangeability is the extent to which the substitution *distorts* meaning. This criterion allows the interchangeability of the tense and aspect of verbs:

> I *shall go* to London tomorrow.
>
> I *go* to London tomorrow.
>
> I *am going* to London tomorrow.

It also allows the interchangeability of INITIAL, MEDIAL AND FINAL linguistic units in larger units, and of DIRECT AND INDIRECT SPEECH. *See also* INDETERMINACY; PARAPHRASE.

interference *(n.)*

The extent to which a person's knowledge of his or her native language influences his or her knowledge of a second or later language.

The term 'interference' is usually applied to errors made in the second language, a process also known as **negative transfer**. For example, some non-native speakers of English have difficulty with English conditional constructions and say:

> If I would go back again

or

> If I will go back again

for

> If I went back again

or

> If I were to go back again

Interference can also take the form of FALSE COGNATES.

interjection *(n.)*

A small word class with the exclamatory function of expressing emotion. Interjections, for example, *oh, ah, ouch, oops*, are often involuntary, spontaneous VOCALIZATIONS, that is, sounds that are uttered almost instinctively. They are more often used in speech, or in written dialogue, than in standard English; because of this, and because of the agitation they express, they sometimes have a comic-strip quality:

> Oops! I've erased a file.

> You walked all the way here? Gosh!

interlocutor *(n.)*

A person who takes an active part in a dialogue or conversation as distinct from persons who are passive observers. *See also* DISCOURSE ANALYSIS.

internal evidence and external evidence

Internal evidence consists of linguistic features in a text that may be used to identify the writer, the writer's knowledge of certain facts or events, or the place or period in which the text was written.

Features include vocabulary, grammar, spelling, punctuation and in some instances handwriting. Dating is sometimes possible by taking key words in the text and using a dictionary to check the period when the words, or particular meanings of words, entered the language.

External evidence consists of non-linguistic features in a text. For example, historical, scientific and other references can be checked in reference sources. The features of the physical media – ink, paper, typescript, type styles, printing methods – can sometimes be identified and dated.

international language
1 A natural LANGUAGE that is used in several countries of the world, for example, English, French, Spanish and Russian.

2 An ARTIFICIAL LANGUAGE (1) such as Esperanto that is designed for international use.

interpersonal and social meaning *see* MEANING.

interpersonal function
The social use of language, especially spoken language, for such purposes as establishing and maintaining relationships and influencing attitudes and opinions. *See also* PHATIC COMMUNION.

interrogative *(adj./n.)*
A word, clause or sentence that asks a QUESTION. Interrogative sentences are sometimes contrasted with declarative sentences, which are designed to convey information, but the interrogative/declarative boundaries are often crossed in English. A declarative construction can be used interrogatively:

> You went to the art club exhibition last week?

And interrogative constructions can be used to make statements. This sentence:

> Aren't those landscape paintings beautiful?

is as much a statement of opinion as a question.

interrogative adjective *see* INTERROGATIVE DETERMINER.

interrogative adverb
An ADVERB that indicates that a question is being asked; the adverbs *where, when, why, how*.

interrogative determiner
A DETERMINER that indicates that a question is being asked; the determiners, *what, which, who, whose*.

Whose portrait is this?

Interrogative determiners, which are also known as **interrogative adjectives**, are placed immediately before the noun, as in the example above, in contrast to INTERROGATIVE PRONOUNS, which are used instead of nouns.

interrogative pronoun

Pronouns, identical in form to the INTERROGATIVE DETERMINERS, that indicate that a question is being asked.

Which of the portraits do you prefer?

intervocalic *(adj./n.)*

1 A consonant that appears between two vowels.

a*p*art, e*l*ephant, u*n*acceptable.

2 The pronunciation of such a consonant, which sometimes differs from the pronunciation of the same consonant in an initial or final position.

intonation *(n.)*

The fluctuations of PITCH, that is, of higher and lower notes, in speech.

The term 'intonation' is usually applied to spoken units of one or more sentences, in contrast to TONE, which is applied to single words or syllables. Intonation is an integral part of the sound system of every language, and of the sub-systems of regional dialects. Further sub-divisions can be made: in British English some intonation patterns are characteristic of particular professions: airport announcers, street traders, university vice-chancellors. In spoken English generally, different patterns of **rising** and **falling** pitch are used in statements, questions and exclamations:

You have read her book. (level > falling)

Have you read her book? (level > rising)

You haven't read her book! (level > rising > rising)

This pattern of rising or falling intonation is known as an **intonation contour**.

Intonation can also reveal a speaker's attitude or emotional state. The words *How beautiful you are* can express sarcasm, infatuation or condescension, depending on the speaker's intonation. *See also* PARALANGUAGE.

intonation contour *see* INTONATION.

intransitive verb *see* TRANSITIVE VERB AND INTRANSITIVE VERB.

intrinsic *see* INHERENT.

introductory *It*
The word *It* appearing at the beginning of a sentence, with the real subject of the sentence appearing in a later *that* clause.

> *It* is rumoured *that the chairman will resign.*
>
> Is *it* not scandalous *that he lied to the board?*

intrusive intervocalic /r/
In some social accents of English, the introduction of the sound /r/ between two vowels, especially after /a/, when there is no /r/ in the written form.

> Russia[r], India[r] and China
>
> the idea[r] of it
>
> Is this a question of law[r] and order or is it just a propaganda[r] exercise?

invariable word *see* VARIABLE WORD AND INVARIABLE WORD.

inversion *(n.)*
A reversal of normal syntax, especially of subject and verb, to form a question and some negative statements. The word order of subject + auxiliary verb + verb + adverb in the sentence:

> We are leaving now

becomes the inversion, auxiliary verb + subject + verb + adverb in:

> Are we leaving now?

Inversion can also be used to form negative statements like:

> Never before has a government been so unpopular

for

> No government has ever been so unpopular before

and

> Quite without precedent is the anti-government feeling

for

> The anti-government feeling is quite without precedent.

Some forms of front focus involve inversion. *See also* END FOCUS AND FRONT FOCUS.

irregular *see* REGULAR AND IRREGULAR.

irregular sentence
An alternative term for minor sentence. *See* SENTENCE.

isochronous language
An alternative term for stress-timed language. *See* STRESS-TIMED LANGUAGE AND SYLLABLE-TIMED LANGUAGE.

isogloss *(n.)*
A line on a map indicating the boundary of an area within which a significant linguistic feature occurs.

The features most often mapped are pronunciation, vocabulary and grammar. In a linguistic map of the Scots language, for example, the isogloss for the word *quine*, a young woman, would limit the word to Aberdeenshire and Angus. *See also* DIALECT; DIALECT CONTINUUM.

isolating language *see* ANALYTIC, SYNTHETIC AND AGGLUTINATIVE LANGUAGES.

isomorph *(n.)*
A morphological isogloss, that is, a linguistic boundary defining an area within which certain forms of words appear. A regional form of a word, for example, *wur* for *our* in some dialects of Scots, and *us* for *our* in parts of Yorkshire, is usually accompanied by a regional pronunciation.

isomorphic *(adj.)*
1 Descriptive of two or more language systems that correspond in form. In a phonetic spelling system, for example, there would be regular correspondence between form as sound and form as writing.

2 A degree of isomorphism exists in different but cognate languages. There are corresponding forms in French, Italian, Spanish and Portuguese, which are descended from Latin, and in Danish, Swedish and Norwegian, which are descended from North Germanic.

3 In psycholinguistics, isomorphism is the correspondence between mental events, for example, various language activities, and the underlying neural events; the abstract linguistic processes and the associated physiological processes are isomorphic.

isosyllabic language
An alternative term for syllable-timed language. *See* STRESS-TIMED LANGUAGE AND SYLLABLE-TIMED LANGUAGE.

iterative *(adj./n.)*
1 A linguistic unit that denotes repetition or frequency of action. The sense of repetition is usually expressed by verbs and adverbials:

> *Painstakingly*, the archaeologists *sifted* the soil.

See also FREQUENTATIVE; HABITUAL.

2 A compound word formed by the repetition of a word:

> can-can, chin-chin, chop-chop, go-go, never-never land, softly softly.

See also REDUPLICATION.

J

jargon *(n.)*
1 The specialist terminology of a particular occupation or interest group.

2 A babel of incomprehensible sounds or unintelligible writing. When the word 'jargon' first appeared in late Middle English it meant the inarticulate twittering of birds and also meaningless talk or writing. Today, the word still has pejorative connotations. Every specialist activity needs terms to express the nature of the activity, but the preferred, and neutral, words for such terms are TERMINOLOGY, NOMENCLATURE or LANGUAGE (4).

journalese *(n.)*
A pejorative term for a particular use of language in some British newspapers. Journalese changes over time. Until the mid-twentieth century it was characterized by euphemism and an inflated use of language. Euphemism was the effect of the moral, and sometimes penal, codes of the time. Male homosexuals, for example, were identified as *men of a certain proclivity*, prostitutes as *women of easy virtue* and brothels as *houses of ill-repute*.

Today, journalese still tends to be cliché-ridden, but the language is now so explicit and the syntax so abrupt that it has been renamed TABLOIDESE.

juncture *(n.)*

1 In spoken language, the transition between two units of speech, or between a unit of speech and a silence. A term like *unit of speech* is needed because speech consists mainly of clusters of words fused together rather than a succession of single, separate words. For example, the three words *in a moment* are normally spoken as a fused cluster whereas the single words *incompatible* and *nonconformist* are often pronounced with a momentary pause between the prefix and the remainder of the word.

2 The transition between two grammatical units of speech, or between a grammatical unit and a silence. A grammatical unit is not always the same as the word cluster that forms a unit of speech. Consider *I love man* and *Isle of Man*. In speech they sound the same, but the first is a complete sentence consisting of subject, verb and object, whereas the second, the place-name, is a noun phrase.

jussive *(adj./n.)*

A verb, clause or sentence that expresses a command or an instruction. The word 'jussive' is largely synonymous with IMPERATIVE, but jussive can include declarative statements:

> You must follow the instructions.

Jussive also includes interrogatives. The two sentences below are expressed as questions, but they are also commands:

> Will you follow the instructions, please?

> You will follow the instructions, won't you?

juxtaposition *(n.)*

Placing two or more linguistic units side by side, especially contrasting units that create a sense of the unexpected or the absurd.

> disgustingly healthy

> remarkably normal

> beautifully simple

> the commonplace atrocities of war.

k

keneme *(n.)*

A minimal unit of writing, or of sound, without meaning. The word 'keneme', also sometimes spelled **ceneme**, was coined in the mid-twentieth century but it did not gain general currency, probably because the similar technical terms MORPHEME and PHONEME were more firmly established.

kernel *(adj./n.)*

The ROOT form of a word that can be inflected into various forms in order to indicate different grammatical functions. The kernel or root form of a verb can be inflected to show tense; the root form of a noun can be inflected to show number and possession; the root forms of adjectives and adverbs can be inflected to show comparison. *See also* INFLECTION; LEXEME.

kernel sentence

A core, or kernel, sentence structure from which other sentences can be generated by TRANSFORMATION.

The term derives from generative grammar and means a sentence of this type: grammatically simple, that is, without subordinate or coordinate clauses; declarative rather than imperative or interrogative; has a verb that is active rather than passive and transitive rather than intransitive.

These rules produce sentences consisting of subject + verb + object (S + V + O):

The fox ate the rabbit

and allow various transformations of the sentence to be generated; the negative transformation:

The fox did not eat the rabbit

the passive transformation:

The rabbit was eaten by the fox

and the interrogative transformation:

Did the fox eat the rabbit?

key sentence

A general term for a sentence that identifies the subject matter of a paragraph or a longer statement. Such a sentence, the metaphorical key that unlocks the meaning of the paragraph, is also known as a **topic sentence**.

key word

A word that identifies the subject matter of a text. Key words in a pamphlet on the environment could be *ecosystem*, *landscape*, *vegetation*, *habitat* and *pollution*.

kinesics *see* NON-VERBAL COMMUNICATION.

kinetic imagery *see* IMAGERY.

King's English, Queen's English

Originally, the speech and writing of the educated and privileged classes of the London–Oxford–Cambridge triangle of southeast England; a prestige form of speech or writing. Today, the Queen's English, or the King's English, means speech or writing that is regarded as grammatically and socially acceptable and correct, that is, RECEIVED PRONUNCIATION in speech and standard English in writing. The actual speech of members of the royal family is not widely regarded as a desirable model. *See also* BBC ENGLISH; PARALECT, STANDARD AND NON-STANDARD ENGLISH.

knowledge *(n.)*

INFORMATION possessed by a person; the body of information possessed by a group of people. The word is usually applied to information that can be recalled from memory rather than information in reference works. Two main forms of knowledge are recognized.

Declarative knowledge, also known as **factual knowledge**, is a conscious awareness of facts about which a person can make declarative statements in speech or writing.

Procedural knowledge, also known as **functional knowledge**, is practical, operational, usually extra-linguistic knowledge about how to perform a task. Driving a car, riding a bicycle, tying a shoelace or necktie – these tasks involve procedural knowledge.

l

labial *(adj./n.)*

Speech sounds that are formed by the partial or complete closure of the lips; the consonants /b/, /f/, /m/, /p/, /v/, /w/ and the rounded vowels /o/ and /u/.

lacuna *(n.)*

A HIATUS (2), or blank or missing section of a manuscript or text. The term can also be applied to gaps in memory or consciousness.

language *(n.)*

1 A system of human communication using particular combinations of words in speech or writing. Languages defined in this way are NATURAL LANGUAGES that have evolved over thousands of years. The origin of natural languages is disputed. The monogenesis theory argues that there was a single original language from which all languages have diverged. The polygenesis theory argues that several different languages emerged separately in different parts of the world. Although the exact origin of language cannot be known, it probably began to develop in the same evolutionary period as the emergence of human consciousness and has continued to evolve as the human race has evolved. *See also* MONOGENESIS AND POLYGENESIS.

2 A set of sentences, each of which is finite in length and is formed from a finite set of linguistic elements. This definition sees language as a set of systems or structures. A theoretically infinite number of sentences can be formed in any natural language, but each sentence has a finite number of linguistic elements because all phonological systems have a finite number of sounds and all WRITING SYSTEMS have a finite number of symbols or characters. *See also* PHONOLOGY.

3 A variety of human communication, as defined in (1) above, used in a particular country or society. All human societies have language in the form of speech; only a minority of languages have writing systems. The majority of NATIONAL LANGUAGES have evolved from parent languages. GERMANIC, for example, was the parent language of English, German, Dutch, the Scandinavian languages and others; Germanic, in turn, was a branch of the Indo-European FAMILY OF LANGUAGES.

4 (a) A range of words used in a particular circumstance or domain. Examples are the language of science, the language of politics and metaphorical language. Depending on the circumstance, such a range of words is known as a VOCABULARY, a REGISTER or as DICTION.

(b) The characteristic use of language by an individual. This use of language is also known as vocabulary and IDIOLECT.

5 Any system of human or animal communication. This general definition includes NON-VERBAL COMMUNICATION, also known as body language, the calls of animals and birds and the dance of the honey bee. *See also* ARTIFICIAL LANGUAGE.

language acquisition *see* ACQUISITION OF LANGUAGE.

language acquisition device (LAD)
The innate capacity of humans to learn language, including grammar, and to produce new, independent utterances; sometimes known as a LANGUAGE ACQUISITION SYSTEM (LAS).

The theory, introduced by Chomsky, is a version of earlier theories that the brain of an infant human is not a *tabula rasa*, an erased writing tablet, but a dynamic, developing system of networks. In 1921 the psychiatrist and philosopher, Carl Gustav Jung, wrote, 'The new-born brain or function-system is an ancient instrument, prepared for quite definite ends', and it possesses 'inherited function-possibilities'.

It is clear that humans are biologically programmed for various forms of cognition, including language, but there is no single language device in the brain; the language faculty is a system of neural networks. *See also* INNATENESS; LANGUAGE CENTRES OF THE BRAIN; NATIVISM.

language areas of the brain
An alternative term for LANGUAGE CENTRES OF THE BRAIN.

language centres of the brain
Those areas of the brain involved in the processing of language, also known as **language areas** and **speech centres**. The processes include the formulation and expression of words in speech and writing, listening and interpreting, reading and interpreting, memorizing and recalling words, and linguistic forms of decision-making and problem-solving. These functions are usually located in the left hemisphere of the cerebral cortex, but a significant number of people, especially left-handed people, have language centres in the right hemisphere.

Recent research suggests that the language centres are not confined to precisely circumscribed areas of the brain but are located in extensive, complex and changing networks. *See also* INNATENESS.

language change

Alteration in a language over time. CHANGE in language is inevitable because language must take account of the changing world and because change, evolutionary and sometimes revolutionary, is part of the human condition.

Vocabulary and pronunciation are subject to continuous change; morphology and syntax change at a much slower rate; spelling is largely resistant to change.

language community

An alternative term for SPEECH COMMUNITY.

language dominance

1 The importance attached to one language in a bilingual or multilingual society. One language may dominate because it is the MAJORITY LANGUAGE in the society, or the OFFICIAL LANGUAGE, or both.

2 Of a bilingual or multilingual person: a greater competence and performance in one language than others; sometimes contrasted with AMBILINGUALISM. *See also* NATIONAL LANGUAGE.

language family *see* FAMILY OF LANGUAGES.

language planning

A deliberate attempt to promote or suppress one or more languages in a society.

In the Highlands and Islands of Scotland, for example, from the late eighteenth to the early twentieth century, attempts were made to eliminate the Gaelic language. In the late twentieth century the policy was reversed and attempts were made to support Gaelic. When the state of Israel was founded in 1948, Hebrew was chosen as the national language and was taught to what was then, and to an extent is still, a multilingual community.

language shift

The displacement of one language by another. Language shift often occurs among second- or third-generation immigrants, who usually abandon the language of their parents or grandparents in favour of the

NATIONAL or MAJORITY LANGUAGE of the country. In Britain, for example, people of Asian origin abandoned Hindi and Urdu for English.

langue and *parole* (n.)

Terms introduced by the Swiss linguist, Ferdinand de Saussure (1857–1913). **Langue** is the complete system of language that is theoretically shared by users of that language; **parole** is the actual use of the language, the linguistic behaviour of the speakers. The concepts are similar to Chomsky's COMPETENCE AND PERFORMANCE.

Latin (n./adj.)

Latin, FRENCH and GREEK are the three languages that have had the greatest influence on English, and derivation from Latin and Greek is a major type of WORD FORMATION in Modern English. The English writing system, based as it is on the Roman alphabet, has been directly affected by Latin, and Latin borrowings and derivations have had a slight influence on the sound system of the English language. The Latin influence on English phonology has been less than the French, but Latin helped to change the sound of English from a GERMANIC to a non-Germanic – in effect, a Germanic–Romance–Italic – system.

Latin was the most dominant of the Italic family of languages. It was the language of Rome and parts of the Roman Empire from around 1000 BC until the empire began to disintegrate at the end of the fourth century AD. A DEMOTIC version of Classical Latin, Vulgar Latin, was the parent language of the Romance languages.

The Anglo-Saxons brought a few Latin words from mainland Europe to England: *pound* (weight), Old English *pund*, Latin *pondo*; *street*, Old English *stræt*, Latin *strata*. And with the gradual conversion of the Anglo-Saxons to Christianity from around 600, other Latin words, for example, *font*, *pope* and *school*, and the Latin alphabet, were adopted. But the main influx of Latin began when the great revival of learning and the arts, the Renaissance, reached England in the fourteenth century. For over three hundred years Latin was the European language of diplomacy, scholarship and, in some countries, of religion.

Latin was taught in British grammar schools and universities, and the rules of Latin grammar were imposed on English grammar in the sincere but mistaken belief that the rules were universally valid. The belief was mistaken because the two languages differ in fundamental ways. English is a partly Germanic language and Latin is Italic; English is, in effect, an analytic, non-inflecting language and Latin is a synthetic, inflecting language; English is a living, changing language and Latin is a dead language. These differences are so great that, despite centuries of promotion, Latin has had comparatively little effect on English syntax.

The lasting effect of Latin is in word formation in general and scientific word formation in particular. Linnaeus, the Latinized name of the Swedish botanist Carl von Linné (1707–78), began the process with his Latin nomenclature; today, many of the sciences derive their nomenclatures from Latin and Greek.

Latin alphabet *see* ALPHABET.

least effort principle

The theory that one of the factors involved in the evolution of language is the human inclination to choose options that require the least mental or physical energy; also known as the least effort theory or hypothesis.

This long-standing but disputed theory is sometimes applied to the use of language generally and to the acquisition of language by children. Some linguists have expressed the principle in a mechanical way, stating that there is a tendency to increase the efficiency of a language in the sense that the length of a linguistic unit is inversely proportional to its probability of occurrence; that is, the longer the word, the less likely it is to be used.

The principle seems to gain support from the fact that the most frequently used words in English are usually short, and that longer words are less frequently used. In the mid-twentieth century it was thought that the principle had been confirmed by Zipf's Law, named after the American scientist George Kingsley Zipf (1902–50). Zipf investigated the frequency of occurrence of words in natural languages and produced statistical evidence showing that a large number of short words occurred with high frequency and that progressively longer words occurred with progressively lower frequencies. The findings confirm a relationship between word length and frequency of occurrence, but similar findings show the comparative frequency of occurrence between Anglo-Saxon and Latinate words, and show that the Anglo-Saxon words are usually shorter. The longer words, Greek and French as well as Latin, were assimilated into English, but according to the least effort principle the language should have resisted the new, foreign, longer and thus 'greater effort' words. Zipf's findings do not prove a principle of least effort.

Such a principle would surely affect irregularities in a language, grammatical complexities and the size of the lexicon as well as the lengths of words. But irregularities, notably in verbs, have survived since pre-Anglo-Saxon times; personal pronouns retain their case endings; the English lexicon continues to grow in size and diversity. In the acquisition of language by children, the determining factor is not a least effort principle but social contact in the immediate speech community of the family and the size and neural network of the child's growing brain.

The least effort principle is an appealing 'common sense' view of language, but the principle has not been proved.

lect *(n.)*

A particular use of a language; a particular variety of a language used by a speech community within the wider community of users of the same language. The word was coined in the late twentieth century to cover the variations – personal, professional, regional, social – in the use of a language. *See also* DIALECT; IDIOLECT; SOCIOLECT.

lemma *(n.)*

1 (a) A word or phrase that is defined in a dictionary or glossary. By this definition, a lemma is similar to a lexical item.

(b) The form of a word chosen to represent all inflectional or spelling variants in a dictionary. By this definition, lemma is similar to CITATION FORM and LEXEME, but the much later introductions 'lexical' and 'lexeme' have made lemma obsolete.

2 An alternative, but now obsolete, term for PROPOSITION. Although the word 'lemma' entered the language in the late sixteenth century, it did not displace the older word 'proposition'.

letter *(n.)*

A character of the ALPHABET; a character representing one or more sounds in the spoken form of a language. *See also* CAPITAL LETTER.

level *(n.)*

1 One of the main areas into which a language can be divided for separate study and analysis; the levels SYNTAX, SEMANTICS, PHONOLOGY, MORPHOLOGY; one of these areas of language.

2 A linguistic unit within a larger, hierarchical, linguistic unit; also known as rank. A sentence, for example, is a hierarchical unit that can be discussed at the level of a clause, a phrase or a word.

3 In generative grammar, surface and deep levels of structure.

lexeme *(n.)*

In the vocabulary, or lexicon, of a language, a lexical unit that may take various forms; also known as a **lexical item**. For example, *walk* is a lexeme that produces the word forms *walks, walking, walked, walker. Book* is a lexeme that produces the word forms *books, book's, books', booking, bookish.*

The term 'lexeme' was coined to define the meaning of 'word' more precisely. A lexeme is the base, or unmarked, lexical unit; the variants derived from that unit can be known as word forms.

lexical *(adj.)*

Referring to the words, or vocabulary, or lexicon, of a language; sometimes used as a contrast to GRAMMATICAL.

lexical collocation *see* COLLOCATION (2).

lexical density

The ratio of the number of different words in a text to the total number of words in the text. The ratio, and thus the lexical density, is calculated by dividing the number of different words by the total number of words and multiplying the result by 100. The end result, expressed as a percentage, is a rough measure of the difficulty of a text. *See also* READABILITY.

lexical entry

A word, phrase or AFFIX entered and defined in a dictionary.

lexical field

An alternative term for SEMANTIC FIELD.

lexical item

An alternative term for LEXEME.

lexical meaning *see* LINGUISTIC MEANING *under* MEANING; SEMANTICS.

lexical memory and semantic memory

Lexical memory is a person's ability to store and retrieve words in their morphological or phonological form, without necessarily knowing the meanings of the words.

Semantic memory, on the other hand, is the ability to store and retrieve the meanings of words. Semantic memory usually includes lexical memory.

lexical stress *see* STRESS.

lexical verb
An alternative term for FULL VERB.

lexical word
An alternative term for CONTENT WORD.

lexicalize *(v.)*
To represent an entity in the lexicon or vocabulary of a language; to identify an entity by a word or words.

Lexicalization is sometimes the same as word formation; a new word must be found to denote a new phenomenon, not only in science and technology but in society generally:

> narcoterrorism, telecottager, viewdata.

Other twentieth-century coinages – ageism, sexism, speciesism – are lexicalizations of the concepts of prejudice or discrimination based on age, sex or biological species.

The process of lexicalization can also be the reduction of a longer linguistic unit to a word or a phrase. Golf commentators, for example, use the terms *carded* and *posted* to refer to a golfer's score. *Carded* is the lexicalization of a form of words such as *the total number of strokes on the scorecard*, and *posted* the lexicalization of *the scores posted on the clubhouse notice board*. Similarly, the widening of a road to a dual carriageway is known by planners as *dualling*.

lexicography *(n.)*
The practice of compiling DICTIONARIES.

lexicon *(n.)*
1 A dictionary; the complete VOCABULARY of a language. Each item in a dictionary is known as a lexical entry.

2 The words in an individual's personal vocabulary, or an individual's personal lexicon.

lexis *(n.)*

1 The diction, or vocabulary, or register, of a piece of writing, in contrast to other levels of language, for example, morphology or syntax, in the same piece of writing.

2 An alternative term for LEXICON.

lingua franca

An auxiliary language; a language used as a common medium by speakers of two or more different languages. Lingua francas are widely used in multilingual societies. Historically, lingua franca was a mixture of Italian, French, Spanish, Greek and Arabic used as a trade language around the Mediterranean in the Middle Ages. Today, English is the main lingua franca in the world.

linguistic determinism *see* SAPIR-WHORF HYPOTHESIS.

linguistic meaning *see* MEANING.

linguistic relativity *see* SAPIR-WHORF HYPOTHESIS.

linguistic science

The systematic study of a language; also known as LINGUISTICS. With the invention of the gramophone, patented by Thomas Edison in 1877, phonetics began to establish itself as a scientific discipline. And since the 1950s, the study of linguistics has been scientific in the sense that it has amassed a body of theory that has been related to observed facts that, in turn, have been systematically classified in general laws. In the process, linguists have developed methods for discovering new facts in the domain.

Linguistics, then, is a science, but as a social rather than a natural science it still poses the unresolved question of objectivity. Many features of language can be measured objectively, but language is an aspect of human behaviour, and we cannot be objective if we are the subjects of our own investigation. We cannot be objective about the source or the cause of linguistic creativity, linguistic play or linguistic irrationality.

Noam Chomsky acknowledged this in the chapter 'Problems and Mysteries in the Study of Human Language' in *Reflections on Language* (1975), but in 1986, in *Knowledge of Language: its nature, origin and use*, Chomsky refers to generative grammar as being concerned with 'the principles and procedures brought to bear to attain full knowledge of a language'. Full knowledge of a language will be attained, if at all, only when we have full knowledge of the conscious and unconscious working of the brain. And even then we would not know how or when language originated in human pre-history.

A question about the scientific nature of linguistics stems, paradoxically, from the growth of linguistics as a professional discipline. Like other sciences, it has divided and multiplied repeatedly so that there are now several sciences of linguistics, some of them dealing with the same phenomena in different, even contradictory, ways. Each branch of linguistics and each system of grammar may be a science, but as long as one branch contradicts another there will be doubt about the kind of science linguistics is.

linguistics *(n.)*
The systematic study of language. Linguistics, like other academic disciplines, expanded, divided and multiplied in the twentieth century. The subdivisions include APPLIED LINGUISTICS, COMPARATIVE LINGUISTICS, PSYCHOLINGUISTICS and SOCIOLINGUISTICS.

linking verb
An alternative term for COPULA.

liquid *(adj./n.)*
A voiced consonant, particularly the letters /l/ and /r/.

literacy *(n.)*
1 The ability to read and write.

2 Knowledge of letters or literature; the condition of being educated.

literate *(adj.)*
1 Able to read and write.

2 Having some knowledge of letters or literature; educated.

litotes *(n.)*
A figure of speech consisting of an ironic understatement of the opposite case. *No mere token effort*, for example, is litotes for *a genuine effort, no small achievement* for *a great achievement*, and the colloquial *no big deal* for *small transaction*. Litotes contrasts with HYPERBOLE.

loan shift

A change in the meaning of a word brought about by the influence of the meaning of a word in another language.

When the Russian word *poputchik* was translated into English as *fellow-traveller*, it changed the meanings of *fellow* and *traveller* in that phrase from a travelling companion to someone who, perhaps secretly, supports communism. The German adjective *ausgezeichnet* (excellent) was translated into the American-English *out of sight*. The meaning of *sympathetic* has been affected by one of the meanings of the French *sympathique*, likeable, attractive. *See also* LOAN TRANSLATION.

loan translation

A form of BORROWING in which a word, phrase or longer linguistic unit is translated more or less literally into another language; also known as **calque**. Among the many loan translations from Latin are:

> Let the buyer beware (*Caveat emptor*)
>
> First among equals (*Primus inter pares*).

Loan translations from French include:

> delusion(s) of grandeur (*folie de grandeur*)
>
> They have learned nothing and forgotten nothing (*Ils n'ont rien appris ni rien oublié*).

The Spanish *el momento de la verdad* gives the English loan translation *the moment of truth*, and the German *Gastarbeiter* gives the loan translation *guest-worker*. *See also* LOAN SHIFT.

loan word

An alternative term for BORROWING.

locative *(adj./n.)*

A word or phrase that indicates a location. Some languages have inflections to express the locative case; in English, location is usually expressed by a preposition:

> at, in, on, above, under

or by an adverb:

> here, there, everywhere, nearby.

locution *see* ILLOCUTION, LOCUTION AND PERLOCUTION.

logocentric (adj.)

Descriptive of a view of culture, philosophy or human behaviour that is based on language; a view that regards language as a fundamental expression of reality. The words 'logocentric' and 'logocentrism' are sometimes associated with the STRUCTURALIST approach to textual analysis.

logogen (n.)

A hypothetical memory unit that forms an intersection of the networks that encode all forms of a word's representation: semantic, auditory and morphological. The hypothesis, proposed by the British psychologist, John Morton, suggests that all relevant information about a word, phrase or concept is integrated by the logogen. Morton's hypothesis is an addition to the body of theoretical work on language and memory, especially the concept of the **engram** (*en* + Greek *gramma*, letter) formulated in Germany at the beginning of the twentieth century. The engram is a hypothetical biological realization of memory, an alteration of neural tissue that represents what has been learned or memorized.

logogram (n.)

1 A sign or symbol that represents a word. Most characters in the Chinese writing system are logograms, as are the outlines in most shorthand systems. A logogram is also known as a **logograph**.

2 A symbol designed to represent the name or nature of a company or organization, for example, the fused V and W of Volkswagen. Such logograms, colloquially known as logos, could also be called logotypes, that is, words or letters written as a single piece of type, or DIGRAPHS (2).

logograph (n.)

An alternative term for LOGOGRAM (1).

loudness (n.)

The degree of audibility of a sound. In discussing speech, the term 'loudness' is preferred to the possibly ambiguous 'volume'.

lower case *see* CAPITAL LETTER.

low variety *see* HIGH VARIETY AND LOW VARIETY.

m

macrolinguistics and microlinguistics *(n.)*

Macrolinguistics is the study of language on a broad scale, usually at national or international level. The areas of study include national languages, language planning, phylogeny and language types or typologies. Macrolinguistics overlaps with COMPARATIVE LINGUISTICS and diachronic linguistics.

Microlinguistics is the detailed study of language in a specific context: accent, idiolect, DISCOURSE ANALYSIS, enclosed speech communities and limited forms of textual analysis.

main verb

The headword in a VERB phrase; the principal, or main, verb in a phrase, clause or sentence, in contrast to an AUXILIARY VERB; usually the minimum requirement of a clause or sentence; in some grammars an alternative term for FULL VERB or lexical verb.

When a clause or sentence contains only one verb that verb is a main verb:

> Eight athletes *ran* in the 100 metres.

When a verb phrase contains two or more verbs, the final verb in the phrase is the main verb, and the other verbs are auxiliary verbs:

> The 100 metres *should have been won* by the French athlete.

major part of speech

A traditional term for a content word. *See* CONTENT WORD AND FUNCTION WORD.

major sentence *see* SENTENCE.

majority language and minority language

A **majority language** is the language spoken by most of the population of a country, for example, the English language in Britain and the French language in France. The majority language is usually the NATIONAL LANGUAGE of a country.

A **minority language** is a language spoken by less than half the population of a country. Minority languages in Britain include Welsh, Gaelic, Hindi and Urdu. Minority languages in France include Breton in Brittany, Basque in the southwest and Arabic.

Majority languages usually offer greater opportunities than minority languages for education, employment and entertainment. *See also* OFFICIAL LANGUAGE.

mandative subjunctive *see* SUBJUNCTIVE.

manner *(n.)*

An ADVERB, adverbial or adverbial clause that indicates the way, or manner, in which something is done. Adverbials of manner normally answer the question *How?* Most adverbs of manner end in *-ly* and are often derived from adjectives:

Opposition Members of Parliament reacted angrily.

Adverbial phrases of manner may have adverbs as the headwords:

Rather reluctantly, the Speaker intervened

but some adverbial phrases of manner do not contain adverbs. In the sentence:

The Prime Minister accused the Opposition of behaving in a childish way

the adverbial is a prepositional phrase consisting of the preposition *in*, the indefinite article and the adjective *childish*, which modifies the noun *way*. *See also* CLAUSE.

marked and unmarked *(adj./v.)*

A linguistic unit is said to be **marked** when it contains an element or feature that is not present in the base, or standard, or **unmarked** linguistic unit. Some nouns can be marked to show gender:

waitress, widower;

to show plurality of number:

formulae, plateaux, symphonies;

and to show possession:

the symphony's composer, the symphonies' composers.

Adjectives and adverbs can be marked for comparison:

slower, slowest.

Verbs can be marked for tense:

walked (past tense and past participle);

for person, number, tense and aspect:

he walks (third person singular present tense);

they were walking (third person plural past continuous aspect).

Sentences, too, can be marked. A declarative sentence consisting of subject + verb + object is regarded as an unmarked, or kernel, sentence:

The magpie builds a nest.

The unmarked sentence can then be marked for the negative:

The magpie does not build a nest

marked for the interrogative:

Does the magpie build a nest?

and marked for the passive:

A nest is built by the magpie.

The term 'marked' can be applied to speech that shows a distinctive form of a regional or social accent. The condition of being marked is known as markedness.

masculine *see* GENDER.

mass noun
An alternative term for uncountable noun. *See* COUNTABLE NOUN AND UNCOUNTABLE NOUN.

matrix sentence *see* EMBEDDING.

mean length of utterance
The measure of the number of linguistic units, usually words but occasionally MORPHEMES, in a sample of speech. Mean length of utterance is a way of assessing a child's acquisition of language. It allows comparisons to be made between different stages in a child's development, and between a child's actual acquisition of language at a certain age and the notional level for children of that age.

meaning *(n.)*
The signification of information that is expressed in speech, writing or another system of communication. Definitions of the word 'meaning' and of various forms of meaning are disputed, but some distinctions can be made.

Generally, the meaning of a message is intentional, inferential and determined to some extent by the medium. That is, the meaning is what the person, the transmitter, intended to convey; it is also what the receiver apprehended and decoded; and because a message is transmitted by a medium – speech, writing or gestures, for example –

there is, in an abstract sense, meaning in the medium-bound message irrespective of the meaning intended by the transmitter or inferred by the receiver.

Meaning can be further subdivided into four broad areas: linguistic meaning; affective meaning; interpersonal and social meaning; and denotative, referential meaning.

Linguistic meaning, which is meaning in a purely linguistic context, includes lexical meaning, grammatical meaning, contextual meaning and figurative meaning. **Lexical meaning** is the meaning attached to a lexical entry in a dictionary and, usually, the meaning attached to such a lexical item in a sentence. **Grammatical meaning** is expressed by the grammatical categories of linguistic units in sentences:

> We shall travel faster without you.

We is the exclusive use of the plural first person pronoun; the MODAL AUXILIARY VERB *shall* adds the meaning of futurity to the main verb *travel*; *faster* is the comparative form of the gradable adverb; *without you* is an adverbial.

Contextual meaning is the meaning of a linguistic unit in a particular context, which is similar to SENSE. **Figurative meaning** is the metaphorical meaning that appears in figures of speech and in some idioms:

> She is starry-eyed.
>
> He has his head in the sand.

Affective meaning, also known as **expressive meaning**, is meaning in a psycholinguistic context and is the particular personal or emotional value that an individual may attach to a word, an image or a concept. Because affective meaning may include associated words and images, it is also known as **connotative meaning**.

Interpersonal and social meaning, also known as **situational meaning**, is meaning in a sociolinguistic context, and is generated by two or more persons in communication with each other. Meaning may be implicit in the nature of the speech act, for example, phatic or suasive meaning or implicature; meaning will also be expressed through the paralinguistic features of speech and the non-verbal communication that accompanies speech.

Denotative, referential meaning is extralinguistic in that it refers to realities beyond language:

> She weighs sixty-eight kilograms.

Denotative, referential meaning is also known as **factual meaning** or **objective meaning**. A particular form of denotative, referential meaning is **ostensive definition** (from Latin *ostendere*, stretch out to view). Ostension is the physical manifestation of a thing, or the exhibition of an example of a class of things, or the physical demonstration of a process.

medial *see* INITIAL, MEDIAL AND FINAL.

medial cluster *see* CONSONANT CLUSTER.

medium *(n.)*
The means, or channel, by which a MESSAGE is transmitted. In many forms of communication there are two or more media: an agreed system of signals and the physical means by which the signals are expressed and transmitted. In speech, for example, the media are the sound system of the language, the vocal tract of the speaker, and the sound waves; the message lies in the particular combinations of fluctuating sound waves. In writing, the media are the writing system of the language and the physical means of ink and paper or computer disk and screen; the message lies in the particular combinations of letters and words. In gesture, the media are the agreed sets of configurations of fingers and hands, and the fingers and hands themselves; the message lies in the combinations of momentary movements.

merging *(n.)*
An alternative term for CONVERGENCE.

mesolect *(n.)*
An intermediate stage, between ACROLECT and BASILECT, in the process of evolution from a CREOLE to the standard form of a particular language.

message *(n.)*
INFORMATION sent from a transmitter to a receiver by means of a messenger or MEDIUM; a combination of signs that denote the thing signified.

The content, or essence, of the message exists in prototypical form before it is encoded; the encoding transmutes the prototype into a form that can be transmitted. Decoding is usually said to change the message back to its original form before it was transmitted, but in speech, writing, non-verbal and other forms of communication the prototypical form in the mind of the transmitter is not normally available to the receiver; it may not even be available to the transmitter after it has been transmitted. *See also* MEANING.

metacognition *(n.)*
A term coined to express a person's awareness of his or her own mental processes, including some language functions. Metacognition is more likely to occur during the act of writing, which is a more conscious and deliberate activity than speech, but metacognition often accompanies the TIP-OF-THE-TONGUE experience.

metalanguage *(n.)*
A language used to describe or analyse language; a TERMINOLOGY used to discuss linguistic features.

Almost all specialist activities generate particular terminologies. The metalanguage of English grammar includes the terms 'main verb', 'auxiliary verb', 'principal clause' and 'subordinate clause'. The study of metalanguage is known as metalinguistics. *See also* JARGON.

metaphor *(n.)*
1 A figure of speech in which one thing or circumstance is expressed in terms of another so that, through the comparison, the thing or circumstance is made more vivid and more memorable. This type of metaphor, which is usually coined deliberately by the writer or speaker, is known as a **poetic metaphor**:

> a flight of geese is a skiff of visible sound
> trailing an audible wake across the sky

but the same type of metaphor is used by politicians:

> the tide of public opinion
>
> the oxygen of publicity

and by advertising copywriters:

> You're always streets ahead with Street Cred shoes.

2 A form of words, often a fixed or idiomatic expression, in which one thing is expressed in terms of another. The difference between this type of metaphor and the type discussed above is that this type is not normally a deliberately coined figure of speech but is a fixed expression, that is, a form of words that already exists in the language:

> Let me put you in the picture.
>
> Must you keep raking up the past?
>
> He launched into his argument.

Such metaphors are common in idiomatic English, and for that reason they are known as **conventional metaphors**. Conventional metaphors also appear in more formal contexts:

> the cut and thrust of debate
>
> a headword
>
> a key word, a key sentence
>
> a kernel word, a kernel sentence.

3 A third type of metaphor, a **mixed metaphor**, is one in which an absurd or contradictory element is added to the comparison:

> Once you're out of the woods it's plain sailing.

See also SIMILE.

metathesis *(n.)*

The transposition of sounds or letters in a word; the result of such transposition. Examples are the Modern English spellings of the Old English words:

> adder/nædre, bird/brid, horse/hros, run/yrnan.

When metathesis is a result of a slip of the tongue it is sometimes known as **spoonerism**, after W.A. Spooner (1844–1930):

> She's very pond of fainting.

metonymy *(n.)*

A figure of speech that uses an essential aspect of a thing to denote the thing itself. The metonym *the classroom* is sometimes used as a term for teaching, or the teaching profession, or education as an actual experience. The metonym *Westminster* is used as a term for the House of Commons, or the House of Commons and the House of Lords, or for parliamentary democracy.

A single example of metonymy is known as a metonym.

microlinguistics *see* MACROLINGUISTICS AND MICROLINGUISTICS.

Middle English

The ENGLISH LANGUAGE from the end of the Old English period to the beginning of early Modern English, that is, from around 1150 to around 1450.

The Middle English period was a time of rapid linguistic change. Most of the grammatical inflections of Old English disappeared; the syntax changed from that of Old English to a form closer to Modern

English; there was extensive borrowing of words from FRENCH and LATIN; the sound of the language began to change in the process known as the GREAT VOWEL SHIFT. *See also* CHANGE.

minimal free form
An alternative term for MINIMUM FREE FORM.

minimal pair
Two words that differ in meaning by one contrasting sound. The contrasts, for example, between the minimum pairs *ban* and *pan*, *mine* and *nine* can be identified as different PHONEMES.

minimum distance principle
An alternative term for ADJACENCY PRINCIPLE.

minimum free form
A definition of WORD offered by the American linguist Leonard Bloomfield (1887–1949); also known as a **minimal free form**. *See also* LEXEME; MORPHEME.

minor part of speech
A traditional term for function word. *See* CONTENT WORD AND FUNCTION WORD.

minor sentence *see* SENTENCE.

minority language *see* MAJORITY LANGUAGE AND MINORITY LANGUAGE.

misrelated participle
A present or past participle form of a verb, the -ING FORM or -ED FORM, that is separated from the appropriate noun, noun phrase or pronoun in a sentence. The meaning of this sentence:

> Driving at night along Princes Street, Edinburgh Castle is silhouetted against the skyline

is clear, but there is a momentary absurdity because the present participle *Driving* and the noun phrase *Edinburgh Castle* are misrelated. Standard English requires that the participial clause be followed immediately by the appropriate noun, noun phrase or pronoun, as in this sentence:

Driving at night along Princes Street, one can see Edinburgh Castle silhouetted against the skyline.

In the sentence:

Convicted of fraud, the judge passed sentence

the past participle *Convicted* and the noun *judge* are misrelated. The sentence could be re-written as:

Convicted of fraud, he was sentenced by the judge

or

The judge passed sentence on the man convicted of fraud.

Misrelated participles, which are also known as **dangling participles** or **hanging participles**, show the importance of the ADJACENCY PRINCIPLE.

mixed metaphor *see* METAPHOR (3).

mobility *(n.)*

The ability of a linguistic unit to change position in a clause or sentence without distorting the meaning. *See also* EMPHASIS; END FOCUS AND FRONT FOCUS; INITIAL, MEDIAL AND FINAL.

modal auxiliary verb

A subclass of verbs that express grammatical MOOD, or mode, of utterance; the verbs:

can, could, shall, should, will, would, may, might, must.

Modal auxiliaries express various concepts, attitudes and modes of thought, such as possibility, capability and permission:

can, could, may, might

futurity, and sometimes determination:

shall, will

likelihood and conditionality:

should, would, may, might

duty, obligation and necessity:

should, must.

Modal auxiliaries differ from full verbs in several ways. As the term 'auxiliary' indicates, they cannot function independently but must precede main verbs. When they seem to function independently, the main verb is always implied:

Finish the climb. You must [finish].

They exist only in their base forms, and have no -ING FORM, -ED FORM or -s forms. The exception is *will* in constructions such as:

He willed himself to finish the climb.

The main verb that follows the modal auxiliary always appears in the base form:

You must leave now. We can meet again tomorrow.

In expressing questions, modal auxiliaries appear before the subject of the sentence:

Must I leave now? Can we meet again tomorrow?

In expressing negation, they appear before the word *not*:

You must not stay here.

The modal property of these verbs is known as modality. *See also* EPISTEMIC AND DEONTIC; SEMI-MODAL AUXILIARY VERB.

Modern English (ME)

The ENGLISH LANGUAGE as it has been spoken and written in the period broadly from around 1450 to the present day. The period can be divided into Early Modern English, from around 1450 to around 1700, and Later Modern English, from around 1700 to the present day. *See also* CHANGE.

modification *(n.)*

The semantic or grammatical influence exerted by one linguistic unit on another.

An adjective modifies a noun by defining the meaning of the noun and by extending a one-word noun to a noun phrase. In the phrase *modern music* the noun *music* is modified by the adjective *modern*.

An adverb modifies a verb. In the sentence:

The music was played repeatedly

the verb *played* is modified by the adverb *repeatedly*. An adverb can also modify an adjective. In the phrase *thoroughly modern* the adjective *modern* is modified by the adverb *thoroughly*. And an adverb can modify other adverbs, as in *supremely confidently*.

Modification can be further defined as premodification or post-modification. **Premodification** occurs when a word or words precede a headword and add information to the headword.

He played thoroughly modern music.

The object of the sentence, *thoroughly modern music*, is a noun phrase with the headword, *music*; the words *thoroughly modern* premodify the noun. Words that premodify in this way are known as premodifiers. A particular category of premodifier is the **noun premodifier**, also known as a **noun modifier**. Nouns are usually premodified by adjectives, but they can also be premodified by other nouns:

> *passenger* seat, *petrol* pump, *windscreen* wiper, *garden* furniture, *government* department.

Although these nouns function like adjectives, they differ from full adjectives in being ungradable:

> *passengerer, *petrolest,

and it is more appropriate to define them as noun modifiers.

Postmodification occurs when a word, phrase or clause follows a headword or key word and adds information to the word. In the sentence:

> The man is armed and dangerous

the adjective phrase *armed and dangerous* postmodifies the noun phrase *The man*. In the sentence

> Police arrested the man, who was armed and dangerous

the subordinate relative clause *who was armed and dangerous* postmodifies the noun phrase. Words that postmodify in this way are known as **postmodifiers**.

modifier *(n.)*
A word, phrase or clause that adds information to, and thus modifies, a headword. *See also* MODIFICATION.

monogenesis and polygenesis *(n.)*
Monogenesis is the theory that all languages originated from a single source. **Polygenesis** is the theory that languages originated from several sources. *See also* INDO-EUROPEAN.

monoglot
An alternative word for MONOLINGUAL.

monolingual *(adj.)*
Of a person, speaking, writing or understanding only one language; of a country, acknowledging only one language. Few countries are monolingual in the sense that only one language is spoken within their

boundaries. Most countries are MULTILINGUAL or BILINGUAL because the countries' populations include speakers of minority languages. The condition of being monolingual is known as monolingualism. An alternative term for monolingual is **monoglot**, one tongue or language.

monophthong *(n.)*

A vowel pronounced as a single sound, as in *pat, pet, pit, pot* and *putt*. *See also* DIPHTHONG.

monosyllable and polysyllable *(n.)*

A **monosyllable** is a word of only one syllable, that is, a single unit of pronunciation. In the preceding sentence the words *A*, *is, word, of, one* and *that* are monosyllables.

A **polysyllable** is a word of three or more syllables. In the first sentence of this entry the words *monosyllable, syllable* and *pronunciation* are polysyllables.

A word of two syllables, for example *only* and *unit* in the first sentence of this entry, is known as a **disyllable**.

English prose is normally a mix of monosyllables, disyllables and polysyllables.

monotransitive *see* TRANSITIVE VERB AND INTRANSITIVE VERB.

mood *(n.)*

A property of verbs that indicates whether their mode of action expresses fact, possibility, command, wish or supposition. Traditional grammar identifies three moods, INDICATIVE, IMPERATIVE and SUB-JUNCTIVE. The term DECLARATIVE is sometimes used as an alternative for indicative.

It can be argued that mood is determined not just by the verb but by the type of sentence in which it appears, and by this argument, sentences that ask questions are INTERROGATIVE in mood, sentences that express exclamations are exclamatory in mood, and sentences that exhort or urge are hortative.

In English, mood is often expressed by MODAL AUXILIARY VERBS. An alternative term for mood is modality.

morpheme *(n.)*

The smallest linguistic unit that expresses meaning. The word *linguistic* consists of three morphemes: the root word *lingua*, the agent suffix *-ist*, and the adjective suffix *-ic*. The word *meaning* consists of two morphemes: the root word *mean*, and the noun suffix *-ing*. The words *The*, *unit* and *that* each consist of one morpheme.

Morphemes can be classified as free or bound. A **free morpheme** can function as a separate word; a **bound morpheme** cannot function separately but must be part of a word. The word *smallest*, for example, consists of the free morpheme *small* and the bound morpheme *-est*. The word *disreputable* consists of one free morpheme, *repute*, and two bound morphemes, the negative prefix *dis-* and the adjective suffix *-able*. *See also* ALLOMORPH.

morphology *(n.)*
The branch of grammar concerned with the form and structure of words, including derivations, inflections and changes of form.

morphophonology *(n.)*
The branch of linguistics that deals with the phonological representation of MORPHEMES, or the morphological representation of PHONEMES. Morphophonology, also known as **morphophonemics**, relates the forms of words to their sounds. *See also* PHONETICS.

morphophonemics
An alternative term for MORPHOPHONOLOGY.

morphosyntax *(n.)*
The combinations of morphological and syntactical properties in some grammatical categories.

The morphology of personal pronouns, for example, expresses the grammatical category of case, and a pronoun's morphological form for case is often an indication of its syntactic function as the subject or object, or the pro-form for the subject or object, of a sentence:

> *She* sent *him* a birthday card.

Nouns express the grammatical category of number morphologically, as singular or plural forms, and syntactically through agreement in number with the verb:

> The temperature *is* falling.

> Snowflakes *are* falling.

multilingual *(adj./n.)*
Of a person, speaking, writing or understanding three or more languages; of a country, acknowledging or accommodating three or more

languages. In Switzerland, for example, there are four official languages, German, French, Italian and Romansch. A fifth language, English, is sometimes used by those involved in international trade and commerce.

The condition of being multilingual is known as multilingualism. The word **polyglot**, meaning many tongues or languages, or a speaker of many languages, is an alternative term for multilingual. *See also* BILINGUAL; MONOLINGUAL.

multiple apposition *see* APPOSITION.

multiple coordination
Three or more coordinate words, phrases or clauses. *See also* COORDINATION.

multiple meaning *see* POLYSEME.

multiple subordination
A SENTENCE with a main CLAUSE and two or more subordinate clauses.

mutation *(n.)*
A change in a vowel brought about by the influence of other PHONEMES in the same word; also known as **umlaut**. Examples of mutation are the plural noun forms:

    men, women, children, feet, geese, teeth, lice, mice.

n

narrative *(adj./n.)*
A written or spoken account of a sequence of events. The word has a much wider application than story-telling. Because all writing is a linear progression, line by line and page by page, and because all writing contains a succession, however random, of incidents, ideas or images, it follows that almost every piece of writing forms a narrative sequence. Every writer plays some role in what he or she writes, even if it is only the role of grammatical person *I*, *you*, *he* or *she*, and so every narrative contains a narrative standpoint or viewpoint. Most sentences, and most

spoken utterances of sentence-length or longer, have some of these narrative features.

narrow transcription *see* TRANSCRIPTION.

narrowing *see* BROADENING AND NARROWING.

nasal *(n./adj.)*

A speech sound produced by a flow of air through the cavity of the nose; the consonants /m/ and /n/ and the /ng/ sound (as in *song*).

national language

The main system of speech and writing in a nation, for example, English in Australia, Italian in Italy.

The national LANGUAGE is often the nation's OFFICIAL LANGUAGE, that is, the language that is formally recognized and used in national government, courts of law, higher education and national broadcasting. A country's national language can sometimes differ from its official language. French was the official language of England from the time of the Conquest until 1362, but the MAJORITY LANGUAGE and the national language was English. Today, the majority language, and in that sense the national language, of Scotland is Scots, but the official language is English.

Some bilingual and multilingual nations acknowledge the linguistic diversity of their populations, and also try to avoid possible linguistic and ethnic conflict, by having two or more official languages. In Canada, for example, the official languages are English and French; in Switzerland the official languages are German, French, Italian and Romansch.

national language noun

The noun that denotes the national language of a country.

Some patterns emerge in the forms of nouns for the national languages of Europe and other countries, but overall the naming process is inconsistent. When the name of the country ends with -*a*, the name of the language ends with -*ian* or -*an*:

> Albanian, Bulgarian, Romanian, Russian.

The noun for the language also ends with -*ian* or -*an* when the name of the country ends with -*y*:

> German, Hungarian, Italian.

When the name of the country ends with *-land*, the noun for the language ends with *-ish*:

English, Finnish, Polish

But the Netherlands (Dutch) and Iceland (Icelandic) break the pattern, while Danish, Spanish and Swedish extend the pattern irregularly. French, Greek, Portuguese and Welsh are isolates among the European national language nouns.

The noun for the national language usually has the same form as the nationality adjective:

Bulgarian, English, Greek.

native language

The language of the speech community or country in which a person is born. The term 'native language' is usually synonymous with FIRST LANGUAGE, that is, the language acquired by a child in the family home. Some children, however, acquire a minority language in the family home; when they go to school they learn a MAJORITY LANGUAGE, or the official or NATIONAL LANGUAGE, and then abandon their first language in favour of the majority language, which usually offers greater opportunities for education, employment, communication and entertainment. Until the early twentieth century, for example, some children in the Western Isles of Scotland acquired Gaelic in the family home and learned English when they went to school. In Britain today some children of Asian parents acquire Urdu or Hindi in the home and learn English at school. *See also* NON-NATIVE VARIETY.

native speaker

A speaker of the language of a particular speech community or country; a speaker whose first language is that of a particular speech community or country. *See also* NATIVE LANGUAGE.

nativism *(n.)*

1 The theory that a person inherently, or innately, understands the relationships of sound and sense in a language. The theories of innateness and a language acquisition device are particular versions of nativism.

2 More generally, a view of language that stresses genetic influence or biological pre-programming rather than BEHAVIOURISM.

See also INNATENESS; SPECIES-SPECIFIC.

natural gender

The biological GENDER, or sex, of a person or animal, as distinct from grammatical gender.

natural language

A LANGUAGE that has evolved through generations of speakers. Natural languages are sometimes contrasted with ARTIFICIAL LANGUAGES.

naturalism *see* NOMINALISM AND NATURALISM.

necessity *see* CONTINGENCY AND NECESSITY.

negation *(n.)*

The act of denying or contradicting a statement. Negation is often expressed through the words *no, no one, nobody, nothing, nowhere, never, not*:

> *No one* else could be as slow as this. There is *nothing* we can do but wait. *Never* again will I trust him.

Negation can also be expressed through negative prefixes:

> apolitical, anticlockwise, contradiction, counterproductive, disagreeable, illegal, immobilize, inadequate, non-verbal, unfortunate.

A widely used negative construction is the verb *do* as an auxiliary verb followed by the negative particle *not*, or the colloquial contraction *n't*, followed by the main verb:

> He *did not have* time to develop the film yesterday.
>
> He *doesn't think* the prints will be ready today.

Other negative constructions are the appropriate form of the verb *be* or *have*, either as a main verb or an auxiliary, followed by *not*:

> Your photographs *are not* ready.
>
> I *have not* developed the film.

negative *(adj./n.)*

A prefix, word, phrase or clause that expresses negation. A **transposed negative**, also known as a **transferred negative**, is one that appears in a main clause but applies to a subordinate clause:

> I *can't believe* that we can trust him

for

> I believe that we *can't trust* him

and

We *can't seem* to convince him

for

It seems we *can't convince* him.

negative pronoun
A term sometimes applied to the pronouns:

none, no one, nobody, nothing, neither.

negative question
A QUESTION expressed as a form of NEGATION:

Have you *nowhere* to go? Is there *no one* who can help?

negative transfer
An alternative term for INTERFERENCE.

negator *(n.)*
A word or AFFIX that expresses NEGATION. *See also* NEGATIVE; NEGATIVE PRONOUN.

neologism *(n.)*
A new word or expression; the process of COINAGE or of using a new word or expression. Neologisms are usually coined to denote new ideas and phenomena. Many neologisms are scientific or medical:

superovulation, videosomatography, zeranol.

Some neologisms identify new social or political phenomena:

ecocide, Eurocrat, surfing, tokenism.

Other neologisms, for example, *nimby* (an ACRONYM for *not in my back yard*), *technophobia*, *glitterati* (an ironic term for 'celebrities', by analogy with *literati*, authors), may be the result of wordplay rather than necessity.

All neologisms are examples of WORD FORMATION, but only a few types of word formation can be classified as neologism. Acronyms, EPONYMS and coinages are clearly new expressions, but other types of word formation use existing words or elements. *See also* AFFIX; BACK-FORMATION; BLEND; BORROWING; CLIPPING; COMPOUND; CONTRAC-TION; CONVERSION; DERIVATION; HYPHENATION; LEXICALIZE; PARASYNTHESIS.

nesting (v./n.)

The inclusion of one linguistic unit, usually a phrase, within a larger linguistic unit of the same type. In the sentence

The bird perched on a branch of a tree in the forest

the words *on a branch of a tree in the forest* form an extended prepositional phrase with the headword *on*. The words *in the forest* form a prepositional phrase that is contained by, or is nesting in, the larger prepositional phrase *of a tree in the forest*; in turn, the phrase *of a tree in the forest* is nesting in the larger unit *on a branch of a tree in the forest*.

The same sentence can be analysed in the same way but in terms of an extended noun phrase, *a branch of a tree in the forest*, with the headword *forest*. The noun phrase *the forest* is nesting in the larger noun phrase *a tree in the forest*, and *a tree in the forest*, in turn, is nesting in the longer noun phrase *a branch of a tree in the forest*.

Both these analyses, the prepositional and the nominal, are ENDO-CENTRIC; that is, each linguistic unit is part of a larger unit of the same type.

Some linguists state that nesting and EMBEDDING are identical, but a clear distinction can be made between the two. Nesting is often an endocentric construction in the sense that the nesting phrase has the same function as its headword. In the example above, each noun phrase has the same function as each noun. Nesting is also a type of RECURSION, that is, a construction in which a particular class of word or type of phrase is repeated.

Embedding, by contrast, involves the complete encapsulation within a sentence of a word, phrase or clause that modifies the subject of the sentence or the subject of the main clause:

Six holidaymakers, *all from Manchester*, were slightly injured in the coach crash.

Coach driver Alf Ramsden (*fifty-four*), escaped without injury.

The coach, *which is owned by NorHols Travel*, was in collision with a lorry south of Heidelberg.

network English

The form of English spoken by announcers and news readers on national, or network, coast-to-coast television programmes in the United States; a national as distinct from a regional American accent; also known as General American.

The term 'network English' is equally applicable in a British context; most broadcasters on the national British network use a form of

RECEIVED PRONUNCIATION that is acceptable and intelligible to a majority of audiences. *See also* BBC ENGLISH.

neurolinguistics *(n.)*

The branch of linguistics concerned with the language activities of the brain. Part of our understanding of vocabulary, grammar, and the associated functions of remembering and forgetting, comes from the work of neurosurgeons. *See also* LANGUAGE CENTRES OF THE BRAIN; PSYCHOLINGUISTICS.

neuter *(adj./n.)*

The GENDER that denotes inanimate things and is neither masculine nor feminine; one of the four categories – masculine, feminine, common, neuter – that classify nouns and pronouns in terms of the sex of the persons, animals or occasionally things, for example, ships, that they denote.

neutralize *(v.)*

1 To nullify the differences in the sounds of some PHONEMES in particular contexts. The sounds of the consonants /p/, /t/ and /k/ are usually distinguishable from the sounds /b/, /d/ and /g/, but after an initial /s/ the differences are neutralized. The /p/ of *speck*, for example, is neutralized to *sbeck, the /t/ of *step* is neutralized to *sdep, and the /c/ of *scan* neutralized to *sgan.

2 Three forms of neutralization occur in editing direct speech to indirect speech.

> (a) She said, 'I told you yesterday that I have resigned.'

> (b) She said that she had told him the previous day that she had resigned.

The back-shifting of verbs neutralizes the simple past tense *told* and the present perfect *have resigned* in sentence (a) to the past perfect, *had told* and *had resigned* in sentence (b). First person and second person pronouns *I* and *you* are neutralized to third person *she* and *him*. Adverbials and other words denoting immediacy of time or place are neutralized so that *yesterday* in sentence (a) becomes the *previous day* in sentence (b).

new information *see* GIVEN AND NEW INFORMATION.

node (n.)

A point of intersection in a TREE DIAGRAM. The misleading term 'root' is sometimes applied to the topmost node of a tree diagram; ambiguity can be avoided by using the alternative term ACRONODE, top node.

noise (n.)

Random or irregular fluctuations that are not part of a signal and may distort or obscure the signal.

This definition applies mainly to electronic communications, and can be applied to speech that is transmitted electronically, for example, by radio, television, audio tape or compact disc. Paralinguistic features of speech such as accent, voice quality, rapid tempo and pausing can also be considered as noise if these features obscure the meaning of an utterance.

nomenclature (n.)

A set of names that designate things and classes of things in a systematic way. The advantage of nomenclatures is that the systematic naming process gives the subject area an order that does not exist in real life; the consistency of the terminology lends a consistency to the subject and creates an orderliness in the development of knowledge. The nomenclatures devised by Linnaeus and Jussieu transformed the study of botany. The lack of agreed nomenclatures in English grammar reflects the fragmented nature of the subject.

nominal (adj./n.)

Concerning NOUNS, noun phrases and noun clauses; a noun, noun phrase or noun clause.

The term 'nominal' can also be applied to words from other word classes, for example, the adjectives *rich* and *poor*, in *the rich* and *the poor*, and the past participles of verbs, as in *the wounded, the defeated*.

nominal clause *see* CLAUSE; RELATIVE CLAUSE.

nominal group

A syntactic unit equivalent to a NOUN PHRASE. The term 'nominal group' is used in those grammars that draw distinctions between a PHRASE and a group; the term can also be applied to some forms of NOMINALIZATION.

nominal relative clause *see* CLAUSE; RELATIVE CLAUSE.

nominalism and naturalism *(n.)*

Nominalism is the view that words have no inherent or necessary connection with the things they denote, and that the connection between words and things is arbitrary and coventionalized. Most linguists accept the nominalist view of language but allow the exceptions of ONOMATOPOEIC and PHONAESTHETIC words and some forms of iconicity.

Naturalism is the view that there is an inherent, or natural, connection between words and the things they denote. *See also* ARBITRARINESS.

nominalization *(n.)*

The process of forming nouns or noun phrases from words of other classes; nouns and noun phrases formed in this way. Nouns formed from adjectives include:

> openness (open), pacifism/pacifist (pacific) sameness (same).

Nouns formed from verbs include:

> seclusion (seclude), teacher (teach) vibration (vibrate).

Some phrases, notably those beginning with or including the -ING FORM of a verb, can be seen as nominalizations. In the sentence:

> Swimming and cycling keep you fit

the subject is the nominal group *Swimming and cycling*. Similarly, in the sentence:

> Being drunk and disorderly is a crime

the subject is the **nominal group** *Being drunk and disorderly*, which consists of the *-ing* form, the adjectives *drunk* and *disorderly*, and the conjunction *and*. Neither of these nominal groups, *Swimming and cycling* and *Being drunk and disorderly*, contains a full noun and yet each functions as a noun phrase.

The verb for the action of nominalizing is nominalize.

nominative *(adj./n.)*

An alternative word for SUBJECTIVE.

non-assertive *see* ASSERTIVE AND NON-ASSERTIVE.

non-count noun

An alternative term for uncountable noun. *See* COUNTABLE NOUN AND UNCOUNTABLE NOUN.

non-defining relative clause *see* CLAUSE.

non-finite clause *see* CLAUSE.

non-finite verb *see* FINITE AND NON-FINITE VERB.

non-gradable *see* ADJECTIVE; ADVERB; ANTONYM; GRADABILITY.

non-literate *(adj./n.)*
Without a writing system. The term can be applied to a society or a person who has no access to a writing system, although the society and the individual may have a rich oral culture. The term can also be applied to a language that has no written form. *See also* ALITERATE; ILLITERATE.

non-native variety
A form of a language that has developed in a country in which it is not the indigenous or NATIVE LANGUAGE. The term can be applied to the variety, or varieties, of English that have developed in India and the variety of French used in Haiti. *See also* NATIONAL LANGUAGE.

non-proximal *(adj.)*
An alternative term for non-proximate. *See* PROXIMATE AND REMOTE.

non-restrictive relative clause
An alternative term for non-defining relative clause. *See* CLAUSE.

non-sentence *(n.)*
An alternative term for minor sentence. *See* SENTENCE.

non-standard English *see* STANDARD AND NON-STANDARD ENGLISH.

non-verbal communication
Communication without the use of speech or writing; communication by signals transmitted by the human body. Non-verbal communication (n-vc), colloquially known as **body language**, consists of several forms of communication: (a) facial expression, including eye-contact (facial movements and gestures are also known as **kinesics**, from Greek *kinesis*, movement); (b) physical contact: touching, embracing, caressing, striking; (c) gestures: movements of the fingers, hands, arms, shoulders and head; (d) proximity, also known as PROXEMICS: the distance

between two or more persons during an interpersonal encounter; (e) orientation: the angle or stance – face to face, side by side, back to back – adopted by one person towards another; and (f) posture: a person's overall bodily configuration when sitting or standing.

This combination of n-vc factors allows subtle and complex patterns of communication. Some n-vc is involuntary or unconscious, for example, the dilating and contracting of the pupils of the eyes; n-vc signals vary in number and intensity from one person to another; and n-vc repertoires vary from one culture to another. Even so, a grammar, or proto-grammar, is implicit in some features of n-vc, especially gesture, which is the basis of the sign languages used by deaf or mute persons.

non-word *(n.)*

A word that is not recorded in dictionaries, including specialist dictionaries. The term is usually applied to errors, that is, to forms that a speaker or writer believes to be correct but that are wrong: *inpenetrable* for *impenetrable*, *resolvement* for *resolution* and, until the form was recorded in the *New Shorter Oxford English Dictionary* in 1993, *irregardless* for *irrespective* or *regardless*.

In written form, a non-word is indistinguishable from a spelling error, but a non-word is not the same as a NONCE-WORD or a **slip of the tongue**. *See also* PARAPRAXIS.

nonce-word *(n.)*

A word deliberately coined for a specific occasion. Examples of nonce-words in Shakespeare include *allotery*, a share or portion, in *As You Like It*; *appertainments*, rights or prerogatives, in *Troilus and Cressida*; and *vizaments*, advisements or deliberations, in *The Merry Wives of Windsor*.

Compound nonce-words are a feature of the poetry of Gerard Manley Hopkins: *dapple-dawn-drawn*, *wilful-wavier*, *dare-gale* and *beadbonny*. And nonce-words are a major feature of the nonsense prose and verse of Edward Lear and the nonsense verse of Lewis Carroll and Ogden Nash. Lear offers a lexicon of nonce-words in 'Mr Lear's Wurbl Inwentions: a little dictionary'; Lewis Carroll's 'Jabberwocky', which begins ''Twas brillig, and the slithy toves', from *Through the Looking-Glass*, is the most ingenious use of nonce-words in the language. The *pecticut* and lack of *ecticut* of Ogden Nash's shameless girl from Connecticut are only two of the many nonce-words in his light verse.

Linguists and lexicographers disagree about the nature of nonce-words, but the meaning of the term is clear and exclusive. A nonce-word is not the same as a NEOLOGISM, which usually meets phenomenological rather than aesthetic or psychological needs. If a nonce-word is assimilated or partly assimilated into the language – Horace Walpole's *serendipity*, for example, or *floccinaucinihilipilification* (Sir Walter Scott credited William Shenstone with the coinage in the slightly different form *floccipaucinihilipilification*) – then it ceases to be a nonce-word. **Slips of the tongue** – the child's *snookermarket* and *flutterby* for *supermarket* and *butterfly*, *syndromatic* from *syndrome* and *symptomatic*, *pompificate* from *pompous* and *pontificate* – are amusing and may be revealing but they are not nonce-words because they are not coinages for specific occasions. These minor accidents of language could better be defined as NON-WORDS or PARAPRAXES. *See also* HAPAX LEGOMENON.

normative *(adj.)*

Establishing a norm or standard; prescribing a norm or standard; prescriptive. The term is used pejoratively in some modern grammars to dismiss the rules of traditional, prescriptive GRAMMAR, some of which were unjustified because they were the rules of Latin grammar and ignored or contradicted the real nature of the English language. But ideas of CORRECTNESS, and perhaps some forms of prescriptivism, are inevitable when a language is standardized because the standards, or norms, come to be seen not simply as neutral points of reference or comparison but as ideal or essential forms. Divergence from the norm comes to be seen not as permissible variation but as deviance. *See also* ACCEPTABLE; USAGE.

Norse *see* OLD NORSE.

notation *(n.)*

An alternative term for TRANSCRIPTION.

notional agreement/concord *see* AGREEMENT.

notional grammar *see* GRAMMAR.

noun *(n.)*

A large and varied open class of words that can be defined in terms of their functions, that is, syntactically, or in terms of their meaning, that is, notionally. Nouns were formerly known as **substantives**.

Functional definitions are: the headword in a noun phrase; the subject, object or complement of a verb; the object of a preposition; a word that inflects for plurals and possessives; a word that can be preceded by the definite or indefinite article; a word that can be modified by an adjective. The traditional definition of a noun, the name of a person, place or thing, is inadequate, but if the phrase *the name of* is understood to mean a word that denotes or signifies, and if the word *thing* is seen as one of the most polysemic words in the language and one that refers to different forms of reality, the traditional definition of a noun could be rewritten as: a word that denotes or signifies a person, place, activity or abstraction, including natural phenomena, ideas, emotions, actions and processes.

This definition is still notional rather than formal and is concerned with semantics rather than syntax, but semantics (meaning) is the essential purpose of a definition. A notional definition also acknowledges our nomenclative impulse, our irresistible need to identify and name everything in our world in order to orientate ourselves in the world. Functional and notional definitions are not mutually exclusive but complementary.

Some nouns can be identified by their suffixes; the Old English suffixes *-dom*, *-er*, *-hood*, *-ness* and *-ship*:

> wisdom, manager, likelihood, goodness, friendship;

the suffixes *-eer*, *-ier*, *-or* and *-ery*:

> mountaineer, soldier, spectator, surgery;

and *-ation*, *-ism*, *-ity* and *-ology*:

> regulation, realism, absurdity, cosmology.

Suffixes also indicate the gender – masculine or feminine – of some nouns:

> bridegroom, widower, horsewoman, midwife, waitress.

The gender of some nouns is expressed by different words for the masculine and feminine persons or creatures:

> girl/boy, daughter/son, aunt/uncle, cow/bull.

Nouns vary for number – singular (one only) or plural (two or more) – normally by adding the inflection *s* for plural nouns, but there are irregular plural forms:

> man/men, knife/knives, medium/media, plateau/plateaux.

Some nouns have the same form for singular and plural:

> aircraft, deer, sheep, oats

and some forms that were once plural are now treated as singular:

> economics, mathematics, physics.

The concept of number is also involved in COLLECTIVE NOUNS, that is, nouns that denote groups or collections:

> an *archipelago* of islands
>
> a *flock* of sheep
>
> a *constellation* of stars.

The collective noun is singular:

> a board (singular) of directors (plural)
>
> a crew (singular) of mechanics (plural)

but collective nouns allow notional AGREEMENT; that is, a collective noun can be followed by a singular or plural form of a verb, depending on whether one wishes to stress the unity or the multiplicity denoted by the collective noun:

> The Cabinet *are* divided.
>
> The committee *is* unanimous.

Nouns are inflected for the possessive case:

> the woman's car, the women's cars;
>
> the car's windscreen, the cars' windscreens.

Nouns can be further classified into the categories:

> common: *street*, proper: *Albert Street*
>
> animate: *passenger*, inanimate: *aircraft*
>
> abstract: *philosophy*, concrete: *apple*
>
> countable/count: *books*, uncountable/non-count: *butter*.

See also PLURALE TANTUM; PREDICATIVE; SINGULARE TANTUM.

noun clause

An alternative term for nominal clause. *See* CLAUSE.

noun modifier *see* MODIFICATION.

noun phrase

A group of words with a noun or pronoun as its headword; a group of words that functions in a sentence like a noun; an equivalent term for NOMINAL GROUP. In the sentence:

> The young writer earns a living reviewing other writers' books

there are three noun phrases: *The young writer*, *a living* and *other writers' books*. Although a phrase is normally considered to be a linguistic unit that is larger than one word but does not contain a predicate or a finite verb and is thus not a clause, some linguists define a single word as a noun phrase.

> *Writers* earn a living reviewing *books.*

The entire subject or object of a sentence is sometimes defined as a noun phrase, even when the subject or the object is a complete clause. In the sentence:

> Writers who cannot earn a living from their own books sometimes review other writers' books

the words *who cannot earn a living from their own books* form a subordinate relative clause modifying the noun *Writers*, but some linguists would define *who cannot earn a living from their own books* as a noun phrase because it can be treated as the subject of the verb *review.*

noun premodifier *see* MODIFICATION.

nucleus *see* SYLLABLE.

number *(n.)*
One of the two mutually exclusive grammatical categories, **singular** (one only) or **plural** (two or more). In English, number applies to nouns:

> table (singular), tables (plural)

to PRONOUNS:

> I (singular), we (plural)

to DETERMINERS:

> this (singular), these (plural)

and to VERBS:

> he walks (singular), they walk (plural).

numeral *(n.)*
The closed class of words that denote numbers. Numerals can be divided into two main sub-classes, cardinal and ordinal; a third sub-class consists only of the adverbials *once, twice* and *thrice.*

The term **cardinal** is from Latin *cardinalis* (hinge), and cardinal numerals take the primary form (the form on which secondary factors hinge)– one, two, three ... .

Ordinal numerals, from Latin *ordinalis* (rank order or position in a series), take the forms *first, second, third* ... .

Traditional grammar placed numerals in three different word classes:

The *second* golfer took *seventy* strokes. (adjectives)

Thirty played in the tournament and *two* equalled the course record. (pronouns)

Don Cameron, who had won *twice* before, was *first*. (adverbials)

The term 'numeral' distinguishes the word class from the grammatical property of NUMBER.

O

object *(n.)*

A noun, noun phrase or pronoun that follows a main verb, especially an active transitive verb; a subordinate nominal clause that follows a verb in another clause; a nominal that follows a preposition in a prepositional phrase; a major component of a sentence or clause, the other components being subject, verb, complement and adverbial. Objects are classified as direct or indirect.

In traditional grammar the **direct object** is defined as the person or thing most immediately, or directly, affected by the action denoted by the verb. In the sentence:

Jenny cooked a mushroom omelette

the noun phrase *a mushroom omelette* is the direct result of the verb *cooked* and is the direct object of *cooked*.

A direct object can often be identified by asking the question *Who?* or *What?* If we apply the test to the example above and ask *Jenny cooked what?* the direct answer, and thus the direct object, is *a mushroom omelette*.

A sentence with an active verb and a direct object can normally be transformed by changing the verb to the passive voice and reversing the positions of the subject and object. The active sentence:

Jenny cooked a mushroom omelette

becomes the passive:

A mushroom omelette was cooked by Jenny.

The direct object of the active sentence becomes the subject of the passive sentence.

An **indirect object** is less immediately, or less directly, affected by the action denoted by the verb. In the sentence:

> She cooked her mother a mushroom omelette

it is clear that, although the noun phrase *her mother* follows the verb *cooked* and is partly influenced by the verb, it was not her mother who was cooked. The noun phrase *her mother* is indirectly affected by the verb and is thus the indirect object.

A verb can have an entire clause as its object. In the sentence:

> She knew what her mother liked

the subordinate nominal clause *what her mother liked* is the object of the verb *knew*. Similarly, in this sentence:

> She had always known that her mother never ate meat

the subordinate nominal clause *that her mother never ate meat* is the object of the verb *had known*.

A nominal can be the object of a preposition:

> She cooked an omelette for her mother.

The noun phrase *her mother* is the object of the preposition *for*. The words *for her mother* form a prepositional phrase, with the preposition *for* as its headword. Similarly, in the sentence:

> She sprinkled chopped parsley around the omelette

the noun phrase *the omelette* is the object of the preposition *around*. *See also* ACTIVE VOICE AND PASSIVE VOICE; CASE.

object complement *see* COMPLEMENT.

objective case
In English the objective, or **accusative**, CASE is inflected only in the personal PRONOUNS:

> me, him, her, us, them.

objective meaning
An alternative term for denotative, referential meaning. *See* MEANING.

obligation *(n.)*

The morally binding duty denoted by the deontic MODAL AUXILIARY VERBS *should* and *must* and by the verb *ought*. *See also* EPISTEMIC AND DEONTIC.

obligatory and optional *(adj.)*
An **obligatory** linguistic item is one that, for reasons of syntax, semantics or correctness, is essential in a given context. In a finite

sentence, for example, obligatory elements are a subject (unless the verb is in the imperative mood) and a finite verb. Commas are usually obligatory to clarify the meaning of non-defining relative clauses, apposition phrases and other constructions. Correctness requires that when a personal pronoun is the object of a verb or a preposition, the pronoun be in the objective case.

An **optional** linguistic item is one that is not obligatory, or one that, if omitted from a longer linguistic unit, would not distort the syntax or semantics of the longer unit. Optional items in sentences are adverbial elements, objects, complements, and coordinate or subordinate clauses.

obscurity *(n.)*

Lack of clarity in expression; a condition of unintelligibility. The term 'obscurity' is more often applied to writing than to speech. Obscurity may be the accidental result of inept writing or of writing that does not take account of the needs of the reader, or it may be a deliberate attempt to impress the reader.

Features of obscurity include elliptical or irregular syntax, unusual or contrived juxtaposition, abstruse allusions, private references, and the use of specialist diction or foreign languages. *See also* READABILITY; TRANSPARENT AND OPAQUE.

obsolete *(adj.)*

Descriptive of a linguistic item that has become outdated or made redundant by changes in a culture or a language. Examples of obsolescence that are the results of cultural change include the feminine suffix *-ix*, as in *curatrix* and *proprietrix*, which has been replaced by the masculine noun suffix *-or*, which now functions as a common gender suffix, as in *curator* and *proprietor*.

The obsolescence of *aerodrome*, *aviator* and *charabanc*, replaced by *airport*, *pilot* and *airman* and *coach* or *bus*, is the result of linguistic preference rather than cultural change. *See also* ARCHAISM.

occupational dialect

A way of speaking that gives an indication of the speaker's social background or status, and may also give an indication of the speaker's occupation. The term 'occupational dialect' is used as an alternative for social dialect or SOCIOLECT; it takes occupation into account only in the general sense of professional and non-professional occupation. *See also* INDEXICAL FEATURE.

of-genitive/of-possessive *see* GENITIVE.

official language

The language formally recognized as the principal language of a country; the language of national government, law, higher education and national communications media in a country.

A language can be the official language of a country without being the MAJORITY LANGUAGE or the NATIONAL LANGUAGE. After the Norman Conquest of England, French became the official language but English remained the majority language and, to the extent that England remained a nation under Norman rule, the national language. Similarly, when England and Scotland colonized Ireland, English became the official language but the indigenous Celtic language, known as Irish or Gaelic, remained the majority language, and thus the national language of Ireland, until the eighteenth century.

officialese *(n.)*

The excessively formal or pedantic language of some official documents; language characterized by abstract, polysyllabic jargon and sentences extended unnecessarily by coordinate and subordinate clauses.

Old English

The ENGLISH LANGUAGE from the time of the ANGLO-SAXON invasion in the fifth century to around the year 1150. *See also* CHANGE.

Old Norse

Old Norse influenced the vocabulary of English and may also have affected English morphology and syntax. A North Germanic language, Old Norse was the parent of the modern Scandinavian languages and has some features in common with modern Icelandic. It also had some features in common with Old English, a West Germanic language and, when the hostilities between the Danes and the Anglo-Saxons ended, there was a pattern of borrowing from Old Norse to Old English that suggests a near-equality of cultures.

Borrowings from Old Norse include the nouns:

anger, birth, brink, dirt, dregs, gap, haven, keel, skin, skull, sky;

the adjectives:

awkward, flat, happy, ill, loose, low, rotten, rugged, ugly;

and the verbs:

cast, droop, drown, gape, gasp, ransack, scrape, scrub, skulk.

The borrowings also include the pronoun forms *they*, *them* and *their*, which replaced the Old English *hie*, *hi(e)ra* and *him*, possibly because the Old English plural forms were similar to the singular third person pronouns.

Old Norse words for topographical features:

beck, -by, fell, garth, gill, rigg, thorp, thwaite

appear in hundreds of place-names and show the patterns of Norse settlement in England and Scotland.

Many Norse loan words denote aspects of ordinary life and suggest an easy transfer of language to Old English, whereas many of the Old French loan words denote a cultural difference between the Normans and the Anglo-Saxons.

The loss of inflections during the Old English period may have been partly caused by the attempts of Norse and Anglo-Saxons to eliminate some of the differences in language in order to make themselves mutually intelligible. And with the loss of inflections came changes in syntax; since subjects and objects of sentences were no longer distinguished by case endings, they had to be indicated in some other way, and this need probably led to the *subject* + *verb* + *object* structure of English sentences. *See also* ENGLISH LANGUAGE; CHANGE; FRENCH.

onomatopoeia *(n.)*

The forming of a word whose pronunciation resembles the sound denoted by the word; words formed in this way.

Examples of onomatopoeia are words like *crash*, *slurp* and *whoosh*, and the animal sounds *miaow*, *woof* and *bah*. The device sometimes assumes more complex forms in poetry:

'Ashes to ashes …' Padre opens his fist:
the ball of loam bursts with the little gasp
and scatters across the oak lid like the rasp
of scurrying rats. Padre says, 'Dust to dust …'

Onomatopoeia is sometimes known as **sound symbolism**. *See also* ECHO; PHONAESTHEME.

ontogeny or ontogenesis and phylogeny or phylogenesis *(n.)*

Ontogeny, also known as ontogenesis, is the study of the origin, or acquisition, of language, and the development and eventual decay of language in the individual. The terms are used mainly in the study of the acquisition of language by children.

Phylogeny, sometimes known as phylogenesis, is the study of the evolution of language in the human race or the evolution of a particular language in a speech community. *See also* DIACHRONIC LINGUISTICS AND SYNCHRONIC LINGUISTICS.

opaque *see* TRANSPARENT AND OPAQUE.

open class *see* CLASS OF WORDS.

open question
An alternative term for a Wh- question. *See* QUESTION.

operator *(n.)*
The first auxiliary verb in a finite verb phrase and thus the element that indicates how the verb phrase is intended to function, or operate, for example, as an affirmative statement, an interrogative or a negative. Operators include all the MODAL AUXILIARY VERBS:

> will, would, shall, should, can, could, may, might, must

which always function as operators, and the verb, *do*, when used as an auxiliary. In the sentence:

> We could have gone to Italy last month

could is the first of two auxiliary verbs – the other is *have* – and so *could* is the operator in the verb phrase *could have gone*. It is the operator that 'operates' interrogatives and negatives. The affirmative statement is transformed to an interrogative by reversing the order of subject and operator:

> Could we have gone to Italy last month?

And the affirmative is transformed to the negative by adding the particle *not*, or the contraction *n't*, after the operator:

> We could not have gone to Italy last month.

An affirmative statement, especially one offered in response to a question, may take an elliptical form that uses the operator without the main verb, but the main verb is always implied. For example, in reply to the question:

> Could you have gone to Italy last month?

the reply could take the elliptical form:

> We could [have gone].

Many affirmative statements have a main verb only. When transforming the affirmative to the interrogative or the negative, the appropriate form of the verb *do* is added as an auxiliary. The affirmative:

She runs three miles every morning

contains the main verb *runs* but no auxiliary. To transform that sentence to an interrogative, the verb *do* is added as an auxiliary and thus an operator:

Does she run three miles every morning?

The negative transformation is:

She does not run three miles every morning.

The verb *do* can also be used to make an affirmative statement more emphatic. In the sentence:

She does run three miles every morning

does functions as an auxiliary and an operator in the verb phrase *does run* and adds emphasis to the main verb.

When *do* is introduced to support the main verb in this way it is known as the do-support, or the do-construction, or the DUMMY OPERATOR. The term 'dummy operator' is misleading. 'Dummy' can be applied to a word that has a syntactic rather than a semantic function, but *does* is an essential part of the meaning of the interrogative and negative sentences above. Modern English does not allow:

*Runs she three miles a day?

*She runs not three miles a day.

In the verb phrase *does run*, *does* is just as valid an operator as any other. Some linguists state that the verbs *be* and *have* function as operators both as auxiliary and as main verbs:

He *has bought* a new car (auxiliary)

He *has* a new car (main)

They *were climbing* in the Cuillin Hills (auxiliary)

They *were* experienced mountain-climbers (main).

opposite *(adj./n.)*
A linguistic unit whose meaning is contrary to that of another unit of the same type.

Oppositeness can be divided into three, sometimes overlapping, categories: antonymy, complementarity and converseness. The categories overlap because some forms of oppositeness defy precise identification. Some linguists reserve the term ANTONYM for gradable adjectives and adverbs, but antonymy is more often a feature of words' meanings than their grammatical category or their word class. The adjectives *innocent* and *guilty* are antonyms and so too are the equivalent nouns *innocence* and *guilt*; the adjectives *lovable* and *hateable* are antonyms and so too are the equivalent nouns and verbs *love* and *hate*.

The term **complementarity** can be applied to pairs of words that are counterparts or two-word sets. Some grammars confuse complementarity and converseness by defining *married/single* and *male/female* as complementarities but *husband/wife* as converses. If the word 'complementarity' is taken to mean one of two counterparts that form a completeness, then the word can be applied to all male/female counterparts, human or non-human:

man/woman, husband/wife, king/queen, boar/sow, cob/pen, ram /ewe.

Complementarity can also be applied to linguistic and grammatical terms and properties that are mutually exclusive but complementary. A variety of a language, for example, can be described by the complementarities:

standard/non-standard, formal/informal, high/low.

Complementary properties of nouns are:

common/proper, abstract/concrete, countable/uncountable

and complementary properties of verbs include:

active/passive, main/auxiliary, transitive/intransitive.

Converseness is a term that can be applied to words that are relational opposites, that is, words that denote actions or conditions that are opposite to each other and yet are partly dependent on or partly implied by each other. The word *obverse*, the other side of a coin – heads or tails – gives a clear indication of this form of oppositeness. Converse verbs include:

arrive/depart, marry/divorce, win/lose.

Converse nouns include:

birth/death, guest/host, writer/reader

and converse prepositions or prepositional adverbs include:

from/to, in/out, over/under, up/down.

Oppositeness is usually discussed in terms of pairs of words or conditions, but a word may have two or more opposites in a gradient set. Antonyms for *slow* are *fast*, *fleet*, *quick*, *rapid*, *speedy* and *swift*. The converse of *over* is given as *under* in the example above, but *below*, *beneath* and *underneath* are also converses of *over*.

opposition *(n.)*

Placing two or more linguistic units with opposite meanings in the same context; the condition of being OPPOSITE. Opposition can be expressed through the juxtaposition of opposites – ANTONYMS, complementarities or converses – in a clause, a sentence or a larger linguistic unit; it can also be expressed through ANTITHESIS and CHIASMUS.

Adversative CONJUNCTIONS and adverbs offer another means of expressing opposition. Options include the adversative coordinating conjunctions *but* and *and yet*:

> She arrived late for the test *and yet* she completed it.

Opposition can be expressed through the adversative correlative conjunctions, *either ... or* and *neither ... nor*; the adversative **subordinating conjunctions**, also known as **subordinators**, *although, however, lest, or else, unless* and *whatever*:

> *Although* she arrived late she completed the test

> I intend to continue *whatever* you say

and the adversative adverbs *despite, even so* and *nevertheless*:

> They worked all afternoon *despite* the intense heat.

> By three o'clock he was tired and thirsty; *even so*, he continued to work.

optative subjunctive *(adj./n.)*

An alternative term for formulaic subjunctive. *See* SUBJUNCTIVE MOOD.

optional agreement/concord *see* AGREEMENT.

oracy *(n.)*

The ability to express oneself fluently in speech. The word was coined in the mid-twentieth century to contrast with LITERACY at a time when increasing attention was being given to the grammar and other linguistic properties of speech.

oral *(adj./n.)*

Uttered in spoken words. The words 'oral' and 'orally' are sometimes used as synonyms for VERBAL (2) and 'verbally', but in grammar and linguistics 'verbal' and 'verbally' are used in the sense of relating to or derived from a verb. Outside these domains, 'verbal' and 'verbally' still mean of or pertaining to written as well as spoken words.

ordinal *see* NUMERAL.

orthography *(n.)*

1 The WRITING SYSTEM of a particular language.

2 An agreed system of SPELLING in a particular language; spelling according to an agreed standard of correctness.

ostensive definition

An alternative term for referential meaning. *See* DENOTATIVE, REFERENTIAL MEANING *under* MEANING.

overcorrection *see* HYPERCORRECTION.

overextension and underextension *(n.)*

Overextension is the use of a word or phrase to express a wider range of meaning than the word or phrase actually denotes. Young children, for example, may apply the word *doggie* not only to dogs but to cats and other animals. Adults, too, occasionally overextend the meanings of words; for example, *book* is sometimes applied to magazines and brochures, and *lemonade* to variously flavoured mineral waters.

Underextension is the application of a word or phrase to a narrower range of meaning than the word or phrase allows. A child may use the word *toy* for one particular toy but fail to understand the wider application of the word. When a word has an abstract or metaphorical meaning as well as a concrete meaning – *dry, icy, polished* – young children are likely to underextend the word to its concrete meaning only.

overgeneralization *(n.)*

The application of a general grammatical rule to words that are not governed by the rule. Two common overgeneralizations by young children are the use of the *-s* inflection for all plural nouns – *mouses* or *mices* for *mice, foots* or *feets* for *feet* – and the use of the *-ed* inflection for all past tenses – *bringed, goed, runned*. Such overgeneralizations seem to confirm the view that children have an innate capacity for grammar, because plurals like *sheeps, *teeths and *tooths and the past tenses *given, *singed and *throwed are formed by children themselves rather than modelled on adult speech. The fact that children independently formulate these *-s* and *-ed* forms strongly suggests that they understand the underlying rules for plurals and past tenses.

Some linguists state that OVEREXTENSION and overgeneralization are synonymous, but a distinction can be made. Overextension is semantic, distorting the meanings of words; overgeneralization is grammatical, or morphological, distorting the forms of words.

oxymoron *(n.)*

A figure of speech, usually a noun phrase, that attracts attention by the immediate JUXTAPOSITION of words with contrary meanings.

Literary examples of oxymorons are Bottom's 'monstrous little voice' in *A Midsummer Night's Dream* and Romeo's 'loving hate' and 'heavy lightness' in *Romeo and Juliet*. A commonplace example is the cliché *a living death*. *See also* PARADOX.

p

palindrome *(n.)*

A word, phrase or longer linguistic unit that reads the same backwards as it does forwards.

Madam, I'm Adam.

Revolt, lover.

paradigm *(n.)*

A list of inflected word forms produced from the base form of a word. The word *walk*, for example, produces the paradigm:

walk, walks, walking, walked

and the word *sing* produces the paradigm:

sing, sings, singing, sang, sung.

The paradigm of subjective, objective and possessive personal pronouns is:

I/me/mine, you/yours, he/him/his, she/her/hers, we/us/ours, they/them/theirs.

Some linguists extend the meaning of paradigm to any set of semantically related words or phrases, for example, synonyms or near-synonyms:

cease, conclude, discontinue, end, finish, halt, stop, terminate

and hyponyms:

Barnacle goose, Bean goose, Canada goose, Greylag goose.

The linguistic units in a paradigm are in paradigmatic relationship with each other.

paradox *(n.)*

A seemingly self-contradictory or absurd statement that has an underlying epigrammatic truth that reconciles the contradictory elements.

Literary examples are Shakespeare's 'The fellow's wise enough to play the fool' in *Twelfth Night* and Wordsworth's 'The child is father of the man' in 'My Heart Leaps Up'.

paradoxical injunction

A command, or injunction, that by its very nature is almost impossible to obey.

> There's an alligator behind you, but don't look back.

> I order you not to imagine a Christmas tree.

paragraph *(n./v.)*

1 A piece of writing, usually two or more sentences in length, with some thematic cohesion such as a particular topic or a particular facet of a topic. Paragraphs are usually indicated by an indented new line or an extra line space. A paragraph is normally analysed as a thematic or stylistic unit, not as a grammatical one.

2 A section, usually numbered, of a legal document, a report, a manual or a textbook.

As a verb, the word 'paragraph' means to arrange in paragraphs. Originally, a paragraph was a short horizontal stroke drawn beneath the beginning of the line in which a change or development of topic occurred.

paralanguage *(n.)*

Audible factors in spoken language other than the PHONEMES and thus other than the lexical meanings of words. Part of the significance of any conversation lies in paralinguistic factors such as intonation, loudness, tempo and voice quality. The words 'You are a devil', for example, can be screamed in terror or whispered seductively.

Some linguists restrict paralanguage to speech, but writing, too, has paralinguistic features: the size and style of type, and the use of white space and colour in the design of a page. In notices warning of the danger of fire, the word *fire* is sometimes printed in red letters with ragged edges to represent flames. The study of paralanguage is known as **paralinguistics**.

paralect *(n.)*

An ACCENT that is close to the prestige form of spoken English, RECEIVED PRONUNCIATION, but retains elements, especially vowel sounds, of a regional or social non-RP accent. *See also* DIALECT; SOCIOLECT.

paralinguistics *see* PARALANGUAGE.

parallelism *(n.)*

Two or more successive linguistic units of the same grammatical type and the same or similar structure. The repetitive effect of parallelism can sometimes be cumulative, adding emphasis to a statement:

> We have the time, we have the knowledge and we have the will. We shall certainly finish the job.

paraphrase *(n./v.)*

A form of words, written or spoken, that is designed to resemble the meaning of another piece of writing or speech. The meaning of a paraphrase cannot be identical to the meaning of the original statement. Even in the strictest forms of paraphrase, the transformations of direct speech to indirect speech and of active sentences to passive sentences, the changes in vocabulary and syntax will produce some change in meaning.

> Jake bought the boat
>
> The boat was bought by Jake

The meanings of the two sentences are similar but not quite identical; the sentences differ in syntax, lexis and narrative viewpoint.

parapraxis *(n.)*

A minor error in speech or writing, especially one that suggests an association of two or more ideas; also known as a **slip of the tongue** and, in some contexts, as a Freudian slip.

> Her new novel was *lunched* at a reception.
>
> All they could afford was rough *mating* on the floor.

parasynthesis *(n.)*

A type of WORD FORMATION that uses compounding and affixation; a word derived from a compound of two or more words and one or more AFFIXES.

> telemarketing: tele[phone] + market + -ing

> userfriendliness: use + -er + friend + -ly + -ness
>
> windsurfer: wind + surf + -er

Words formed in this way are parasynthetic.

parataxis and hypotaxis *(n.)*

Parataxis is the omission of conjunctive links between coordinate phrases, coordinate clauses or subordinate clauses, usually to create a sense of urgency through the compressed syntax.

> This is the place. Yes, this is it. I saw the skid marks, the broken glass. I was driving to work. I was driving within the speed limit.

In that example there is a paratactic relationship between the first two sentences, between the two noun phrases *the skid marks* and *the broken glass*, and between the last two sentences.

Hypotaxis is the subordination of one linguistic unit to another, or the syntactic relationship between a dependent and independent linguistic unit. A main clause and its subordinate clause are in hypotactic relationship. In the example:

> This is the place where I saw the skid marks

the subordinate clause *where I saw the skid marks* is dependent on, and hypotatactic to, the main clause *This is the place*.

The term 'hypotaxis' can also be applied to the words other than the headword in a phrase:

> The broken glass was scattered in small, glittering fragments.

In the noun phrase *The broken glass*, the words *The broken* are hypotactic to the headword *glass*; in the verb phrase *was scattered* the auxiliary verb *was* is hypotactic to the main verb *scattered*; in the second noun phrase *small, glittering fragments* the words *small, glittering* are hypotactic to the headword *fragments*. *See also* ASYNDETON AND POLYSYNDETON.

parenthesis *(n.)*

A word, phrase or clause placed within a sentence and offering additional information, usually in the form of an aside, an explanation or an evaluation.

The parenthetical information is usually punctuated by commas, but can also be punctuated by round brackets or dashes:

> Unfortunately, the young reporter, who acted, no doubt, sincerely, did not check the facts of the case carefully enough before he came to write his report.

The embedded subordinate clause *who acted, no doubt, sincerely* is a parenthetical statement within the main clause. A parenthesis can usually be removed without distorting the syntax of a sentence.

parole *see* LANGUE AND PAROLE.

paronym *(n.)*

A word derived from the same root as another word, especially one borrowed from another language and partly changed. The English word *barbarism*, for example, is derived from the Old French word *barbarisme*, which is also the modern French spelling. The Old French was derived from Latin *barbarismus*, which in turn was derived from Greek *barbarismos*, from *barbarizein*, to behave or speak like a foreigner. *See also* DOUBLET.

parse *(v.)*

1 To describe a word by identifying its word class, its inflections, if any, and their significance, and the word's syntactic function in the sentence.

2 To analyse a sentence in terms of its component parts – subject, verb, object, complement and adverbial – or in terms of clauses, phrases and words.

The practice of parsing is rejected as obsolete by some linguists, but parsing, as outlined above, remains a fundamental concern to most grammarians. *See also* ANALYSIS; CONSTITUENT ANALYSIS.

part of speech

The traditional term for the grammatical category to which words with similar functions are assigned; an alternative term for CLASS OF WORDS. The term is an echo of the Latin *pars orationem*.

participant *(adj./n.)*

1 A person involved in an act of communication: writer or reader, speaker or listener, television broadcaster or viewer. A speaker or broadcaster may use material scripted by another person, a source, in which case the source can also be regarded as a participant. *See also* INTERLOCUTOR.

2 The grammatical function of a noun phrase in a sentence.

The student wrote her final essay and gave it to the lecturer.

The noun phrase *The student* is the agent of the sentence and can be defined as the *agent participant*; the second noun phrase *her final essay* is the object of the verb *wrote*, is directly affected by the verb and can be defined as the **affected participant**; the noun phrase *the lecturer* is the recipient and can be defined as the **recipient participant**. *See also* PATIENT.

participial *(adj./n.)*

Pertaining to a participial form of a verb; an -ING FORM and an -ED FORM.

participial adjective *see* ADJECTIVE.

participial clause

An alternative term for non-finite clause. *See* CLAUSE.

participle *(n.)*

Either of two non-finite forms of verbs: the -ING FORM, traditionally known as the **present participle**, and the -ED FORM, traditionally known as the **past participle**.

Modern grammars use the terms *-ing form* and *-ed form* because these forms can function as nouns and adjectives as well as the participles of verbs.

particle *(n.)*

A short linguistic element that is not normally assigned to a class of words; a word that is subordinate to, and subsumed by, another linguistic unit. Examples include the infinitive particle *to – to swim –* the negative particle *not*, and the adverbial particle subsumed in a phrasal verb, *looked out, wandered off*.

partitive *(adj./n.)*

A word or phrase that denotes part of a whole, part of a larger, undifferentiated quantity, one of several forms or types, or part of an abstract quality. In these phrases:

a *page* of a book, a *section* of motorway, a *member* of the audience

the nouns *page*, *section* and *member* are **quantity partitives**. Other quantity partitives, for example:

a *pint* of blood, a *note* of music, a *veil* of mist

are units from larger, undifferentiated quantities denoted by the mass, or uncountable, nouns *blood, music* and *mist*, and to that extent the partitives make the uncountable nouns quantifiable.

The partitives in these examples:

> a *form* of agriculture, a *make/model* of car, a *type* of computer

are **quality partitives** denoting particular versions from general classes of things. And in these examples:

> a *whiff* of corruption, a *trace* of honesty, a *line* of argument

the partitives are aspects of abstract states.

Some COLLECTIVE NOUNS are partitives, but only when they are parts of greater quantities:

> a *class* of words, a *cluster* of shrubs, a *row* of spectators.

passive vocabulary *see* VOCABULARY (2).

passive voice *see* ACTIVE VOICE AND PASSIVE VOICE.

past continuous *see* PAST TENSE.

past in the future

An alternative term for future perfect. *See* FUTURE TENSE; PAST TENSE.

past participle *see* -ED FORM; PARTICIPLE.

past perfect *see* PAST TENSE.

past perfect continuous *see* PAST TENSE.

past perfect progressive

An alternative term for past perfect continuous. *See* PAST TENSE.

past progressive

An alternative term for the past continuous. *See* PAST TENSE.

past simple

An alternative term for simple past. *See* PAST TENSE.

past subjunctive *see* SUBJUNCTIVE MOOD.

past tense

The words 'past time' normally mean the period prior to the present era or, more immediately, the period prior to the instantaneous 'now' of the moment of utterance or the moment of thought. And the words 'past

TENSE' are applied to verbs that denote events that have already happened or conditions that previously existed. But when we consider the ways in which we speak and write about the past we find, paradoxically, that the past is not a single, closed time-state but a continuum that reaches into the present and the future. We find, too, that past tense is not a single grammatical category but several: the simple past; the past continuous; the present perfect; the present perfect continuous; the past perfect; the past perfect continuous; and the future perfect.

The **simple past**, also known as the **preterite**, is the form that is marked for the past tense, the -ED FORM, and indicates an event that took place at a particular time in the past, or a condition or circumstance that is now complete:

> She *hurried* to the station but she *missed* the train.

The **past continuous**, also known as the **past progressive**, always takes the form of a verb phrase that consists of the simple past of *be* as an auxiliary and the -ING FORM of the main verb. The past continuous is used to express ASPECT, that is, duration or repetition over a period of time in the past:

> Because they *were laughing* so loud, they did not know that the telephone *was ringing*.

The past continuous and the simple past can be used in the same sentence to indicate the occurrence of a specific event within a wider time-context:

> They were still laughing when the police arrived.

The **present perfect** tense always takes the form of a verb phrase consisting of *have* as an auxiliary verb and the *-ed* form, or simple past, as the main verb. The present perfect, as the term suggests, implies a link between the present and the past; the form denotes events or conditions in the past as it, the past, relates to the present, or denotes past events or conditions that lead into the present:

> The skies *have cleared*, the sun *has appeared* and the test match *has begun*.

The **present perfect continuous**, also known as the **present perfect progressive**, is a verb phrase that consists of *have* as an auxiliary verb; *been*, the past participle of *be*, as a second auxiliary; and the *-ing* form of the main verb. The present perfect continuous is used to denote an event or condition that began in the past and is still continuing now, or an event or condition that continued for some time and ended only recently:

Rain *has been falling* incessantly and the river levels *have been rising* all day.

The **past perfect** tense, also known as the **pluperfect**, consists of *had* as an auxiliary and the *-ed* form of the main verb. The past perfect refers to an event that occurred or a condition that existed before a particular time in the past:

By midnight he *had finished* the task. He *had painted* the woodwork and [*had*] *varnished* the floorboards.

The **past perfect continuous** or **past perfect progressive** is a verb phrase consisting of *had* and *been* as auxiliaries and the *-ing* form of the main verb. The past perfect continuous is used to refer to an event or condition that continued or was repeated before a particular time in the past:

While she *had been studying* for the final examination he *had been playing* golf.

The **future perfect** is also known as the **past in the future** because it looks forward to a time in the future when an action or state will have been completed. The future perfect is a three-word verb consisting of the modal auxiliary *shall* or *will*, followed by the bare infinitive *have* and the *-ed* form of the main verb:

I *shall have travelled* 10,000 miles by the end of the month.

In addition to the sequence of past tenses outlined above, four more constructions can be used to express some feature of past time: the **future in the past**; the HYPOTHETICAL PAST; the HISTORIC PRESENT AND the **present in the past**.

The future in the past can be expressed in several constructions: the simple past of *be* followed by a *to*-infinitive; *would be*; *would* and a main verb; *was going to* and a main verb; *was about to* and a main verb. The future in the past usually functions as a narrative focus that adopts a viewpoint in the remote past and anticipates the more recent past:

They were close friends at school but later they *were to drift apart.*

When he joined the team he did not imagine that he *would be captain within two years.*

The present in the past, sometimes known as **social distancing**, is the use of the past tense for events that are occurring at the present time:

Did you have something to say?

for

Do you have something to say?

I *had been hoping* to meet her

for

>I *hope*/I *am hoping* to meet her
>
>I *should have thought* you were right

for

>I *think* you are right.

The effect of this construction is, as the alternative term makes clear, a form of social distancing in which the speaker is less assertive than the occasion allows.

See also MODAL AUXILIARY VERB.

patholect *(n.)*

A generic term for speech or writing that is impaired by mental illness or injury to the brain. No suitable single word exists, and the word 'patholect' was coined to meet that need.

patient *(n.)*

In some systems of grammar, the noun phrase that is affected by the action denoted by a verb and that is usually the direct object of the verb:

>Mary planted *crocus bulbs*

and can also be the subject of a passive sentence:

>*Crocus bulbs* were planted by Mary.

See also PARTICIPANT (2).

patois *(n.)*

A non-standard local dialect. The term is sometimes used pejoratively, implying that the speakers of the patois are socially or intellectually inferior to speakers of the standard form of the language.

pause *(n./v.)*

A temporary break in speech. Pauses can be divided into three types: a filled pause, a silent pause and a hesitation pause.

A **filled pause** is one in which the speaker makes a hesitation noise, which may be a vocalization or a word: *um, er, well*, and which usually indicates that the utterance is incomplete.

A **silent pause** is one without audible vocalization.

A **hesitation pause** is sometimes used as an alternative term for silent pause, but a distinction can be made if hesitation pause is applied to a deliberate break that is designed to emphasize part of an utterance or to regain the attention of a listener.

The usual function of a filled pause or a silent pause is to allow the speaker to select an appropriate word or to plan the next stage of the utterance.

pejoration *(n.)*

A change in the meaning of a word from a favourable or neutral meaning to an unfavourable one. The word *lavatory*, for example, once meant a spiritual and ritual cleansing or purification but now means a place for urinating and defecating, and because of its pejorative meaning *lavatory* is often replaced by the euphemism, *toilet*.

Propaganda can still be used with its earlier meaning, the promotion of religious faith, but it is now more often used pejoratively to mean ideology or even misinformation. The word *rhetoric* has undergone a similar transformation. Rhetoric was once an art form and a university discipline but the word is now more often used pejoratively in such phrases as 'mere windy/empty/hollow rhetoric'. Pejoration is often contrasted with AMELIORATION.

perfect *(adj./n.)*

A verb form that denotes a completed action or condition that has some implication for the present, or a habitual action that extends from the PAST into the present. *See also* ASPECT.

perfect/perfective aspect *see* ASPECT.

perfect infinitive

A verb phrase consisting of the particle *to*, the auxiliary verb *have* and the past participle of the main verb.

> to have visited, to have written

performance *see* COMPETENCE AND PERFORMANCE; LANGUE AND PAROLE.

performative *(adj./n.)*

Speech or writing that performs an act simply by being spoken or written.

The words *I beg you to give me another chance* constitute an act of begging. Similarly, *I apologize* is an apology, and *I promise to do better* is a promise. A notice with the words *You are warned not to cross this line* delivers a warning to the reader. *See also* ILLOCUTION; SPEECH ACT.

period *(n.)*
An alternative term for full stop. *See* PUNCTUATION.

periphrasis *(n.)*
1 The use of two or more words rather than a single, inflected word to express a grammatical category. The comparison of adjective and adverbs, for example, can be made by inflections:

slow, slower, slowest,

or by periphrasis:

straightforward, more straightforward, most straightforward.

The verb forms:

writes, writing, wrote, written

are inflectional whereas the forms:

was writing, have written

are periphrastic as well as inflectional.

2 A roundabout way of speaking or writing. *See also* CIRCUMLOCUTION.

perlocution *see* ILLOCUTION, LOCUTION AND PERLOCUTION.

person *(n.)*
A grammatical category of PRONOUNS, and to a lesser extent of DETERMINERS and VERBS, that partly identifies persons and their relationship to one or more linguistic units in a sentence.

English has three categories of person, which are often associated with the categories of NUMBER or GENDER or both.

First person is the speaker or speakers, or writer or writers, who identify themselves with the pronouns, *I*, *me* (singular) or *we*, *us* (plural).

Second person is the person or persons being addressed by the speaker or writer and identified as *you*.

Third person is the person, persons or things being spoken or written about. People in this category are identified by the pronouns *he*, *him* (masculine, singular), *she*, *her* (feminine, singular), *they*, *them* (common gender, plural).

Things are identified by *it* (neuter gender, singular), or *they*, *them* (neuter, plural).

personal pronoun

A word used instead of a noun to identify someone; a word that exhibits the grammatical categories of person, number, gender or CASE.

person	singular		
	subjective	objective	possessive
first	I	me	mine
second	you	you	yours
third	he, she, it	him, her, it	his, hers, its

person	plural		
	subjective	objective	possessive
first	we	us	ours
second	you	you	yours
third	they	them	theirs

See also PRONOUN.

personification *(n.)*

A figure of speech that is based on metaphor and attributes human qualities to inanimate things and abstractions. Personification appears in the epigrammatic sayings:

> Justice is blind.

> The law never sleeps.

It also appears in poetry:

> Despair's corrupt, voluptuous embrace.

phatic communion

Casual, informal, everyday exchanges that help to maintain social cohesion.

> Isn't it a fine day?

> How are you?

The term was coined by the Polish-born British anthropologist, Bronislaw Malinowski (1884–1942), whose use of the word 'communion' indicates that this use of language has a general social function rather than the function of transmitting information.

philology *(n.)*

The study of the structure and development of a language or languages; the comparison of two or more languages.

As the study of language came to be seen as a social science rather than a branch of the arts or humanities, so the word 'philology' was replaced by the terms historical LINGUISTICS and comparative linguistics. *See also* LINGUISTIC SCIENCE.

phonaestheme *(n.)*

One or more PHONEMES that recur in words with similar meanings. Examples include the occurrence of a vowel and the letter /p/ in *hop*, *leap*, *skip*, *step* and other words, and the occurrence of /gr/ and a vowel in *gripe*, *groan*, *growl*, *gruff*, *grumble* and *grunt*.

The use of phonaesthemes is known as phonaesthesia or phonaesthesis; the study of phonaesthemes and their poetic or aesthetic properties is known as phonaesthetics.

phoneme *(n.)*

The smallest unit of sound in the sound system of a language. The actual sound of a phoneme varies from one dialect of a language to another and from one speaker to another. These variations in the sound of a phoneme are known as ALLOPHONES.

RECEIVED PRONUNCIATION (RP), the prestige dialect of British spoken English, has forty-four phonemes: twenty-two consonants, twelve pure vowels, two semi-vowels and eight diphthongs. RP phonemes are an attempt to attach fixed values to what are, in fact, sets of variables.

phonemic transcription *see* TRANSCRIPTION.

phonetic alphabet

A set of symbols to represent speech sounds, each symbol having an agreed acoustic value. *See also* ALPHABET.

phonetic spelling

A SPELLING system in which each symbol represents a single sound.

phonetic transcription *see* TRANSCRIPTION.

phonetics *(n.)*

The study of speech sounds. Phonetics is sometimes divided into three areas of study. **Acoustic phonetics** deals with the transmission of speech sounds and the measurement of speech sound waves. **Articulatory phonetics** is concerned with the ways in which speech sounds are produced. **Auditory phonetics** deals with the ways in which speech sounds are heard by the listener. *See also* PHONOLOGY.

phonogram *(n.)*

In a WRITING SYSTEM a written character that represents a spoken sound. The characters in ALPHABETIC and SYLLABIC writing systems are phonograms. *See also* GRAPH; GRAPHEME.

phonological component *see* COMPONENT (1).

phonology *(n.)*

The branch of linguistics concerned with the structures and patterns of the **sound systems** in human language. Phonology and PHONETICS are closely related disciplines but a distinction can be made. Phonetics is the study of the articulatory and acoustic properties of speech sounds; phonology is the study of the principles that underlie the distribution of speech sounds in a language or languages.

phrasal auxiliary verb *see* PHRASAL VERB.

phrasal prepositional verb *see* PHRASAL VERB.

phrasal verb

1 A generic term for a verb that consists of a main, or lexical, verb, one or more particles and, in the case of phrasal auxiliary verbs, an auxiliary. A phrasal verb, also known as a multi-word or compound verb, functions as a single linguistic unit. As a generic term, 'phrasal verb' covers several types of multi-word verb: phrasal auxiliary verb; phrasal prepositional verb; and prepositional verb. By contrast, a verb phrase consists of a main verb and one or more auxiliary verbs.

2 More precisely, a phrasal verb is sometimes defined as a verb that consists of a main, or lexical, verb and an adverb particle.

> As one aircraft touched down, another took off.

In that example the phrasal verbs *touched down* and *took off* consist of the main verbs *touched* and *took* and the adverbial particles *down* and *off*.

Touched down and *took off* are intransitive. In this example the phrasal verbs are transitive:

He handed over a cheque to make up the full price.

The object of *handed over* is *a cheque*, and the object of *make up* is *the full price*. The object can sometimes appear between the verb and the adverbial particle:

He handed *a cheque* over.

Other phrasal verbs include:

give in, give up, get by, get away, hurry up, die down, lie down.

Other constructions that are sometimes defined as phrasal verbs are: phrasal auxiliary verb, phrasal prepositional verb and prepositional verb.

A **phrasal auxiliary verb** is a verb that consists of two or more words. Only the first word is a true auxiliary verb, but the entire phrase functions as an auxiliary preceding a main verb:

I am going to try again.

The words *am going to* form a phrasal auxiliary verb preceding the main verb *try*. Similarly, in this example:

The director is prepared to meet the delegates

the phrasal auxiliary is *is prepared to*, and the main verb is *meet*. Other phrasal auxiliary verbs are:

be able to, be about to, be supposed to, be willing to, had better, have to.

A **phrasal prepositional** verb is a verb that consists of a main verb, an adverb particle and a preposition particle.

When he comes in from the garden he looks forward to a glass of ice-cold beer.

In that example, *comes in from* and *looks forward to* are phrasal prepositional verbs; the main verbs are *comes* and *looks*; the adverb particles are *in* and *forward*; the preposition particles are *from* and *to*. Other examples of phrasal prepositional verbs are:

look in on, look out for, look up to, look down on, put up with, get away with, face up to, stand up for.

A **prepositional verb** is a verb that consists of a main verb and a preposition particle.

He approved of the work but he objected to the cost.

In that example the prepositional verbs are *approved of* and *objected to*. The noun phrases *the work* and *the cost* are the prepositional objects of *of* and *to*. Some prepositional verbs can have two objects, one after the verb and one after the preposition:

> She sent a birthday card to her friend.

The noun phrase *a birthday card* is the object of the verb *sent*, and the noun phrase *her friend* is the object of the preposition *to*. Other prepositional verbs are:

> apply for, ask for, call for, call on, send for, comment on, look at, refer to, deal with.

The two constructions, a transitive phrasal verb and a prepositional verb, are sometimes confused, but there are clear differences between the two. A phrasal verb consists of a verb and an adverb particle that modifies the verb; a prepositional verb consists of a verb and a prepositional particle that is the headword in a prepositional phrase and also modifies or 'governs' a noun phrase. The object of a transitive phrasal verb can appear between the verb and the adverb particle.

These sentences, for example:

> She cleared her room out and gave her old toys away

> She looked the addresses up and sent the invitations out

are acceptable alternatives for:

> She cleared out her room and gave away her old toys.

> She looked up the addresses and sent out the invitations.

The object of a prepositional verb cannot appear between the verb and the preposition particle. This sentence:

> Because he could not cope with the volume of work he called on his colleague to deal with the problem

cannot be rewritten as:

> *Because he could not cope the volume of work with he called his friend on to deal the problem with.

phrase *(n.)*

A **group** of words that includes a headword but does not include the subject + verb + predicate structure of a clause or sentence; a linguistic unit at a level between a word and a clause. A nominal group, for example, is a noun phrase.

Some linguists claim that a group is an expansion of a word whereas a phrase is a contraction of a clause. *See also* ADJECTIVE PHRASE *under* ADJECTIVE; ADVERBIAL PHRASE; NOUN PHRASE; PREPOSITIONAL PHRASE; VERB PHRASE; VERBLESS CLAUSE.

phrase-marker *(n.)*

A means of identifying and analysing, or marking, the syntactic structure of a phrase or a clause. The marking can take the form of BRACKETING or a TREE DIAGRAM.

phrase structure grammar

A GRAMMAR that contains rules of phrase structure. The rules can be written as formulae:

S → NP VP

where S means sentence, → means consists of, NP is noun phrase and VP is verb phrase. The formula, $S \rightarrow NP\ VP$, means: a sentence consists of a noun phrase and a verb phrase.

Another phrase structure rule is:

NP → Art (Adj) N

that is, a noun phrase consists of an article, an optional adjective, and a noun.

Phrase structure rules can generate large numbers of sentences and shorter linguistic units, and also allow a CONSTITUENT ANALYSIS to be made of the sentences and units.

phylogeny *see* ONTOGENY AND PHYLOGENY.

pictogram *(n.)*

A pictorial symbol that represents a word or group of words in a writing system; also known as a pictograph.

pictography *(n.)*

The study of pictographs or PICTOGRAMS; the practice of using pictographs or pictograms.

pidgin *(adj./n.)*

A simplified form of a language used by two or more communities who do not understand each others' native languages; also known as a **trade language**.

pitch *(n.)*

The property of a tone of voice that allows the tone to be placed on a frequency scale, or pitch, of sound waves and to be classified from high to low. The pitch of a single word is usually referred to as a TONE; the pitch of longer linguistic units is referred to as an INTONATION.

place *(n.)*

A location or position, usually indicated by an adverbial, a preposition, an adjective or an adjective and preposition together. The adverbial can be a single adverb:

> Fruit trees grew *nearby*

or an adverbial clause of place:

> Apples lay *where they had fallen*

or a prepositional phrase:

> They gathered apples *in the orchard.*

Place can be expressed by an adjective:

> a *near* miss, a *remote* village

or by an adjective and preposition together:

> adjacent to, far from.

pleonasm *(n.)*

A superfluous or redundant use of words; the use of more words than are necessary to express a thought. The REDUNDANCY (2) may be involuntary; it may be an attempt to inflate the importance of the occasion or the self-importance of a speaker or writer; or the redundancy may be part of a deliberate attempt to explain or clarify a meaning. *See also* CIRCUMLOCUTION; PERIPHRASIS (2).

plosive *(adj./n.)*

A consonant pronounced with an abrupt release of breath; the consonants /p/, /b/, /t/, /d/, /k/ and /g/.

pluperfect *(adj./n.)*

An alternative term for past perfect. *See* PAST TENSE.

plural *see* NUMBER.

plurale tantum

A noun that is used only in the plural form. *Pluralia tantum* can be divided into several categories. Implements and instruments:

> scissors, shears, tongs, binoculars, spectacles;

clothing (the chestnut is that these garments are singular at the top and plural at the bottom):

> trousers, shorts, pants, knickers, pyjamas, dungarees, clothes;

professions and academic disciplines:

> electronics, linguistics, mathematics, physics;

illnesses:

> measles, mumps, shingles, staggers (in animals).

See also SINGULARE TANTUM.

plurisign *(n.)*

A word or sign that expresses more than one meaning simultaneously; a deliberate form of ambiguity. The terms 'plurisign', 'plurisignation' and 'plurisignative' were coined in the mid-twentieth century. Although these words are not synonymous with 'polysemy' and 'polysemous', which were coined in the late nineteenth and early twentieth centuries, 'polysemy' and 'polysemous' are the usual terms for words with two or more meanings. *See also* POLYSEME.

poetic metaphor *see* METAPHOR (1).

polarity *(n.)*

The contrast created by two semantically OPPOSITE linguistic units of the same type, especially positives and NEGATIVES. Polarity can be expressed through AFFIXES:

> *mono*lingual/*multi*lingual, merci*ful*/merci*less*;

through ANTONYMS:

> hot/cold, rough/smooth;

or through ANTITHETICAL clauses or sentences:

> She told the truth but he lied.

See also ADVERSATIVE.

polygenesis *see* MONOGENESIS AND POLYGENESIS.

polyglot *(adj./n.)*

An alternative term for MULTILINGUAL.

polyonymy *(n.)*

The condition of having many words or phrases denoting the same thing.

The term 'polyonymy' is sometimes used in discussing the SAPIR-WHORF HYPOTHESIS, which suggests that polyonymous sets indicate that the things denoted by them – for example, running water in the form of a *river*, *rivulet*, *stream*, *brook*, *rill* or *freshet* – have a greater importance, or greater frequency of occurrence, in a country or a culture.

A related form of polyonymy is the heaping up of titles or epithets in order to emphasize someone's importance. A British Prime Minister, for example, is not only Prime Minister but also First Lord of the Treasury and Minister for the Civil Service.

polyphony *(n.)*
The representation of different sounds by the same letter of the alphabet. The letter /i/, for example, is a polyphone:

> critic, criticize, critique

and /s/ is polyphonic in:

> sand, sugar, measure, lose.

polyseme *(n.)*
A word that has several meanings, all of them related to an earlier meaning. As the English language evolves, some words acquire **multiple meanings**, for example, *head*, *eye*, *face*, *hand* and *arm*. These words also appear in many compound words and in associated phrases. The word *straight* has over twenty-five meanings as a noun, adjective and adverb, and over fifty additional meanings in associated phrases.

The condition of having several meanings is known as polysemy; the associated adjective can take three forms: polysemous, polysemantic, polysemic.

polysyllable *see* MONOSYLLABLE AND POLYSYLLABLE.

polysyndeton *see* ASYNDETON AND POLYSYNDETON.

portmanteau word
A word that is coined by BLENDING the sounds, spellings and meanings of two other words. The word 'portmanteau' entered the English language in the mid-sixteenth century, but the term 'portmanteau word' was probably coined by Lewis Carroll, who wrote of his NONCE-WORD *slithy*, which appears in *Through the Looking-Glass* (1872): 'You see it's like a portmanteau – there are two meanings packed up into one word.'

positive *(adj./n.)*
1 An alternative term for AFFIRMATIVE.

2 The base, or unmarked, form of a gradable adjective or adverb; also known as **absolute**:

> angry (positive/absolute), angrier (comparative), angriest superlative)

> high (positive/absolute), higher (comparative), highest (superlative).

See also COMPARATIVE (1).

possessive *(adj./n.)*
The CASE of nouns, pronouns or DETERMINERS that denotes possession, ownership or occupancy; also known as the GENITIVE case. The possessive case of nouns is indicated by an APOSTROPHE and the letter s, or s and an apostrophe.

PERSONAL PRONOUNS in the possessive case are:

> mine, ours, yours, his, hers, theirs;

possessive determiners are:

> my, our, your, his, her, their.

postdeterminer *see* DETERMINER.

postmodification *see* MODIFICATION.

postmodifier *see* MODIFICATION.

postmodifying genitive/possessive *see* GENITIVE.

postponement *(n.)*
Placing a word or phrase at the end of a clause or sentence and thus creating end focus or end weight. *See* END FOCUS AND FRONT FOCUS.

postpositive adjective
An ADJECTIVE that is postposed, or placed, immediately after a nominal.

> the man *implicated*, the person *concerned*.

One group of adjectives, all beginning with the letter *a*, always appears after the noun or pronoun, and sometimes after the verb, in a sentence:

> The children are *alone* and *afraid*.

Other adjectives used in this way include:

> abroad, agog, alike, alive, ashamed, astray, awake, aware, away.

Postpositive adjectives also appear in a few fixed expressions:

court *martial*, chairman *designate*, heir *apparent*, inspector *general*, president *elect*, lion *rampant*, princess *royal*.

Adjectives that modify indefinite pronouns appear as postpositives:

anyone *special*, no one *important*, someone *brave*, something *odd*.

postpositive preposition

A preposition that is placed immediately after a nominal. The construction was once acceptable in poetry: 'Their hats they swam aboone' for 'They swam *above* their hats' in 'sir Patrick Spens', but it is now limited to a few phrases such as:

the long night through/through the long night

the whole world over/over the whole world

homewards, northwards/towards home, towards the north.

pragmatics *(n.)*

The branch of linguistics concerned with ways in which people communicate through speech in various circumstances, for example, in teaching, counselling, interviews and conversations. *See also* FUNC-TIONALISM.

predeterminer *see* DETERMINER.

predicate *(n.)*

The part of a clause or simple sentence that contains a verb and may also contain an object, a complement or an adverbial; the part of a clause or simple sentence that follows the subject; traditionally, the part of a clause or simple sentence that contains what is said about the subject.

The woman bought a rocking-horse for her niece.

The predicate *bought a rocking-horse for her niece* consists of a verb, *bought*, an object, *a rocking-horse*, and an adverbial, *for her niece*. In this example:

Her niece seemed delighted with the gift

the predicate *seemed delighted with the gift* consists of a verb, *seemed*, a complement, *delighted*, and an adverbial, *with the gift*.

predication *(n.)*

1 The assertion or proposition about the subject of a sentence that is made by the predicate of the sentence; that which is predicated. By this definition, predication is similar to PREDICATE.

2 In some grammars, predication is defined as the part of a clause that follows the subject and the operator. By this definition, the predicate is the part of a clause that contains a main verb that follows an auxiliary verb functioning as an operator, and may also contain an object, a complement or an adverbial. This second definition acknowledges the particular function of the operator in forming questions and in coordinating double predications:

> Can you meet me tomorrow evening?

In that example, the operator *Can* is isolated from the rest of the predication *meet me tomorrow evening.* In this example:

> You should change your plans and [you should] meet me

the operator *should* 'operates' the two main verbs, *change* and *meet*; it also coordinates the two objects *your plans* and *me*, and allows the elliptical construction, *and meet me* for *and you should meet me.*

An even more elliptical and idiomatic predication is made possible by an operator. The question:

> Must I meet you tomorrow?

could elicit the reply:

> Yes, you must.

predicative *(adj./n.)*

An ADJECTIVE or NOUN that follows a linking, or copular, verb and forms a predicate or predication, or is contained in a predicate or predication.

> They called him a failure at first but he became a highly successful chef.

The noun phrase *a failure* is the predicative object of the COPULA or linking verb *called*, and the noun phrase *a highly successful chef* is the predicative subject complement of the linking verb *became.*

prefix *see* AFFIX.

prelingual *(adj.)*

1 Descriptive of the hypothetical stage in cognition or ideation that precedes the act of speaking or writing; descriptive of thought that has not been formulated into words; also known as prelinguistic.

2 In the human evolutionary process, descriptive of the period before the development of language; also known as prelinguistic.

3 In language acquisition by children, descriptive of the stage that immediately precedes the use of words; also known as prelinguistic.

preliterate *(adj./n.)*

A person or culture without a written form of their language; a child who has not developed the skill of writing. *See also* ALITERATE; ILLITERATE.

premodifier *see* MODIFICATION.

preposition *(n.)*

A small, closed class of function words that relate two linguistic units to each other, the second unit being a nominal, which is traditionally said to be 'governed' by the preposition. Most prepositions denote location:

> along the shore, over the waves, under the pier.

Other prepositions of place include:

> above, across, among, at, below, on, off, towards, upon, with.

Some prepositions denote time:

> before the match, during the interval, after the final whistle.

Prepositions that consist of two or more words are known as **complex prepositions**:

> away from the crowd, in accordance with the rules, out of the rain, over and above your normal duties.

There is no objection to ending a sentence with a preposition:

> Which channel is the programme *on*?
>
> This is the team we are *up against*.
>
> What are you staring *at*?

Sentences like these reflect the real nature of the English language and are acceptable in written standard English.

preposition group

A group of words that functions as a preposition and contains a preposition and one or more other words, usually adverbials.

> shortly before, right along from, directly above, straight across from.

prepositional adjective

An adjective that is normally followed by a preposition.

> allergic to, capable of, exempt from

See also PREDICATIVE ADJECTIVE *under* ADJECTIVE.

prepositional adverb

A word that is usually a preposition but that can function as an adverb.

He jogged along for half an hour, waving to friends who drove past.

Along and *past* are prepositional adverbs modifying the verbs *jogged* and *drove*, whereas in this sentence:

He jogged along the street, waving to friends who drove past him

along and *past* are prepositions, the headwords in the prepositional phrases *along the street* and *past him*.

prepositional complement

The nominal in a prepositional phrase; the nominal that is said to be governed by a preposition.

They climbed over the ten-foot-high boundary fence and ran towards the forest.

The noun phrase *the ten-foot-high boundary fence* is the complement of the preposition *over*, and the noun phrase *the forest* is the complement of the preposition *towards*.

Words from other classes can function as nominals in prepositional phrases. In this example:

They fled from the unbearable to the unknown

the adjectives *unbearable* and *unknown* function as nominals and as the complements of the prepositions *from* and *to*. And in this example:

They were aware of being hunted

the nominal phrase consisting of an -ING FORM and an -ED FORM functions as the prepositional complement after *of*.

prepositional phrase

A group of words with a preposition as its headword and a nominal as its object, or complement:

among the many incidents; until the final scene

Prepositional phrases often function as adverbials by modifying verbs:

They rowed *up the river*, struggling *against the current*.

They can also appear after a noun phrase and thus postmodify the noun phrase:

the face *behind the mask*; a man *with a secret*.

prepositional verb *see* PHRASAL VERB.

prescriptive *(adj.)*

Laying down rules of English USAGE, especially in GRAMMAR, vocabulary and pronunciation; laying down *pro*scriptive rules, that is, prohibiting certain spoken and written forms.

Prescriptivism is often contrasted with descriptivism, but the two sets of attitudes are not polar opposites. Some descriptive grammars lay down rules, and some descriptions include notions of CORRECTNESS and acceptability. Some forms of prescription, for example, house styles, are essential in most branches of the publishing industry.

Prescriptions based on LATIN grammar are not appropriate for English because the two languages function in different ways, the most obvious differences being that Latin is an inflecting, or synthetic, language and English a non-inflecting, or analytic, language, and that English remains to some extent a GERMANIC language.

Prescriptivism that is based on social values and excludes linguistic principles may well misrepresent the real nature of the English language. *See also* NORMATIVE.

present continuous *see* PRESENT TENSE.

present in the past *see* PAST TENSE; PRESENT TENSE.

present participle

A traditional term for the -ING FORM.

present perfect *see* PAST TENSE.

present perfect continuous *see* PAST TENSE.

present perfect progressive

An alternative term for present perfect continuous. *See* PAST TENSE.

present progressive

An alternative term for present continuous. *See* PRESENT TENSE.

present simple

An alternative term for simple present. *See* PRESENT TENSE.

present subjunctive *see* SUBJUNCTIVE MOOD.

present tense

The present, like the PAST and the FUTURE, is not one time-state but several, and the present TENSE of verbs is used not only to denote the various present time-states but also past time and future time.

One form of present time is the immediate, instantaneous Now, a time that is contemporaneous with the moment of utterance or the moment of thought. This form of time can be expressed in the **simple present** tense of a verb:

We stop here and wait for the green light

or by the **present continuous** tense, also known as the **present progressive**:

I *am writing* these words and [I *am]* *thinking* about time.

The present is also a period of time over which an event or condition recurs, or a time-span that reflects frequency or repetition. The simple present is used to express this form of present time:

They *go* to France every year, and because they hate flying they *travel* by ferry.

Another meaning of present time is the present age, the current epoch, or an existing state or condition. The simple present or the present continuous tense can be used in these contexts:

We *live/are living* in an electronic age

but the present continuous is used to denote a change from one condition to another:

Computers *are taking over* our lives. We *are becoming* the servants of machines.

A fourth form of present time is a perpetual, absolute 'timeless' state or condition, for which the simple present is used:

The earth *revolves*.

The origin of language *remains* unknown.

The present tense is also used to discuss the past and the future.

When the present tense of a verb is used as the HISTORIC PRESENT, the verb can take the simple present form or the present continuous form:

Last week I'*m standing* in the garden when I *see* this hedgehog.

Three constructions that use the present tense – *be going, be going to* and *be about to* – are used to discuss the future:

They are going back to Canada next week.

The *to* of *be going to* can be a preposition:

We are going to the match on Saturday

or it can be the particle of the *to* infinitive:

We are going to buy tickets for the match.

The *to* of the *be about to* construction is always the infinitive particle of the verb that is added to *be about to*:

I am about to leave the office.

The *be about to* construction refers to a more immediate future than *be going to*:

I am about to leave now because I am going to a concert at eight o'clock.

Events in the present can be referred to in the form of the past tense that is known variously as the **present in the past** or **social distancing**, or the **attitudinal past**:

I was thinking of going home. Did you want to see me before I left?

for

I am thinking of going home. Do you want to see me before I leave?

presupposition *(n.)*

An idea or belief that is assumed by someone before he or she has knowledge or experience of what is assumed; an assumption implicit in a piece of writing or speech. Presupposition is sometimes discussed in relation to ENTAILMENT.

I know he broke his promise.

The statement presupposes that a promise has been broken. If a promise has, in fact, been broken, that would entail that a promise had been made in the first place.

He broke no promise.

This second statement may presuppose that a promise was made and kept, but it does not entail this. The statement could mean that no promise was broken because none was given.

preterite *(adj./n.)*

An alternative term for simple past. *See* PAST TENSE.

primary verb

A verb that can function as a MAIN VERB or as an AUXILIARY VERB; the verbs *be*, *have* and *do*. These three verbs are called primary because they are the three most frequently used verbs in English, and because of their dual function as main and auxiliary verbs.

Be is used in all continuous verb constructions, for example:

is loving, was loving, has been loving

and in all passive verb constructions, for example:

is loved, was loved, has been loved.

Have is used in all perfect verb forms, for example:

has loved, have loved, had loved.

Do is the DUMMY OPERATOR, the do-support, in questions and negatives:

do love, did you love? did not/didn't love.

Do is also the do-support for *do*:

Do you do maths at school?

Did you do that drawing?

No, I didn't do it.

principal clause

An alternative term for main clause. *See* CLAUSE.

principal parts of verb

The base form, the simple past form, and the past participle, or -ED FORM, of a verb.

talk, talked, talked

take, took, taken

speak, spoke, spoken

sing, sang, sung.

The *-s* form for the simple present tense and the -ING FORM for the present participle follow from the base forms of all verbs except *be*, which has the irregular present tense forms *am*, *are* and *is* and the irregular past tense forms *was*, *were*, and *have*, with the irregular present form *has* and the irregular past form *had*.

procedural knowledge *see* KNOWLEDGE.

proclitic *see* ENCLITIC AND PROCLITIC.

productive and unproductive *(adj.)*

1 A **productive** linguistic unit is one that can be used to produce new examples of the same kind. The prefix *poly-*, for example, has been used in the production of dozens of scientific and technical terms, from

polyacrylic to *polyvinylidene*. The use of *Euro-* as a prefix has produced several nouns, including *Eurocrat, Eurocurrency* and *Europhobe*.

An **unproductive** linguistic unit is one that does not produce new examples of the same kind. The diminutive suffix *-ock* – *bullock, hillock, paddock* – seems to have produced no new nouns since the slang *pillock* in the mid-twentieth century.

2 The words 'productive' and 'productivity' can be applied to the process of word formation, as in *polyacrylic* and *Eurocrat*.

3 The wider generative process of projecting a theoretically infinite number of sentences from a finite number of words is another form of productivity.

pro-form *(n.)*

A linguistic unit, or form, that takes the place of another; a linguistic unit that represents, or is a substitute for, another. The main pro-forms are pronouns, which can be said to represent nouns. The indefinite pronoun *it* can be a pro-form for simple objects:

> You asked for the menu? Here *it* is

and for complex, sometimes abstract, processes:

> I said I would pass, and I've done *it*.

Several pro-forms denote identical or equivalent action:

> Emma joined the police, and her brother *did too/followed suit/did likewise/did the same*.

A similar effect is produced by the pro-form, *so*:

> Emma joined the police, and *so* did her brother.

> Has Emma been promoted? I think *so*.

progressive form

An alternative term for CONTINUOUS FORM.

pronominal *(adj./n.)*

Pertaining to a PRONOUN; characterized by the presence of a pronoun. *See also* PRO-FORM.

pronominalization *(n.)*

The replacement of a noun phrase by a PRONOUN.

pronoun *(n.)*

A closed class of function words that operate as nominals.

Pronouns function as the subjects and objects of verbs, as the complements of prepositions, and occasionally as the headwords in pronominal phrases such as:

> I myself, lonely old me, we few, you others, silly little you, anyone else, almost everyone.

PERSONAL PRONOUNS have more grammatical properties – person, number, gender and CASE – and more inflections than any other word class than verbs.

Pronouns are usually divided into a number of sub-classes, as follows: DEMONSTRATIVE PRONOUN; EMPHATIC PRONOUN; INDEFINITE PRONOUN; INTERROGATIVE PRONOUN; PERSONAL PRONOUN; REFLEXIVE PRONOUN; RELATIVE PRONOUN.

pronunciation *(n.)*
The way in which speech is sounded, usually with reference to a known or agreed standard of pronunciation; the phonological quality of speech. Almost everyone's pronunciation is uniquely distinctive and also exhibits regional, national or social qualities of sound. *See also* ACCENT; BBC ENGLISH; DIALECT; DICTION; KING'S ENGLISH; RECEIVED PRONUNCIATION; SOCIOLECT.

proper noun *see* COMMON NOUN AND PROPER NOUN.

prop *(n.)*
A word that completes the syntax of a sentence but adds little to the meaning.

> *It* was midnight when he finally left.

> *There* is nothing we can do.

See also DUMMY.

property
An alternative term for CATEGORY.

proposition *(n.)*
The MEANING of a statement expressed as an affirmation that can be either true or false; a meaning, usually expressed as an affirmation in a declarative sentence, that can be proved or disproved; an axiom, or generally accepted principle, that is used in an argument as proof.

The term 'proposition' was borrowed from logic and has proved ambiguous in linguistics. Many sentences in English have some propositional content but few sentences are propositions in the sense that they invite the reader to prove or disprove the truth of their contents. The usefulness of the concept of proposition is that it allows a further distinction to be made about the nature of meaning. Propositional meaning, true or false, is different from lexical and grammatical meaning, and is also different from most other forms of meaning. *See also* ANALYTIC PROPOSITION AND SYNTHETIC PROPOSITION.

proscriptive *(adj./n.)*
Characteristic of the prohibition, or rejection, of particular uses of language. The term is usually applied to those rules in traditional, PRESCRIPTIVE grammar that declared certain USAGES to be incorrect or unacceptable. *See also* ACCEPTABLE; CORRECTNESS.

prosody *(n.)*
1 The fluctuations in intonation, rhythm, loudness and tempo that occur in speech; also known as prosodic features. Prosody is similar to PARALANGUAGE, that is, the audible features of speech other than the sounds of the PHONEMES.

2 Originally, the study or practice of versification, including diction, rhythm, rhyme and stanza pattern.

protolanguage *(n.)*
1 A hypothetical parent language from which actual languages have evolved. *See also* INDO-EUROPEAN.

2 In the acquisition of language by children, descriptive of the stage at which vocalizations precede words.

prototype *(n.)*
1 A typical representative of a class or a concept.

2 A hyponym that is regarded as one of the most representative, or typical, examples of a hypernym. *Chair* and *table* (hyponyms), for example, are prototypes of *domestic furniture* (hypernym), whereas *chaise longue* and *fire-screen* are atypical. *See also* HYPERNYM AND HYPONYM.

pro-verb *(n.)*

A verb that functions as a PRO-FORM for another verb. The term is usually applied to the verb *do* when it functions as an operator or a substitution:

> Do you have the money? Yes, I *do*

but other verb forms can also function as pro-verbs:

> Please check the brake lights. Yes, I'll *do/take care of/see to/look after* that.

proxemics *(n.)*

The study of the amount of space that a participant feels it necessary to maintain between himself or herself and other people during an interpersonal encounter. The degree of proximity, like other features of NON-VERBAL COMMUNICATION, varies from one culture to another and is also affected by the formal or informal nature of the occasion.

proximal *(adj.)*

An alternative term for proximate. *See* PROXIMATE AND REMOTE.

proximate and remote *(adj.)*

A **proximate** linguistic unit is one that denotes nearness, or proximity, in space or time. A **remote** linguistic unit is one that denotes distance, or remoteness, in space or time. The terms, **proximal** and **non-proximal**, or **distal** (from distant), are alternatives for proximate and remote. The transformation from proximate to remote is a feature of the conversion from direct speech to indirect speech. *See also* DIRECT SPEECH AND INDIRECT SPEECH; NEUTRALIZE.

psycholinguistics *(n.)*

The study of the mental processes associated with language; the study of people's linguistic behaviour. Psycholinguistics began to be recognized as an academic discipline in the 1950s. The subject now covers a wide field, including the acquisition of language by children; learning, remembering and forgetting language; dyslexia; aphasia and other patholectic conditions.

punctual *see* DURATIVE VERB AND PUNCTUAL VERB.

punctuation *(n.)*

The application of a set of marks to a piece of writing in order to clarify its meaning; the division of a text into paragraphs, sentences, clauses and phrases by means of such marks.

Punctuation marks also act as a guide to the structure, rhythm and tone, and thus the prose style, of a text by indicating syntactic and semantic units and also pauses and stresses. A partial exception is the hyphen, which is the only punctuation mark that links rather than separates linguistic units. Although there is some flexibility in the use of punctuation marks – for example, a parenthetical statement like this can be punctuated by commas, round brackets or dashes – the main applications of punctuation marks are agreed.

The **full stop** [.], also known as the **period**, marks the end of a sentence and, optionally, an abbreviation.

The **comma** [,] punctuates several linguistic units:

a sentence adverbial, or disjunct:

> Normally, spoken English is less formal than written English

a participial clause at the beginning of a sentence:

> Having won the race, the sprinter felt elated

a non-defining embedded clause:

> The Australian bowler, who took six wickets, was named man of the match

the vocative case of nouns:

> Let's see, Fred.
>
> Drink up, John

apposition phrases:

> Percy Smith, the club chairman, was re-elected

parentheses:

> Four batsmen, including the team captain, were dismissed in the morning session

two or more items in a list:

> Fog delayed flights to Amsterdam, Brussels, Essen and Cologne

two or more adjectives modifying the same noun:

> A crowd of impatient, angry, noisy fans demonstrated outside the stadium

three or more clauses of the same type when the last two clauses are linked by a conjunction:

> He asked if they had that particular printer in stock, how much it cost and whether it was compatible with his computer.

A **semicolon** [;] marks two or more main clauses in a sentence or two or more coordinate clauses that are not linked by a conjunction:

> His only aim was to finish the marathon; his time was not important.

A **colon** [:] is used in British newspapers to separate introductory indirect speech from the direct speech that follows:

> The editor asked: 'Why didn't you interview the manager?'

The colon can also be used to separate introductory or explanatory information from the illustrative material that follows:

> The selectors have chosen three new players: Andrew Butts, Graham Earnshaw and James Loveridge.

A **question mark** [?] must appear at the end of a QUESTION.

An **exclamation mark** [!] in standard English is used only after genuinely exclamatory material:

> What a farce!

> He was covered in spaghetti!

In informal written English the exclamation mark is often an invitation to the reader to supply missing information or to guess at an outcome:

> Just imagine! I'm meeting him tonight!

Inverted commas ['...' or "..."] punctuate direct speech. They can also be used for the opposite purpose of indicating that the words in inverted commas are not what the writer means but are intended as an allegation or an irony:

> He 'relaxes' by going rock-climbing.

An **apostrophe** ['] indicates a contraction and the possessive case of nouns.

A **hyphen** [-] links two or more words into a compound word, including compounds for specific contexts:

> The long-suffering, rain-soaked spectators saw a low-scoring game with too much time-wasting.

A **dash** [–] can be used to punctuate a parenthesis:

> Four batsmen – including the captain – were dismissed in the morning session.

It can mark the end of a series of examples and the beginning of an explanation of, or comment on, the examples:

> Yachts, cabin cruisers, power boats, lobster boats – dozens of craft were torn from their moorings.

The dash can be used to indicate an ironic or dramatic – sometimes melodramatic – pause:

> After the storm Fred Vedley found his yacht – in the marina car park.

And it is used to disrupt a linguistic unit in order to signal a sudden change in thought:

> When I was in Norwich last week – Tea or coffee? – I met and old colleague of yours.

Round **brackets** ( ) can be used, like commas and dashes, to punctuate parentheses, or to mark information that is supplementary rather than essential:

> T.S. Eliot (1888–1965) won the Nobel prize for literature in 1948.

Square **brackets** [ ] mark an addition to, or comment on, a writer's text:

> I sent the contract to E.P. [Edwin Palfrey, the author's literary agent] for his advice.

The **ellipsis** […] has three functions, two of which are similar: to mark that an utterance is left unfinished by a speaker, or to mark an aposiopesis, a statement that is syntactically incomplete but intelligible to the reader:

> He switched off the light, lay back on the pillows, closed his eyes and …

An ellipsis can also indicate that a section of text, anything from a single word to several paragraphs, has been omitted. This is a rather crude editing technique; a more readable result can be achieved by summarizing and paraphrasing the text. *See also* APOSTROPHE; DIRECT SPEECH AND INDIRECT SPEECH.

purpose *(n.)*

An adverbial that signifies the aim, intention or purpose of an action.

Adverbials of purpose include:

> in order that, in order to, so that, so as to, with the intention of, with the aim of

and the *to* infinitive when it follows another verb:

> He went out to buy a newspaper.

putative *(adj./n.)*

The use of the MODAL AUXILIARY VERB *should* to express uncertainty, possibility or polite disagreement as distinct from the deontic use of *should* to show duty or obligation.

> I'm sorry you *should* say that. I *should* have thought you would agree. Perhaps I *shouldn't* be surprised by anything you say.

See also EPISTEMIC AND DEONTIC.

q

qualifier *(n.)*

1 A word, phrase or clause that adds information to, or qualifies, the meaning of a headword. By this definition, 'qualifier', 'qualify' and 'qualification' are the same as 'modifier', 'modify' and 'MODIFICATION'.

2 More narrowly, the terms 'qualifier', 'qualify' and 'qualification' are sometimes applied only to words, phrases or clauses that are placed after the headword. By this definition 'qualifier', 'qualify' and 'qualification' are the same as 'postmodifier', 'postmodify' and 'postmodification'.

3 Traditionally, an adjective that qualifies the noun in a noun phrase. Ambiguity can be avoided by using the terms 'modifier', 'modify' and 'modification'; 'premodifier', 'premodify' and 'premodification'; 'postmodifier', 'postmodify' and 'postmodification'.

quality partitive *see* PARTITIVE.

quantifier *(n.)*

A word or phrase that indicates a quantity. Quantity can be expressed by indefinite DETERMINERS:

> all, enough, few, many, several.

Cardinal numerals and numerical measures can be used to express quantity:

> four, five, a fifth, three-quarters,

and ordinal numerals can be used as determiners in phrases such as:

> the first time, a second chance, the third man.

PARTITIVES, too, express quantity:

> a slice of cake, a plank of timber, a handful of coins.

The action of a quantifier is to quantify, and the nature of a quantifier is quantitative. Quantifiers are sometimes contrasted with IDENTIFIERS.

quantity partitive *see* PARTITIVE.

Queen's English *see* KING'S ENGLISH.

question *(n.)*

A clause or sentence that asks for information or for a response from a listener or reader; a clause or sentence containing an INTERROGATIVE construction. Several types of question can be identified: yes/no; Wh-?; rhetorical; tag; and direct and indirect.

Yes/no, sometimes known as a closed question or a direct question:

Have you read Robert's new novel?

Wh- questions, that is, questions beginning with *Who, What, Where, When, Why* or *How*:

What do you think of the book?

Wh- questions are sometimes known as **open questions** because they are open to a wide variety of responses.

Alternative questions or either/or questions:

Do you prefer his new novels or his earlier work?

Rhetorical questions, a form of thinking aloud rather than a request for information:

Who would have thought it?

Tag questions, also known as **question-tags**, which are tagged on to the ends of declarative sentences:

You enjoyed the book, did you?

Another type, the **exclamatory question**, can be punctuated by a question mark or an exclamation mark, depending on whether the writer wants to convey the interrogative or the exclamatory nature of the sentence:

Isn't that sickening!

What on earth are you doing?

Some declarative sentences can have interrogative or exclamatory functions:

The concert begins in ten minutes and you've forgotten the tickets[?]/[!]

He wants to be a professional musician[?]/[!]

An **indirect question** is one that is expressed in indirect speech. This question in direct speech:

'Why do you want to see me?' she asked

can be rewritten as the indirect question:

She asked why he wanted to see her.

A yes/no direct question:

He asked her, 'Do you intend to submit your report today?'

becomes the indirect question:

> He asked her if she intended to submit her report that day.

The transformation from direct question to indirect question is a transformation from interrogative to declarative; as a declarative, an indirect question is not punctuated with a question mark. *See also* DIRECT SPEECH AND INDIRECT SPEECH.

question mark *see* PUNCTUATION.

question-tag *see* QUESTION.

quotation marks *see* DIRECT SPEECH AND INDIRECT SPEECH; PUNCTUATION; QUESTION.

r

radical *(n./adj.)*
Pertaining to the root of a word; an alternative term for ROOT and STEM.

range *(n.)*
The number and nature of the CONTEXTS or COLLOCATIONS in which a word or phrase can appear.

Range is determined SEMANTICALLY rather than syntactically. The word 'range' itself is polysemous and can be used in several contexts: references to scope and extent, to a selection or cross-section, to mountains and hills, to pasture or grazing land, and to a cooking oven. The word *mange*, by contrast, has a restricted range; it refers only to itching skin diseases unless the word is used metaphorically. *See also* SEMANTIC FIELD.

rank *(n./v.)*
1 A level in a hierarchical syntactic relationship; a level or stage on a syntactic scale; an alternative term for HIERARCHY and LEVEL (2). In a sentence, for example, the ranks, or levels, are clause, phrase, word and MORPHEME.

2 Traditionally, the level of semantic importance of words in a phrase or clause. For example, in the noun phrase *dark blue wooden chair* the

headword and semantically the most important word is *chair*; second in importance is the inherent, or intrinsic, adjective *wooden*; third in rank is the colour adjective *blue*; fourth is the qualitative adjective *dark*. *See also* SUPERORDINATE (2).

readability *(n.)*

The ease with which a piece of writing can be read and understood. A text is more likely to be readable if it has certain features: a VOCABULARY that contains a higher proportion of monosyllabic and disyllabic than polysyllabic words, a higher proportion of concrete words than abstract, and a higher proportion of words drawn from general vocabulary than from specialist or regional vocabulary; SENTENCES that are generally short, grammatically simple and thus make only limited use of coordination, subordination, recursion and embedding, in contrast to sentences that are compound, complex or compound-complex; PARAGRAPHS that are comparatively short, cohesive and coherent, and develop a theme in a logical progression; and uses standard GRAMMAR and SPELLING.

Two problems may arise if the writer strives too hard for readability. The text may be simplified to the point where it misrepresents the real nature of the subject matter and also antagonizes the reader. The unvarying use of simple techniques may become repetitive and boring. Repetition can be avoided if the writer uses a mix of monosyllabic, disyallabic and polysyllabic words, and of concrete and abstract words. Some variety in the lengths and structures of sentences and paragraphs will also help to make the text more readable. *See also* LEXICAL DENSITY; OBSCURITY; TRANSPARENT AND OPAQUE.

ready-made expression

A FIXED EXPRESSION that can be used in various contexts; an expression that already exists in a language. Ready-made expressions in English include idioms, proverbs, sayings and clichés:

> Blood is thicker than water
>
> Running around like a headless chicken

and social exchanges or PHATIC COMMUNION:

> Lovely weather. How do you do? Excuse me.

realization *(n.)*

1 The physical expression in writing or speech of a linguistic form; an actual example of a phonetic, graphic or syntactic form, a class of words or grammatical category. Grammatical categories such as mood, voice and case, for example, are abstract concepts until they are realized in physical expression.

2 LEXICALIZATION is a particular type of realization.

reason *see* CAUSATIVE VERB; CAUSE; CLAUSE.

rebus *(n.)*
A writing system in which pictures or logograms represent words, phrases or ideas, or in which two or more homophones are represented by the same sign. The word is taken from the phrase *de rebus quae geruntur* (concerning the things that are happening), applied to sixteenth-century picture puzzles and riddles. Modern examples are often equally light-hearted:

O, I C U R Y Y (Oh, I see you are wise).

Received Pronunciation (RP)
A form of British English spoken by a minority of speakers; a middle-class British social ACCENT (1). The word 'received', which is used here in the sense of handed down and accepted as authoritative, is a reminder that RP was once the accent of a privileged social class. RP is still the most widely understood British accent, but it has lost some of its authority and prestige. *See also* BBC ENGLISH; KING'S ENGLISH; PARALECT; STANDARD AND NON-STANDARD ENGLISH.

recipient *(n.)*
The person, or sometimes an animal, who receives what is denoted by the action of a verb. The recipient is usually the indirect object of a verb:

She presented the cup to *the captain* and gave *each player* a cup-winner's medal.

See also PARTICIPANT (2); PATIENT.

recipient participant *see* PARTICIPANT (2).

reciprocal *(adj./n.)*
Descriptive of a pronoun or a verb that expresses mutual action or relationship. Reciprocity is expressed in the pronouns:

each other, one another;

in the set of verbs synonymous with *meet*:

assemble, associate, come together, congregate, gather, join, partner;

and in the set of verbs:

> apportion, exchange, interchange, reciprocate, share.

See also COMITATIVE.

reclassification *(n.)*
An alternative term for CONVERSION.

recovery *(n.)*
The retrieval or restoration of information required to interpret an incomplete or corrupt text, or an incomplete or erratic utterance. A HIATUS or incoherence in a text can be recovered by using INTERNAL EVIDENCE AND EXTERNAL EVIDENCE. Ellipses, contradictions and slips of the tongue in speech can be recovered by the listener's competence in the language of the speaker or by a self-initiated REPAIR by the speaker.

The condition of being recoverable is known as recoverability.

recursion *(n.)*
The generation of a theoretically infinite number of similar linguistic units from a finite set of rules; the use of a particular type of linguistic unit to extend a phrase, a clause or a sentence; the application of recursive rules.

A succession of noun phrases, for example, can be followed by a succession of relative clauses:

> This the cow with the crumpled horn that tossed the dog that worried the cat that killed the rat that ate the malt that lay in the house that Jack built.

redesignation *(n.)*
An alternative term for CONVERSION.

reduction *(n.)*
Shortening, or reducing, a clause or sentence by omitting one or more component parts; reducing a syntactic unit by means of ellipsis or pro-forms. In this sentence:

> One athlete, obviously exhausted, dropped out of the marathon

the adjective phrase *obviously exhausted* can be regarded as a reduction of the relative clause *who was obviously exhausted*. This sentence:

> Emma's brother may join the police

could elicit the elliptical response:

> He did

or a response with the reductive pro-form *so*:

> He did so/He has already done so.

reductionism *(n.)*

The principle of analysing, or reducing, complex linguistic units to simpler constituents in the belief that an understanding of the separate constituents will lead to an understanding of the whole; the view that the meaning of the sum of the parts of a linguistic unit is the meaning of the complex whole.

Reductive componential analysis in the form, say, of BRACKETING or a TREE DIAGRAM can clarify the syntax of a complex unit but is unlikely to reveal the meanings of ambiguous, idiomatic, metaphorical or figurative linguistic units.

The terms 'reductionism' and 'reductive' are sometimes used with the pejorative connotation that a structure or a concept has been falsified by oversimplification.

redundancy *(n.)*

1 A degree of predictability that is present in a written or spoken message, either because of the nature of language and grammar or because predictability has been deliberately added in order to clarify the message.

> He is about to buy a gift for her.

In the example above, the nature of English grammar makes it predictable that the subject, the singular personal pronoun *He*, will be followed by the singular form of a verb; that *is about to* will be followed by the base form of a verb; that the indefinite article *a* will be followed by a singular noun beginning with a consonant; and that a personal pronoun after the preposition *for* will be in the objective case.

In other circumstances, for example, lectures and demonstrations, redundancy may be a deliberate feature of the content of the message. In order to clarify and reinforce the message, the speaker may repeat some key words and phrases, may offer several examples or case studies, and may use visual aids.

2 Superfluous information in a written or spoken message. By this definition, redundancy can be viewed as a pejorative term that suggests unnecessary repetition, over-elaboration or CIRCUMLOCUTION in speech or writing.

reduplication *(n.)*

1 A word or phrase that is formed by repetition of a word, a syllable or a sound. Most reduplicative words have a colloquial ring and clearly suggest wordplay:

> flip-flop, hum-drum, mish-mash, riff-raff, tit-for-tat.

See also ITERATIVE (2).

2 Repetition of a letter, syllable or word in the formation of some tenses in Latin and Greek verbs.

reference *(n.)*

1 The relationship between a word, a phrase or a longer linguistic unit and the physical or abstract reality to which the unit refers. The relationship is also known as **referential meaning**, and the thing referred to is known as the referent. All signs and signals represent something other than themselves; the 'something other' is the referent, and the act of representation is the reference. *See also* DENOTATIVE, REFERENTIAL MEANING *under* MEANING.

2 The relationship between one grammatical unit and another. A pronoun, for example, refers to a noun. In the relationship between the pronoun and the noun phrase, the noun phrase is the referent.

> *See also* PRO-FORM.

referential meaning *see* DENOTATIVE, REFERENTIAL MEANING *under* MEANING; REFERENCE (1).

reflexive pronoun

A pronoun that refers back to, or reflects, a noun phrase; the pronouns *myself, yourself, himself, herself, itself, ourselves, yourselves* and *themselves*. A reflexive pronoun is not normally acceptable as the subject of a clause or sentence:

> *He and *myself* will wait while *themselves* go on ahead

but in its dual function as reflexive and emphatic pronoun, it can be used to emphasize the subject:

> The players *themselves* admitted they performed badly.

Reflexive pronouns also appear as the objects of verbs:

> Angela taught *herself* to play the clarinet

and as the complements of prepositions:

> He bought the wine for his hosts, not *for himself*.

reflexive verb

A verb that has a reflexive pronoun as its object. Many transitive verbs can have reflexive pronouns as their objects:

> The losing finalist admired/comforted/excused/forgave/injured/killed *himself*

but there are few verbs that normally require reflexive pronouns, as distinct from other nominals, as objects. The following verbs are usually followed by reflexive pronouns:

> abase, absent, disgrace, perjure, preen, unburden.

regional dialect *see* DIALECT.

register *(n.)*

1 The variety and level of language required to discuss a particular subject or professional discipline. A scientific register, for example, is likely to include complex, polysyllabic nominal groups, many of them derived from Latin and Greek; frequent use of the passive rather than the active voice of verbs; formal, impersonal VOCABULARY and syntax.

2 The variety and level of language used by a particular writer or speaker. By this second definition, register is partly determined by a person's education, IDIOLECT and social or professional status, by the formal or informal nature of the occasion, and by the size and nature of the audience.

See also DICTION; ELABORATED CODE AND RESTRICTED CODE.

regular and irregular *(adj./n.)*

A **regular** linguistic form is one that conforms to a standard pattern, norm, rule or set of rules. An **irregular** linguistic form is one that differs from the pattern or rule established by other linguistic units of the same kind.

Irregular verbs are those that do not form the past tense and past participle by adding the inflection, *-ed*:

> arise/arose/arisen, go/went/gone, hurt/hurt/hurt.

Irregular nouns are those whose plural does not end in *-s*:

> men, women, children, lice, mice, feet, teeth.

The plural forms of some foreign nouns are, in an English-language context, irregular:

> cherubim, data, plateaux, termini.

Irregular adjectives and adverbs are those that do not have the inflection, *-er*, or the premodifier, *more*, for the comparative forms, and do not have the inflection, *-est*, or the premodifier, *most*, for the superlative forms:

> bad/badly, worse, worst; good/well, better, best.

A verbless clause or sentence is syntacically irregular:

> *In love with life*, he sings in the bath.

See also NORMATIVE.

relationship *(n.)*

A connection between two or more units in a linguistic system.

This general definition assumes that language consists of systems of interdependent, or interrelated, units. Relationship can take several forms.

Semantic relationships exist in sets of synonyms, antonyms, hyponyms and polyonyms; between the modifier and the headword of a phrase; a pronoun and its antecedent; words or phrases in apposition; a LEXEME and its associated word forms.

There are syntactic, or structural, relationships between the components of a sentence, for example, between subject and verb, verb and object. There are coordinating relationships, or co-relationships, between the clauses of a compound sentence, and there are subordinate, or dependent, relationships between main clauses and subordinate clauses.

Grammatical relationships link the forms in a paradigm. The relationships of components in a sentence are grammatical as well as semantic, for example, the relationship between a MODAL AUXILIARY VERB and the main verb in a sentence.

Transformational relationships link the declarative, interrogative and negative forms of a sentence, and also link active and passive sentences.

relative adverb

An adverb that introduces a relative clause; the adverbs *when* and *where*, signifying *at which*, *in which* or *on which*.

> Midnight is the time *when* he feels most awake.

> He sold the house *where* he had lived for twenty years.

relative clause

1 A subordinate CLAUSE, previously known as **adjective clause**, that modifies a noun phrase in another clause by adding information about the headword in the noun phrase; a clause that begins with a relative pronoun or relative adverb and functions like an adjective. Also known as a **subordinate relative clause**.

2 A subordinate CLAUSE that functions as the object or subject of a verb in another clause; a clause, also known as a **nominal relative clause** or **nominal clause**, that begins with a relative pronoun or relative adverb and functions like a noun:

> I know who you are and I know where you live.

The two nominal relative clauses *who you are* and *where you live* are the objects of the verb *know* in the two main clauses. In this sentence:

> What you say makes sense

the nominal relative clause *What you say* is the subject of the verb *makes* in the main clause.

relative determiner *see* DETERMINER.

relative pronoun

A pronoun that introduces a relative clause; a pronoun that relates to the headword in a noun phrase in another clause; the pronouns *who*, *whom*, *whose*, *that* and *which*.

The headword to which a relative pronoun refers is known as an ANTECEDENT. When the antecedent is human, the relative pronouns *who*, *whom* or *whose* are used. Increasingly, *whom* tends to appear only in formal written English unless it follows a preposition:

> The young musician, *about whom* critics are divided, gave a concert last night.

When the antecedent is not human, the relative pronouns *that* and *which* are used. *That* is sometimes used to refer to human antecedents, perhaps because of the vacuum and uncertainty caused by the vanishing *whom*. Traditionally, *that* is used in defining relative clauses:

> Cradle Bay hotels that depend on tourism are doing less business this year

and *which* is used in non-defining relative clauses:

> The Black Horse Hotel, *which was sold last year*, is up for sale again.

The relative pronouns *that* and *whom* are sometimes omitted, and the omission is known as a ZERO RELATIVE PRONOUN:

The hotel [that] they chose was the Black Horse.

The man [whom] I met was the hotel manager.

See also CLAUSE.

relativity *see* SAPIR-WHORF HYPOTHESIS.

remote *see* PROXIMATE AND REMOTE.

repair *(n./v.)*

The attempt by one or more participants in a discourse to clarify, or repair, a discontinuity in the discourse. Discontinuity may be caused by several factors: ambiguity, ellipsis, slip of the tongue, mispronunciation, mishearing or exceptionally long pauses.

A repair made by the speaker is known as a self-initiated repair; a repair made by a listener is an other-related repair. *See also* DYAD; RECOVERY.

reported speech *see* DIRECT SPEECH AND INDIRECT SPEECH.

reporting verb

A verb that signifies the act of speaking, and occasionally of writing.

said, stated, asked, demanded, shouted, whispered, argued, claimed.

representative speech act *see* SPEECH ACT.

restricted code *see* ELABORATED CODE AND RESTRICTED CODE.

restriction *see* SEMANTIC RESTRICTION.

restrictive clause

An alternative term for defining clause. *See* CLAUSE.

result *(n.)*

An adverbial clause that expresses the consequence, or result, of the action denoted by a verb in another clause in the sentence.

He was so tired that [as a result] he fell asleep in the chair.

Result can also be expressed by an adverbial that indicates the consequence expressed in the same clause:

Leadership was weak. Consequently, staff became demoralized.

See also CLAUSE.

rewrite rule *see* RULE.

rheme *see* THEME AND RHEME.

rhetorical question *see* QUESTION.

rhythm *(n.)*
In speech the sense of movement produced by the tempo of the speaker's delivery, the occurrence and duration of stressed and unstressed syllables, and the occurrence and duration of pauses between word-clusters.

In writing the sense of movement produced by the writer's syntax, for example, the length and structure of sentences, by the use of punctuation, the occurrence of stressed and unstressed syllables, and the occurrence of monosyllabic, disyllabic and polysyllabic words. *See also* CADENCE; PROSODY.

rise/rising *see* INTONATION; PITCH; TONE.

Roman alphabet
An alternative term for Latin alphabet. *See* ALPHABET.

root *(n.)*
1 The form of a word or element after the removal of any AFFIXES; the core MORPHEME of a word; also known as STEM. The word *spell*, for example, is the root of *misspell* and *spelling*.

A distinction can be made between the root form of a word and the base form. The verb *port*, is the root of *deport*, *export*, *import* and *transport*, but the base form of *transportable*, *transporter* and *transportation* is *transport*.

2 The earliest known form of a word. By this second definition, the root of *alley* is Old French *alee*, from Latin *ambulare* (to walk); the root of *road* is Old English *rad*; the root of *track* is Old French *trac*.

3 An alternative term for **acronode**, the topmost node of a TREE DIAGRAM.

rule *(n.)*
1 A description of the forms and functions of linguistic units and their relationship with other linguistic units; a description of the ways in which language functions in agreed contexts. By this definition, rules

are observed in, rather than imposed on, all written linguistic units from the MORPHEME to the sentence, and in all spoken units from the PHONEME to the discourse. Different rules operate in different varieties of written and spoken English: standard and non-standard, formal and informal, regional and national, specialist and general.

2 In generative grammar, the principles and predictive formulae for producing a theoretically infinite number of sentences. For example, the **rewrite rule** S→ NP VP means that a sentence consists of a noun phrase and a verb phrase, and that any sentence can be replaced by, or rewritten as, a noun phrase and a verb phrase.

3 In transformational GRAMMAR, formulae or principles that determine the conversion of one syntactic structure into another, for example, the conversion of an active sentence to a passive sentence.

4 In traditional grammar, the prescription and prohibition, often unjustified, of certain linguistic forms in speech and writing. *See also* CORRECTNESS; NORMATIVE; PRESCRIPTIVE.

run-on sentence *see* COMMA SPLICE.

S

sandhi *(n.)*
A change in the sound and form of a MORPHEME because of the influence of a preceding or following sound. Examples of this kind of change are the fusions of personal pronoun and verb:

> we've, you'll, they're;

the fusion of a verb and the negative particle *not*:

> can't, hasn't, won't;

the change of the indefinite article from *a* to *an* before a vowel, and the INTRUSIVE INTERVOCALIC R between certain vowels. *See also* ASSIMILATION.

Sapir-Whorf Hypothesis
A theory proposed by the American linguists and anthropologists, Edward Sapir (1884–1939) and Benjamin Lee Whorf (1897–1941). The theory combines the concepts of **linguistic determinism** and **linguistic**

relativity. Linguistic determinism is the belief that our native language partly determines the way we think and the way we perceive or comprehend the world. Linguistic relativity is the belief that perception of the world is relative and differs from speakers of one language to speakers of another.

The hypothesis, prompted partly by studies of the Hopi Native Americans, raises questions about the role of language in perception, cognition and cultural conditioning. *See also* POLYONYMY.

schema *(n.)*

1 A particular type of READY-MADE EXPRESSION or ready-made structure that can be adapted to meet the needs of particular circumstances. The term was borrowed from philosophy by the British linguist, John Lyons, and applied to such constructions as:

> What's the point of ...?
>
> Up with ...! Down with ...!
>
> Has anyone seen my ...?

2 More generally, the ability to apply concepts to what is perceived by the senses.

Linguistic schemata are abstract mental plans or frameworks against which speech and writing can be interpreted. A schema is usually unconscious or intuitive, but it can also function at a conscious level, especially in the act of writing. *See also* IDEATION.

scope *(n.)*

The extent of the influence of a linguistic unit in a sentence. The scope of a sentence adverbial, for example, extends to the entire clause or sentence:

> *Slowly*, he turned the key and opened the door.

By contrast, the scope of an adjective extends only to the noun it modifies:

> The *black door* swung open, and he stepped inside.

second language

1 A language acquired in addition to a speaker's FIRST LANGUAGE or NATIVE LANGUAGE.

2 A language given a degree of official recognition in addition to a country's national or majority language. French, for example, is in effect the second language of Canada, although its status as an OFFICIAL

LANGUAGE is equal to that of English. English is a second language in India.

second person *see* PERSON.

segment *(n.)*
A minimal unit in speech, that is, a PHONEME; a minimal unit of writing, a GRAPHEME; an identifiable and isolatable unit in the sound system or writing system of a language.

The term 'segment' is applied mainly to speech and phonemes, but it can also be applied to writing and graphemes. The division of speech into segments is known as segmentation. When more than two phonemes are considered as a unit, for example, in the study of intonation, the unit is **suprasegmental**.

semantic change
A gradual change in the meaning of a word; also known as **semantic shift**. *See also* AMELIORATION; BROADENING AND NARROWING; CONVERSION; PEJORATION.

semantic component *see* COMPONENT (1).

semantic differential
A variation in the connotative meanings attached to a word by two or more persons. Semantic differentials can be surveyed by inviting people to assess the connotative effects of words and rate them on scales that range, say, from good to bad or active to passive. A large-scale survey of such differentials may reveal patterns in the use and understanding of emotive, or affective, language, and also differences in the use or understanding of emotive language by different social groups.

semantic feature
One of a set of defining characteristics, or meanings, that can be assigned to a word. The phrase 'semantic feature' is part of the terminology of COMPONENTIAL ANALYSIS, where semantic features are discussed in terms of kinship and gender. The word *grandfather*, for example, has the semantic features:

    male, adult, with one or more children and with one or more grandchildren.

semantic field

A network of linguistic units that have some similarity in meaning; also known as a **semantic network** and a **lexical field**.

A semantic field may take the form of sets of coordinates, collocations, hyponyms, synonyms or polyonyms. The mental lexicon, at least in part, is a system of semantic, phonological and referential fields; we assimilate and remember, or store and retrieve, words according to their meanings, sounds and referents rather than alphabetically or as separate units. *See also* LOGOGEN.

semantic memory *see* LEXICAL MEMORY AND SEMANTIC MEMORY.

semantic network

An alternative term for SEMANTIC FIELD.

semantic primitives *see* COMPONENTIAL ANALYSIS (2).

semantic relationship *see* RELATIONSHIP.

semantic restriction

A limit to the number and to the nature of contexts or COLLOCATIONS in which a word or phrase can appear. *See also* RANGE; SEMANTIC FIELD.

semantic satiation

The paradoxical sense of loss of meaning when a word or phrase is thought, spoken or written repeatedly.

semantic shift

An alternative term for SEMANTIC CHANGE.

semantics *(n.)*

The study and analysis of the MEANINGS of MORPHEMES, words, phrases and sentences, and their influence on each other in interrelated networks of meaning. Distinctions can be made between lexical meaning, grammatical meaning and utterance meaning.

Lexical meaning, and semantic relations, are found in antonymy, homonymy, hyponomy, polyonymy and synonymy.

Grammatical meaning is the extent to which grammatical categories such as case, gender, number and person, or mood, tense and voice affect the meanings of sentences.

Utterance meaning is the extent to which the meaning of the spoken word is affected by redundancy or ellipsis, by paralinguistic features such as accent, intonation, pitch, stress, loudness, tempo and pauses, or by features of non-verbal communication.

sememe *(n.)*

The unit of meaning expressed by a MORPHEME; a minimal unit of meaning. Almost all AFFIXES are sememic; for example, the morpheme *neo*, from Greek *neos*, means new:

> neoclassical, neologism, neoplasm.

The morpheme *-ity*, from Old French *ité*, denotes a condition or state:

> humanity, humidity, plurality.

The English suffixes for conditions or states *-dom*, *-hood* and *-ness* produce the nouns:

> freedom, childhood, kindness.

semi-auxiliary verb

A verb phrase that has some of the properties of an AUXILIARY VERB; a verb phrase that begins with the verb *be* or *have*. Semi-auxiliaries include:

> be able to, be about to, be going to, be likely to, be supposed to, have to.
>
> We may be able to finish the job tomorrow.
>
> You were supposed to have finished it yesterday.

semicolon *see* PUNCTUATION.

semi-modal auxiliary verb

A VERB that has some of the properties of a MODAL AUXILIARY VERB; the verbs *dare*, *need*, *ought to* and *used to*.

> He does not dare repeat what he said.
>
> You need not reply to his challenge.
>
> We ought to warn him about his rudeness.
>
> He used to behave more courteously.

Dare and *need* can also function as main verbs followed by a *to* infinitive:

> He dared to challenge the director.
>
> We need to discuss the problem.

As a main verb, *need* can be followed by a noun phrase:

> We need an answer to the problem.

semiology *(n.)*

The study of sign systems, their production and control, meanings and interrelationships; also known as semiotics. Semiology is concerned with sign systems in cinema, television, advertising, popular culture and sometimes literature. Semiologists are also interested in the production, control and social impact of sign systems and the cultural forms in which they appear.

semi-passive *see* ACTIVE VOICE AND PASSIVE VOICE.

sense *(n.)*

1 The MEANING of a linguistic unit as determined by its semantic relationships with other linguistic units in a particular CONTEXT. By this definition, sense relations are CONTEXT-DEPENDENT. Sense is sometimes contrasted with denotation, or referential meaning. Sense is intralinguistic, that is, a meaning that lies within language alone; denotation is extralinguistic, that is, a meaning that lies not in language but in some other form of reality. A word can be discussed in terms of its sense relations or its denotation. *Cup*, for example, has a hyponymous sense relationship with the words *saucer* and *plate*; the denotative meaning of *cup* is an actual, physical object. Similarly, *lake* has a synonymous sense relationship with *mere* and *loch*, but the denotative, referential meaning of *lake* is an actual geographical feature.

2 The meaning of a linguistic unit in the vocabulary of a language. By this second definition, sense is the same as lexical meaning.

sentence *(n.)*

A linguistic unit that normally includes a verb (V), a subject (S) or zero subject, and may also include an object (O), a complement (C) and an adverbial (Adv), usually in the order: S + V + O + C + Adv; usually, the largest linguistic unit that can be analysed grammatically; a unit that, in a given context, forms a complete item of information; a unit that begins with a capital letter and ends with a full stop or other end-punctuation mark – question mark, exclamation mark, ellipsis or dash.

Sentences are so variable in content and structure that even that lengthy definition is incomplete. A sentence without a verb is sometimes acceptable in written standard English. For example, the question:

> Can I give you a lift into town?

could elicit a verbless but acceptable reply:

> Oh, how kind of you. And what a welcome offer on such a dull day as this. Yes, thank you.

Two sets of criteria, functional and syntactic, can be used to classify sentence types.

Functionally, sentences that make statements are classed as DECLARATIVE; sentences that ask questions as INTERROGATIVE; sentences that give commands as IMPERATIVE; sentences that are exclamations as EXCLAMATORY or exclamative. Syntactically, sentences can be classed as simple, compound, complex and compound-complex.

A **simple sentence** consists of one clause and contains one, usually finite, verb:

> City councillors made a difficult decision.

A **compound sentence** consists of two or more main, or principal clauses, each of which normally contains a finite verb, and one or more conjunctions:

> Some councillors opposed the plan/but a majority supported it/and the planning application was approved.

The oblique strokes show the division into three main clauses.

A **complex sentence** consists of one main clause and one or more subordinate clauses, which are usually linked by a relative pronoun or relative adverb:

> City councillors made a difficult decision/when they approved the plan.

A **compound-complex sentence** consists of two or more main clauses and one or more subordinate clauses:

> City councillors made a difficult decision/and caused some controversy/ when they approved the plan/that had been attacked in the press.

A distinction is sometimes made between a **major sentence** and a **minor sentence**.

A major sentence, also known as a **full sentence**, is one that has a subject and a verb, especially a finite verb, and may also have an object, complement or adverbial. Imperative sentences usually have a zero subject. Major sentences can be classified as one of the types: declarative (or indicative), interrogative, imperative, exclamatory; and also one of the types: simple, compound, complex, compound-complex.

A minor sentence is one that may form a semantically complete linguistic unit but is irregular in form, usually because it lacks a finite verb. A minor sentence is also known as an **irregular sentence** and sometimes as a **non-sentence**.

What an embarrassment! How kind of you.

On Tuesday at five o'clock, then.

See also VERBLESS CLAUSE.

sentence adverbial

An alternative term for DISJUNCT or DISJUNCTIVE.

sentence disjunct *see* DISJUNCTIVE.

sentence stress

An alternative term for contrastive stress. *See* STRESS.

set expression

An alternative term for FIXED EXPRESSION.

sibilant *(adj./n.)*

A fricative consonant; the consonants /s/ and /z/.

sign *(n.)*

A distinct unit in an agreed sign system; an image or symbol that represents a referent, or that which is signified. In a writing system, signs are letters of the alphabet, other GRAPHEMES and words. In a sound system, the signs are PHONEMES, syllables and words. In non-verbal communication, the signs are visual, auditory and kinetic images. *See also* SIGNIFICATION; SIGNIFIER AND SIGNIFIED.

signal *(n.)*

1 A SIGN in a system of signs.

2 In the electronic transmission of speech, the audio wave-form that carries information from the human and electronic source to the human and electronic receiver.

signification *(n.)*

The referential meaning of a SIGN; the fact of having or expressing the meaning denoted by a sign; the conceptual relationship between the SIGNIFIER AND SIGNIFIED.

Signification can take the form of denotation, which is sometimes defined as the first order of signification, or it can take the form of connotation, sometimes defined as the second order of signification. See *also* REFERENCE (2).

signifier and signified *(n.)*

A signifier is the physical medium that expresses the meaning of a sign such as a speech sound, a written symbol or a visual image. The signified is the thing to which the sign refers; in an abstract context, the signified is a person's concept of the thing referred to.

The relationship between the signifier and the signified is the sign, which can be arbitrary or iconic. ARBITRARINESS in a sign, like arbitrariness in language, is a lack of similarity or correspondence between the signifier and the signified. An extralinguistic example is musical notation, which is an arbitrary or conventionalized way of indicating sounds.

ICONICITY is a similarity between signifier and signified, for example, pictorial road signs that warn of possible hazards such as a railway crossing or a lane closure.

silent pause *see* PAUSE.

simile *(n.)*

A figure of speech that compares one thing to another of a different type in order to stress the similarity or the difference or both, and thus to make the comparison more striking than a reference to one thing only.

> John looked like a startled rabbit.

Many similes are fixed expressions:

> as prickly as a porcupine
>
> like a bat out of hell.

See also METAPHOR.

simple future *see* FUTURE TENSE.

simple past *see* PAST TENSE.

simple sentence *see* SENTENCE.

simple stem *see* STEM.

singular *see* NUMBER.

singulare tantum

A word, especially an UNCOUNTABLE or mass noun, that has a singular form only. *See also* PLURALE TANTUM.

situational meaning

An alternative term for interpersonal and social meaning. *See* MEANING.

slang *(adj./n.)*

An informal variety of language characterized by non-standard vocabulary; the non-standard vocabulary of a particular occupational, social or regional speech community. Slang is more volatile than standard English and varies from one sub-culture to another and from one generation to another. It is a way of defying taboos, and can be regarded as an antonym of, and antidote for, EUPHEMISM. Slang expressions for death, for example, include *go for a burton* (a *burton*, or *barton*, was a block and tackle for lifting 'dead' weights), *go west* (and into the setting sun), *push up daisies, kick the bucket, pop your clogs* and *snuff the candle*.

slip of the tongue *see* NON-WORD; NONCE-WORD; PARAPRAXIS.

social dialect *see* DIALECT; SOCIOLECT.

social distancing

An alternative term for the present in the past. *See* PAST TENSE; PRESENT TENSE.

sociolect *(n.)*

A variety of spoken language that partly reflects the speaker's social background, social status, profession or occupation; an alternative term for social DIALECT. *See also* INDEXICAL FEATURE.

sociolinguistics *(n.)*

The branch of linguistics concerned with the ways in which language, especially speech, is used in society. Sociolinguistics includes such areas of study as the use of language by particular speech communities, language and region, language and nationality, language and social class.

sound symbolism

A similarity between the pronunciation of a word and the sound the word denotes. The similarity is clearest in ONOMATOPOEIA, and can sometimes be detected in PHONAESTHEMES:

whimper, whine, whinge; groan, growl, grunt.

See also ECHO.

sound system

An alternative term for PHONOLGY.

source *(n.)*

The origin of a signal or a message. In speech, writing and non-verbal communication, the source is usually the sender, the person who encodes and transmits the signal.

source language

1 The language from which a loan word is borrowed. The source of the borrowing *catamaran*, for example, is Tamil *kattumaram* (tied wood); the source of *dinghy* is Hindi *digi, degi*; the source of *yacht* is Dutch *jaghta*, now *jacht*.

2 The language from which a translation is made; the language that is translated into another language.

species-specific *(adj.)*

Descriptive of a faculty or quality that is particular, or specific, to one biological group, or species. The terms 'species-specific' and 'species-specificity' are used in discussing the INNATENESS of LANGUAGE, the likelihood that only humans are biologically programmed for language, and that the language faculty is genetically transmitted.

speech *(n.)*

Humans probably began to develop speech in the same period as the evolution of the modern brain and the emergence of consciousness. We are biologically programmed for speech, and in that sense it is a natural, innate, faculty, but since it has to be acquired, or learned, it is not an instinct.

Once acquired, speech can be used in most circumstances with little or no planning except at the moment of utterance; indeed, it can be uttered spontaneously and involuntarily at times of sudden pain or fear. In normal delivery, speech consists mainly of clusters, or 'chunks', of words, with pauses between the clusters rather than between individual words. Although EGOCENTRIC SPEECH is a normal activity, in adults as well as children, speech is usually a social activity that is influenced by circumstances, for example, formal or informal occasions, large groups or small.

Speech is much more variable than WRITING. The form of a **spoken language** can vary according to country, region, social status, education or the age of the speaker; it can also vary through paralinguistic features such as pitch, tempo, loudness and voice quality. The spatial and temporal limitations of speech – the human voice can be projected only so far, and the sound disappears as soon as it is uttered – began to be overcome with the invention of the gramophone and telephone in the nineteenth century. And with the development of magnetic sound tape, radio and satellite transmission in the twentieth century, it became possible to store and transmit the spoken word as effectively as the written word.

Since the middle of the twentieth century, the linguistics of spoken English has developed rapidly as an academic discipline. *See also* ACQUISITION OF LANGUAGE; INNATENESS; LANGUAGE ACQUISITION DEVICE; PARALANGUAGE.

speech act

An utterance that is delivered with a particular intention and for a particular effect. Speech acts such as instructing, negotiating, assuring and apologizing can be assessed in terms of the act's illocutionary quality, that is, the speaker's intention, and its perlocutionary quality, that is, its effect on the listener.

Speech acts are sometimes classified as five main types: commissive, declarative, directive, expressive and representative.

A **commissive speech act** is one in which the speaker makes a commitment, usually in the form of a promise, guarantee, warning or threat:

> I give you my word that I won't repeat the offence.

A **declarative speech act** is a declaration that, by the fact of being uttered, brings about a change of circumstance:

> I now pronounce you Master of Arts/husband and wife/a Member of the Society.

A **directive speech act** is a suggestion, instruction, command or request.

An **expressive speech act** is one in which the speaker exhibits emotions, attitudes or opinions, and can take the form of a compliment, congratulations, an apology or complaint:

> What a wonderful performance!
>
> I'm sorry about the interruption.
>
> I don't like the noise.

A **representative speech act** reports, or represents, a fact or circumstance in the form of an account, assertion or claim:

> The road ahead is flooded.

Prices have risen five per cent this year.

See also ILLOCUTION, LOCUTION AND PERLOCUTION; PERFORMATIVE.

speech centres of the brain

An alternative term for language centres of the brain.

speech chain

The alternating stages, or links, in a sequence of exchanges between two or more speakers. In this model of communication the main stages are speech production, speech transmission and speech reception.

The production stage involves the neurological process of transforming electro-chemical activity in the brain into language. The transmission stage consists mainly of the physiological formation and projection of speech by means of the vocal tract. Reception involves the physiological mechanism of the ear and the neurological process of interpreting the sounds.

speech community

A group of people who speak the same language or the same dialect of a language; a group of people who use language in the same way; also known as **language community**. The term 'speech community' can be applied to national or even international groups, for example, speakers of English or French, but the term is more often used to refer to specific regional, social or occupational groups. The more tightly knit and isolated the community – people in prison, for example, or in a remote boarding school – the more distinctive the speech of that community is likely to be.

speech continuum

An alternative term for DIALECT CONTINUUM.

speech disorder

A general term for various abnormalities of speech. The natures and definitions of speech disorders are disputed, but they can be divided into two broad classes: acquired and congenital.

An acquired speech disorder is one that appears as the result of a brain injury or lesion some time after the person's birth. A congenital speech disorder is one that is present from the time of birth. Cerebral palsy, for example, can cause congenital speech disorders.

speech marker
An alternative term for INDEXICAL FEATURE.

spelling *(n.)*
Writing or naming the letters of words; also known as ORTHOGRAPHY (2).

The adoption of the Roman ALPHABET by the Germanic-speaking Anglo-Saxons was the first in the long series of accidents that determined the spelling of Modern English.

Old English writing was phonetic in the sense that every letter of a word was sounded and no letters were silent, but with the arrival of the Normans the phonetic base began to be undermined. When the Normans colonized England, Old French, with a spelling system different from that of Old English, became the official language. French was never the majority language but it transformed English and English spelling. Old English *cwacian*, *cwen* and *cwencan*, for example, became *quake*, *queen* and *quench*.

English spelling was no longer phonetic, and differences between speech and spelling, between the phonology and the morphology of English, continued to appear in the fifteenth century when the sound of the ENGLISH LANGUAGE was transformed in the process known as the GREAT VOWEL SHIFT.

The sound system changed but there was no equivalent change in spelling. There was, however, a development that eventually led to the standardization of spelling. The first printed book in England appeared from William Caxton's Westminster press in 1477, and by the time Caxton died in 1491 he had printed almost a hundred books. Printing gave the written word, and the spelling of the written word, a permanence and a wider readership; it also created a new awareness of writing and spelling.

A similar kind of awareness was fostered by the English-to-Latin dictionaries that began to appear from the mid-fifteenth century, and by the English dictionaries from Robert Cawdrey's *A Tale Alphabeticall* in 1604 to Samuel Johnson's *Dictionary* in 1755, by which time spelling was standardized.

Spelling was stabilized but pronunciation varied from one generation of speakers to another and from one geographical area to another. And it is the diversity of spoken English – along with the limited number, twenty-six, of alphabetical characters to represent hundreds of thousands of words – that makes it impossible to create a strictly phonetic system of English spelling. Even if there were agreement on the sound system – RECEIVED PRONUNCIATION, North American network English – to be adopted as the model for a revised spelling system, the system would not represent the speech of the vast majority of speakers. And the system would be out of date within a century because the model speech-pattern would have changed. *See also* ACCENT; CHANGE; DICTIONARY.

split infinitive
A TO-INFINITIVE with an adverbial between the particle and the verb. The old, unjustified prohibition lingers on, but in some contexts the split infinitive is a means of avoiding ambiguity or awkwardness of style and rhythm. This sentence with the split infinitive:

>He decided *to quickly end* arguing with colleagues

could be ambiguous if it were written as:

>He *decided quickly* to end arguing with colleagues

>He decided to end *quickly arguing* with colleagues

>He decided to end *arguing* with colleagues *quickly*.

The italic type highlights the possible ambiguities. The prohibition against the split infinitive is the result of the mistaken application of Latin grammar to the English language. The infinitive form of a Latin verb is a single word, for example, *findere* (to split), but the English *to*-infinitive, unlike the bare infinitive, is already split.

spoken language *see* SPEECH.

spoonerism *see* METATHESIS.

standard and non-standard English
1 Written standard English observes the current norms of spelling, morphology, semantics and syntax. Standardization of written English, which was achieved mainly by printers and publishers rather than grammarians and authors, makes the language intelligible to everyone who is literate in English.

Non-standard written English ignores some or all of the norms outlined above. Instead, it may include regional folk grammar, such as *we have drove* for *we have driven*, or *wus* or *wur* for *our*, and other non-standard features such as irregular sentences.

2 Spoken standard English observes – in a modified form that acknowledges differences between speech and writing – the norms of grammar and semantics, irrespective of accent. Alternatively, spoken

standard English can be defined as above but with RECEIVED PRONUNCIATION or with a PARALECT of RP that is a social as well as a linguistic standard.

Non-standard spoken English takes a wide variety of regional and national forms, and is likely to include folk grammar and regional dialect uttered in a regional or national accent. Non-standard spoken English is likely to include social as well as linguistic features.

See also NORMATIVE; USAGE.

statement *(n.)*

A clause or SENTENCE that expresses a declaration, proposition or statement. Sentences that express statements, that is, declarative sentences, are sometimes contrasted with sentences that express questions (interrogative), commands (imperative) and exclamations (exclamatory).

stative verb *see* DYNAMIC VERB AND STATIVE VERB.

stem *(n.)*

Usually, an alternative term for ROOT. Distinctions can be made between a simple stem, a compound stem and a complex stem. A **simple stem** consists of one root MORPHEME:

> man, wife, boy, girl.

> A **compound stem** consists of two root morphemes:

> ringside, shotgun, timetable, workman.

> A **complex stem** consists of a root morpheme and an AFFIX:

> manly, boyish, timeless, worker.

stop *(n./v.)*

A consonant formed by a closure of the vocal tract followed by an abrupt release of breath; the consonants /p/, /b/, /d/ and /t/.

stress *(n./v.)*

The ACCENT, or emphasis, given to syllables in speech. Stress varies according to the amount of force used to articulate syllables and the rate of air flow from the vocal tract. Changes in stress are usually accompanied by changes in the pitch or in the loudness of the spoken word.

A distinction is made between contrastive stress and lexical stress. **Contrastive stress**, also known as **sentence stress**, is the emphasis placed on one or more syllables in order to reinforce a particular meaning:

> *This* is the right answer.
>
> This is the *right* answer.

Lexical stress, also known as **word stress**, is the agreed pattern of stress for almost every word in English, or for every word in a given context:

> '*con*tract (noun), con'*tract* (verb)
>
> a'*big*, '*blue*'*bott*le; a big'*blue*bottle.

stress-timed language and syllable-timed language

A **stress-timed language**, also known as an isochronous (equal time) language, is one in which syllables are stressed at fairly regular intervals, irrespective of the number of intervening unstressed syllables.

A **syllable-timed language**, also known as an isosyllabic (equal syllable) language, is one in which the syllables occur at fairly regular intervals of time. English is a stress-timed language; French is syllable-timed language. *See also* ACCENT (2); MONOSYLLABLE and POLY-SYLLABLE; STRESS.

strong verb and weak verb

Traditional grammar defined a strong VERB as one that changes its root vowel to indicate past tense.

> bought, flew, swam

Strong verbs, most of which are Germanic in origin, are irregular, but some irregular verbs, those with the same form in past and present tense, are not strong:

> put, slit, upset.

A **weak verb** is one that has its past tense ending in -*ed*. All weak verbs are regular verbs, and most new verbs in English are regular:

> computerized, televised, transduced.

The terms 'strong' and 'weak' have partly been replaced by the terms, REGULAR AND IRREGULAR. *See also* ABLAUT.

structuralism *(n.)*

1 The study of linguistic and ideational systems in language. Structuralism in this general sense involves the study of syntactic and semantic networks in sentences.

2 More narrowly, the study of grammatical and phonological forms and patterns, with little or no concern for semantics. *See also* DEEP STRUCTURE AND SURFACE STRUCTURE.

structure *(n./v.)*

An organized pattern of interrelated linguistic units. The term can be applied to a variety of linguistic units and associated features.

Sentence structure is the syntactic relationship of clauses, phrases and words in sentences.

Clause structure is the syntactic relationship of phrases and words in clauses.

Morphological structure is the pattern of roots, inflections, AFFIXES and compounds in words.

Semantic structure is the organization and development of meaning in sentences, paragraphs and longer units.

Information structure is the pattern of GIVEN INFORMATION AND NEW INFORMATION in units of information.

stylistics *(n.)*

The analytical study of particular uses of language; the analytical study of style in language. A distinction can be made between general stylistics and literary stylistics.

General stylistics is the study of any use of language, formal or informal, written or spoken, the spoken form usually being recorded or transcribed for analysis. The analysis could include such features as vocabulary, sentence structures and grammar.

Literary stylistics is the study of the aesthetic linguistic features of creative writing. Poetry, for example, can be analysed in terms of stylistic poetic devices such as diction, imagery, rhythm and rhyme.

suasive verb

A verb that denotes an attempt to persuade or influence. A suasive verb is usually followed by a *that* clause, in which the putative *should* can precede the base form of the non-suasive verb, or in which the verb can appear in the subjunctive or indicative mood.

Are you *suggesting* that he should resign? (suasive + *should* + base form)

Are you *suggesting* that he resign? (suasive + subjunctive)

Are you *suggesting* that he resigns? (suasive + indicative)

subject *(n.)*

A major, usually obligatory, component of a sentence or a clause; the component that appears before the verb in a sentence or clause, and with which the verb agrees in number and person.

The subject of a sentence is often a noun phrase:

Seven candidates contested the by-election.

The subject can be a nominal relative clause:

What the voters want is a conscientious Member of Parliament

or a non-finite clause:

Contesting the by-election was exhausting.

When no subject is available, the dummy *it* is sometimes used:

It snowed on polling day.

The term ZERO SUBJECT can be applied to the implicit subject, usually the pronoun *you*, of an imperative construction:

Fight hard but fight fairly.

In passive sentences, a distinction can be made between the grammatical subject and the logical subject, which is often the actor.

The by-election was contested by seven candidates.

The grammatical subject is *The by-election*; the logical subject is *seven candidates*, and the noun phrase *seven candidates* is the actor.

subject complement *see* COMPLEMENT.

subjective case

The CASE of a noun or pronoun when it is the subject of a sentence; an alternative term for **nominative**.

subjunctive mood

The mood that expresses a hypothetical relationship between the subject and predicate of a sentence, or between the main clause and subordinate clause of a sentence. Verbs in the subjunctive mood always appear in the *base* form. Subjunctives can be divided into three classes: formulaic, mandative and past.

The **formulaic subjunctive**, expressing a wish, desire or choice, appears in set expressions, or formulae, such as:

So be it.

God bless this ship.

Long live the king.

The **formulaic subjunctive** is also known as the **optative subjunctive**.

The **mandative subjunctive** is the verb in a nominal clause or *that* clause, following a main clause expressing an assertion, request or suggestion:

> We insist that he *appear* in person.

> The director recommended that her assistant *undertake* new duties.

The word 'mandative', which means of or pertaining to a command, could be misleading; the mandative subjunctive mood, unlike the imperative mood, does not, in fact, express a command.

The **past subjunctive** takes the form *were* in expressions of wishing or supposing:

> I wish I *were* fitter than this.

> Imagine the outcry if a newspaper *were* to publish the story.

subordinate clause *see* CLAUSE.

subordinate relative clause
An alternative term for RELATIVE CLAUSE.

subordinating conjunction *see* OPPOSITE.

subordination *(n.)*
1 The relationship between a linguistic unit that operates at a lower level than another, SUPERORDINATE, unit.

2 Adding a subordinate CLAUSE to a main clause or to another subordinate clause, usually by means of a relative pronoun, relative adverb or subordinating conjunction.

Subordination, which is sometimes contrasted with superordination and with coordination, is not only a relationship between a subordinate and a main clause; it can also be a relationship between subordinate clauses. In this example:

> The removal men worked/until all the furniture was in the van,/which had been bought/to replace an older vehicle.

only the subordinate adverbial clause of time *until all the furniture was in the van* is directly related to the main clause *The removal men worked*; the main clause is superordinate to the subordinate adverbial clause. The subordinate relative clause *which had been bought* modifies the noun phrase *the van* in the adverbial clause, and so the adverbial clause is superordinate to the relative clause. The non-finite clause *to replace an older vehicle* modifies the verb *had been bought* in the relative clause; the relative clause, therefore, is superordinate to the non-finite clause in the example above.

3 The relationship between a HYPERNYM AND HYPONYM. The hyponym is subordinate to the hypernym.

subordinator *(n.)*
An alternative term for subordinating conjunction. *See* OPPOSITE.

substantive *(adj./n.)*
Formerly, an alternative term for NOUN.

substitution *(n.)*
The replacement, or substitution, of one linguistic unit for another; an alternative term for PRO-FORM. *See also* PRO-VERB.

substrate/substratum and superstrate/superstratum
A **substrate** or **substratum** is a linguistic unit or variety that is the result of the influence of a socially or politically subordinate language. Gaelic, for example, has for centuries been subordinate to English and Scots, and because of this reduced status relatively few Gaelic words, apart from place-names, appear in English. Gaelic words in English include *clan*, from Gaelic *clann* (children); *ingle*, from *aingeal* (fire, fireside); *slogan*, from *sluagh* (multitude) + *gairm* (call, cry; originally, a war cry).

A **superstrate** or **superstratum** is a linguistic unit or variety that is caused by the influence of a socially or politically dominant language. Old FRENCH was a superstrate language in England from around the year 1100 to around 1350 and influenced English vocabulary, spelling and pronunciation. Particular forms of superstrate are the use Italian in music – *adagio, allegro* and *presto* – and the use of French terms in *haute cuisine*.

sub-vocalization *(n.)*
An alternative term for INNER SPEECH.

suffix *see* AFFIX.

superlative *(adj./n.)*
A word or inflection that denotes the highest degree of a quality or attribute; a gradable ADJECTIVE or ADVERB that expresses the highest

degree; a gradable adjective or adverb ending with the *-est* inflection – *straightest* – or preceded by the intensifier, *most* – *most desirable*. *See also* GRADABILITY.

superordinate *(adj./n.)*

1 A linguistic unit that operates at a higher level than another, subordinate or dependent, unit.

2 A main, or principal, clause in relation to a subordinate clause.

3 A word, a hypernym, whose meaning implies that of another word, a hyponym. *See* HYPERNYM AND HYPONYM.

   See also CLAUSE; SUBORDINATION.

superstrate/superstratum *see* SUBSTRATE/SUBSTRATUM AND SUPERSTRATE/SUPERSTRATUM.

suppletion *(n.)*

Placing one or more words with different roots in a grammatical or morphological paradigm; a paradigm with one or more irregular forms. Suppletive forms include *better* and *best* as grades of *good* or *well*; *worse* and *worst* as grades of *bad*, *badly* or *ill*; *went* as the past form of *go*; *was* and *were* as past forms of *be*.

suprasegmental *see* SEGMENT.

surface structure *see* DEEP STRUCTURE AND SURFACE STRUCTURE.

syllabary *(n.)*

A WRITING SYSTEM in which the characters represent syllables in a language. Most syllabic writing systems, for example, Japanese, have a greater number of characters, from around fifty to several hundred, than alphabetic writing systems.

syllable *(n.)*

A unit of pronunciation that forms the whole or part of a word; a unit of intonation and rhythm in speech. A syllable includes a nucleus, usually a vowel, and may also include an initial or final margin, usually a consonant, before or after the **nucleus**.

   Vowels have greater sonority, or loudness, than consonants. A syllable ending with a vowel is known as an open syllable; a syllable ending with a consonant is known as a closed syllable. *See also*

MONOSYLLABLE AND POLYSYLLABLE; STRESS-TIMED AND SYLLABLE-TIMED LANGUAGES.

syllable-timed language *see* STRESS-TIMED AND SYLLABLE-TIMED LANGUAGE.

symbol *(n.)*
A written mark or SIGN with an agreed value in a system of marks or signs; a written sign or group of signs representing a sound or a word. *See also* CHARACTER.

synchronic *see* DIACHRONIC AND SYNCHRONIC.

syncretism *(n.)*
The merging of two or more inflectional forms into a single form after the loss of inflections. Regular verbs, which have the same form for the past tense and the past participle:

> I *walked*, I have *walked*

show syncretism, in contrast to irregular verbs:

> I *ran*, I have *run*.

Regular nouns, which are inflected only for plural and possessive, are syncretic.

syncope *see* APOCOPE AND SYNCOPE.

synechdoche *(n.)*
A figure of speech in which a part represents the whole so that the words uttered represent more than they actually denote. Newspaper and magazine proprietors are said to own *titles*, a synechdoche for the entire company; recording companies are said to own *labels*; farmers are said to own a number of *head* of cattle.

synonym *(n.)*
A word or phrase with a similar meaning to that of another word or phrase. Synonyms are sometimes defined as words with the same meaning but few, if any, synonyms mean exactly the same as one another. The closest correspondence is probably to be found in pairs such as *equine/horse-like*, *herbivorous/plant-eating*, *stellar/starry* or *star-like*.

Words in synonymous sets are not interchangeable in some contexts; a meeting can be described as *brief* or *short*, but a person below average height can be described as *short* but not *brief*.

Synonyms are said to be in a synonymous relationship with each other, and the quality of being synonymous is known as synonymy. *See also* GRADIENCE.

syntagm, syntagma *(n.)*

A syntactic unit consisting of two or more signs; a linear, or chain, relationship of linguistic units. The word tends to be used loosely. A syntagm can consist of the sequence of letters in a word, or words in a sentence, or sentences in a paragraph, and so on. A linguistic unit, for example, a polysemous word, can change its meaning from one syntagm, or context, to another.

syntactic component *see* COMPONENT (1).

syntax *(n.)*

The order and interrelationship of words in sentences and clauses; the rules of grammatical construction and the branch of grammar that deals with those rules. Syntax includes the components of sentence structuring: the order of subject, verb, object, complement and adverbial, and the order of words, phrases and clauses. It also includes the processes of transformation from active to passive, and from declarative to interrogative and negative, and such features as subordination, coordination, superordination, embedding and recursion.

The word syntax ultimately derives from the same Greek root as syntagm: suntassein, arrange.

synthetic language

1 An alternative term for an inflected, or inflecting, language. *See also* ANALYTIC, SYNTHETIC AND AGGLUTINATIVE LANGUAGES.

2 An alternative term for ARTIFICIAL LANGUAGE (1).

synthetic proposition *see* ANALYTIC PROPOSITION AND SYNTHETIC PROPOSITION.

synthetic speech

Speech sounds produced by a synthesizer, that is, a computerized system that combines signals of different frequencies to produce different sounds. *See also* ARTIFICIAL LANGUAGE (2).

t

tabloidese *(n.)*

A use of language particular to British tabloid newspapers. Tabloidese can be a forceful and economic prose form, but it is often characterized by simple, sometimes colloquial vocabulary, frequent use of ready-made expressions, and simplified sentence and paragraph structures; sentences and paragraphs sometimes consist of only one word. The diction is often emotive, especially in headlines:

> New heartbreak for agony mum

and the prose style sometimes combines compression and clichés in a distinctive way:

> Factory foreman Ken Smith, ex-Para and keep-fit fanatic, had his dreams come true last night.

See also HEADLINE ENGLISH.

tag question *see* QUESTION.

tag statement

A brief comment that is added, or tagged, to a statement in order to reinforce the meaning. A tag statement can be added by a speaker:

> He's a promising fast bowler, *young Ashton*

or by a second speaker, usually to indicate agreement:

> 'Higgins is too impetuous a batsman.' '*Much too impetuous.*'

tangentiality *(n.)*

An indirect response to a question or treatment of a topic. The indirectness can be deliberately allusive or evasive, or unintentionally tangential. *See also* IMPLICATURE.

tautology *(n.)*

The repetition of the same idea in different words in a single context. Tautology is regarded as highly redundant and stylistically unacceptable:

> The scholarship was established in 1979 following a bequest by Mr William Barclay who *left money in his will in order to set up the scholarship.*

telegrammatic *(adj.)*

1 A drastically simplified form of speech or writing that consists mainly of nouns and verbs; also known as telegraphic. In linguistics, the term 'telegrammatic' refers not to distance (*tele-*, far off), but to the terse, elliptical prose of a telegram, a short written message paid for by the word:

> Uncle Horace dead. Funeral St Mark's Friday 3pm.

2 The speech of young children, who acquire nouns, verbs, the determiner *more* and the particle *no* before they acquire function words and inflections:

> Want Teddy. More milk. No bed.

This form of telegrammatic speech, in which the child's utterance consists mainly of key words, or content words, and omits function words, suggests that children have an underlying understanding of some principles of language. For example, if a parent asks:

> Shall we have lunch now or later?

the child's reply may take a form like:

> Want lunch. Lunch now.

See also INNATENESS; LANGUAGE ACQUISITION DEVICE; OVER-GENERALIZATION.

telesis *(n.)*

A planned use of language to achieve a specific objective. Examples of telesis include job applications, political speeches and appeals by charities. *See also* ILLOCUTION, LOCUTION and PERLOCUTION; PER-FORMATIVE.

tense *(n.)*

The form a verb takes in order to relate the occurrence of the action, condition or state denoted by the verb to the time at which a speaker or writer refers to that action, condition or state. By this definition, tense is the expression of temporal narrative viewpoints, ways of fixing events and states in time, of relating the narrator to the events and states and thus orienting the narrator in time. It is a definition that overlaps with ASPECT.

The traditional terms of tense, PAST, PRESENT and FUTURE, are neither three separate time-states nor three mutually exclusive grammatical categories. The terms cover a variety of time-states, some of them interrelated, as in the historic present, the hypothetical past, the future in the past and the past in the future.

This variety of tenses, along with the aspects and moods of verbs, allow us to make complex and subtle distinctions about time. And just as the terminology of grammar in general expresses some of the ways in which we think about language, so the terminology of tense expresses some of the ways in which we think about time.

Morphologically, English verbs have three forms that express tense: the unmarked form for the present tense:

> I/you/we/they walk,

the -*s* form, which is marked for present tense, third person singular:

> he/she walks,

and the -ED FORM, *walked*, which is marked for the past tense. The -ING FORM is marked for continuity but the continuity can be past, present or future:

> is walking, was walking, will be walking.

The future tense is formed by using the MODAL AUXILIARIES *shall* or *will* before the main verb:

> I shall walk; you will walk

or by using the constructions *be going to* and *be about to*:

> She is going to walk.

terminology *(n.)*

A set of specialist terms belonging to a particular subject. The word 'terminology' was originally applied to the languages of science and technology, but the word can be applied to the particular language of most subjects and professions. *See also* JARGON; NOMENCLATURE.

text *(n.)*

A printed or written work; the actual wording of a printed or written document. The word 'text' is sometimes used loosely to refer to any form of writing or speech, but *text* normally refers to a specific piece of writing, including transcriptions of speech, that is studied for its meaning, and sometimes for its style, rather than its grammar.

The study of texts in these ways is known as text linguistics.

theme and rheme

The **theme** is the part of a sentence that expresses the topic, which is then followed and developed in the **rheme**, the part of a sentence that offers new information about the theme. The relationship of theme and rheme is similar to that of GIVEN INFORMATION AND NEW INFORMATION.

third person *see* PERSON.

time adverbial
An ADVERB, ADVERBIAL PHRASE, prepositional phrase or adverbial CLAUSE that indicates when, how frequently or for how long an event occurred or a condition existed. Time ADVERBIALS usually answer the question *When?*

> Police raided the warehouse *recently*.

In this example:

> The raid took place at three in the afternoon.

the adverbial consists of two prepositional phrases, *at three* and *in the afternoon*. And in this example:

> The police acted *as soon as they had enough information*.

the question *When?* is answered by the subordinate adverbial clause of time.

Some time adverbials indicate the frequency of an occurrence:

> *Every summer*, the Martins visit the Isle of Skye.

Other time adverbials indicate the duration of an event or condition:

> The Martins go there *for the first two weeks of June. During that time*, they go climbing and sailing.

tip-of-the-tongue
Descriptive of the mental state in which one cannot quite recall a word or phrase, including names.

The tip-of-the-tongue experience is common. A person may recall the sense, sound or rhythm of a word, or the word's overall structure, including the initial, medial or final letter, or synonymous or antonymous words but be unable to recall the particular word.

The phenomenon supports the SEMANTIC FIELD theory of language storage and retrieval. *See also* LEXICAL MEMORY AND SEMANTIC MEMORY.

to infinitive
The base form of a verb preceded by the particle *to*.

to read, to write, to listen

See also FINITE AND NON-FINITE FORMS OF VERBS; INFINITIVE; SPLIT INFINITIVE.

tone *(n.)*

1 The PITCH at which a word or syllable is uttered. The tone in which a word is spoken can be high or low, **rising** or **falling**.

2 In written English, tone is determined mainly by vocabulary, syntax and punctuation. For example, a piece of writing with a high proportion of polysyllabic, abstract words in sentences with multiple coordination or multiple subordination and embedding is likely to have a solemn, perhaps a pompous, tone. *See also* INTONATION.

topic and comment *(n.)*

Topic is the part of a sentence that indicates the theme (*see* THEME AND RHEME), which is then developed in the **comment**, or rheme, in the remainder of the sentence; an alternative term for theme. *See also* GIVEN INFORMATION AND NEW INFORMATION; KEY SENTENCE.

topic sentence

An alternative term for KEY SENTENCE.

trade language

An alternative term for PIDGIN. *See also* LINGUA FRANCA.

transcription *(n.)*

The systematic written notation of speech sounds; also known as 'transcript' and **notation**. Transcription can take either of two main forms: phonetic or phonemic. **Phonetic transcription** uses phonetic symbols to record actual speech sounds, including particular pronunciations in the speaker's accent, in order to produce what is known as a **narrow**, or highly detailed, transcription.

   Phonemic transcription uses only one symbol for each PHONEME of the language and does not indicate the speaker's actual pronunciation. Phonemic transcriptions, which are also known as **broad transcriptions**, lack the precise detail of phonetic transcriptions.

transferred negative

An alternative term for transposed negative. *See* NEGATIVE.

transformation *(n.)*

1 The conversion, or transformation, of one syntactic structure into another by the application of transformational rules. The main transformations are the conversions of active sentences to passive sentences, and the conversion of declarative to interrogative or negative sentences. Such transformations are centuries-old but the main transformational rules began to be formulated by Noam Chomsky and other linguists only the 1950s.

2 The elucidation, or 'disambiguation', of deep syntactic structures that cannot be achieved solely by the analysis of surface structures; the transformation of surface structure to deep structure in order to interpret a sentence correctly. The surface structure of the sentence:

> Mr Jones keeps racing pigeons

could be ambiguous because a word that ends in *-ing* can function as a verb, a noun or, in the example above, an adjective, and because the verb *keeps* could mean *continues to* or *owns*. But it is not clear that these or other ambiguities are eliminated by reference to a deep structure of grammar or of language.

The nature of the English language makes occasional ambiguity almost inevitable.

> Jack heard Jean sing from inside the house.

Who was inside the house: Jack or Jean?

> Jack left Jean to pay the bill.

Who paid the bill? Did Jack step forward to pay, or did he hold back while Jean paid?

> Jean spent the money she had saved in Norwich.

Did she spend the money in Norwich, save it in Norwich, or save and spend it in Norwich?

> Jean was not invited to the meeting because she was a local councillor.

Did Jean's membership of the local council disqualify her from attending the meeting, or was she invited to attend, but for reasons other than her membership of the council?

Unless additional, unambiguous information is available, these and other ambiguities are resolved by inferring the most likely meaning from the circumstance in which the ambiguity occurs; that is, by reference to non-linguistic forms of reality. A transformation certainly takes place as the ambiguous words are decoded and then re-encoded through a series of electro-chemical impulses in the brain, but it is a process that, initially at least, is non-linguistic or prelinguistic. The entire transformation may be as much the result of reference to these non-linguistic factors as reference to a DEEP STRUCTURE of grammar. *See also* AMBIGUITY; UNDERLYING STRUCTURE AND DERIVED STRUCTURE.

transformational relationship *see* RELATIONSHIP.

transitive verb and **intransitive verb**
A transitive verb is a main verb that takes a direct OBJECT, without which the sentence would be incomplete. In traditional grammar a verb is said to be transitive when the action indicated by the actor, or subject, of the sentence is transmitted through the verb to the direct object:

> The company sold the old furniture and bought a new one.

The condition of being transitive is called transivity. Transivity can take three main forms: monotransivity, ditransivity and complex transivity.

A **monotransitive verb** takes a direct object:

> The removal men lifted the piano.

A **ditransitive verb** takes a direct object and an indirect object. In this example:

> The householder gave the removal men tea and biscuits

the phrase *the removal men* is the indirect object, and *tea and biscuits* is the direct object of the verb *gave*.

A **complex transitive verb** is one that takes a direct object and a complement or an adverbial. In the sentence:

> The men named the new van Juggernaut

the new van is the direct object of *named*, and *Juggernaut* is the object complement. In this sentence:

> The men cleared the house room by room

the house is the direct object of *cleared*, and the phrase *room by room* functions as an adverbial.

An **intransitive verb** is one that does not take a direct object:

> Twilight ebbed. Stars glittered and the moon shone.

Intransitive verbs can, however, take adverbials:

> The sun rose *slowly*. Skylarks soared *into the air*.

Some verbs can function transitively and intransitively:

> The removal men dropped the piano.

> The price of shares dropped.

Anna plays the clarinet.

While the adults talked, the children played.

transliteration *(n.)*

Replacing the letters or characters of one language by those of another language; converting written words in one writing system into written words in another writing system. The Russian writing system in the Cyrillic alphabet is transliterated into the English writing system in the Latin alphabet.

transparent and opaque *(adj.)*

Transparent language is writing, occasionally speech, in which the meaning is clear. Transparency of meaning is unambiguous meaning that can usually be inferred from the surface structures of sentences.

Opaque language is language in which the meaning is not clear and cannot be inferred from the surface structure. Opacity has several causes, including failure to consider the needs of the reader, poor language skills or wilful OBSCURITY. *See also* READABILITY.

transposed negative *see* NEGATIVE.

tree diagram

A triangular, or tree-shaped, structure that shows the hierarchical syntactic levels of a sentence or clause. The word or letter – sentence or S, for example – at the acronode of the diagram, the tree-top, identifies the superordinate syntactic unit, usually a sentence or a clause. Diagonal lines, or branches, lead downwards from the superordinate level to lower-level units, for example, to the subject, verb or object of a sentence. Additional branches can lead downwards to the level of phrases, words or even inflections. Each junction of branches, from the acronode downwards, is known as a node.

Tree diagrams can be used to illustrate both traditional and more recent GRAMMAR. This sentence, for example:

The removal men loaded the van carefully

can be presented in a series of tree diagrams.

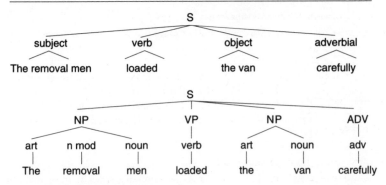

Code: S sentence, NP noun phrase, VP verb phrase, ADV adverbial, art article, n mod noun modifier, adv adverb

See also BRACKETING.

typology *(n.)* *see* ANALYTIC, SYNTHETIC AND AGGLUTINATIVE LANGUAGES.

u

ultimate constituents *see* CONSTITUENT ANALYSIS.

umlaut *(n.)*
An alternative term for MUTATION.

unacceptable *see* ACCEPTABLE.

uncountable noun *see* COUNTABLE NOUN AND UNCOUNTABLE NOUN.

underextension *see* OVEREXTENSION AND UNDEREXTENSION.

underlying structure and **derived structure**
An underlying structure is a deep system of meaning or syntax that is said to lie beneath a surface structure.

A derived structure is a system of meaning or syntax that is said to be the result of the TRANSFORMATION of an underlying structure.

   (a) Racing pigeons are expensive

(b) Racing pigeons is expensive

In sentence (a) the phrase *Racing pigeons* is said to be derived by the transformation of the structure of an underlying sentence such as:

Pigeons are racing

so that the derived structure of *Racing pigeons* consists of a verbal adjective and a noun. In sentence (b), by contrast, *Racing pigeons* is said to be derived by the transformation of the structure of an underlying sentence such as:

The Pigeon Club races pigeons

so that the derived structure *Racing pigeons* now consists of a verbal noun and a noun.

In this view of grammar, each sentence is said to have both a deep, or underlying, structure and a derived, or surface, structure. The view assumes that transformations are made by reference to a deep or surface structure of language and grammar rather than by reference to extra-linguistic forms of reality. *See also* DEEP STRUCTURE AND SURFACE STRUCTURE.

ungradable *see* ADJECTIVE; ADVERB; ANTONYM; COMPARISON; GRAD-ABILITY.

ungrammatical *(adj.)*
Descriptive of a USE of language that does not observe the rules of morphology or syntax in a system of GRAMMAR. By this definition, the statement *I never done nothing* is ACCEPTABLE in a system of folk grammar but not in standard English. *See also* NORMATIVE; PRE-SCRIPTIVE.

universal grammar *see* GRAMMAR.

unmarked *see* MARKED AND UNMARKED.

unproductive *see* PRODUCTIVE AND UNPRODUCTIVE.

upper case
An alternative term for CAPITAL LETTER.

usage *(n.)*
The established use of language in a society. The term *usage* covers several linguistic areas: semantics, morphology, syntax, idiom and

pronunciation. Among linguists, the practice is to note the nature of a linguistic feature and how it is used in a linguistic context, including the context of a speech community.

The practice of some other professional language users, in teaching, broadcasting and publishing, for example, and the comments of non-specialists are often prescriptive and may include some of the set-piece debates: *disinterested* or *uninterested*; *It is I* or *It is me*; the split infinitive; whether a sentence can begin with a conjunction or end with a preposition; whether the idiomatic English of the United States is acceptable in Britain; whether *controversy* is pronounced *'con*troversy or con*'troversy*.

These topics excite attention for several reasons. Most people end the systematic acquisition of language in their mid or late teens, after which their use of language is more or less fixed for the rest of their lives. The lessons we learn about the use of language are sometimes so firmly imprinted that they become simple absolutes; differences in usage are then seen as differences between right and wrong. Language, especially speech, is a form of social behaviour, and all social behaviour attracts notions of conformity and deviance. And for linguists and non-linguists alike, language is inescapably part of our personal, social, regional or national identity; a challenge to our use of language may be seen as a challenge to our selves. Concepts of usage, then, are often social or psychological as well as linguistic concepts, and they tend to invite strong views as to what is right or wrong.

See also ACCENT (1); ACCEPTABILITY; CORRECTNESS; DIALECT; IDIOLECT; NORMATIVE; SOCIOLECT; UNGRAMMATICAL.

utterance *(n.)*
An uninterrupted sequence of words spoken, or uttered, by one speaker. Utterance is sometimes contrasted with sentence or text in order to focus attention on the distinctive properties of speech – for example, loudness, tempo, pitch and the tolerance of ellipsis, redundancy and pauses – in contrast to the grammatical properties of the written sentence. When an utterance is transcribed, then, of course, it becomes a sentence or a text. *See also* DISCOURSE; DISCOURSE ANALYSIS; SPEECH ACT.

utterance meaning *see* SEMANTICS.

V

valency *(n.)*
The power of a grammatical unit, especially a verb, to govern other grammatical units in the same sentence.

In **dependency grammar** the concept of valency regards the verb as the superordinate unit in a sentence. The valency of a verb is measured by the number of noun phrases, including the subject, that are said to be dependent on the verb. An intransitive verb, for example, is usually monovalent because it can have only one associated noun phrase, the subject of the sentence. A verb with a direct object, an indirect object and a complement would have a valency of four. *See also* GRAMMAR.

variable *(adj./n.)*
A linguistic feature that changes, or varies, in different varieties of a language. The British English idiom, for example, *Going by tube* differs from idiomatic American English *Riding the subway*. Other variable features include the particular vocabulary and the non-standard grammar and pronunciation of regional dialects in contrast to standard English. *See also* INDETERMINACY.

variable word and invariable word
A **variable word** is one that can change its form, usually by inflection. Variable words include most nouns, which have singular, plural and possessive forms; personal pronouns, with variations for case, person, number and gender; gradable adjectives and adverbs; verbs, with variations for third person singular present tense and past participle; the DETERMINERS *this/these* and *that/those*. A few words have variant spellings, for example, *inflection/inflexion, jeweler/jeweller, amuck/amock/amok*.

An **invariable word**, also known as a **constant word**, is one that does not change its form. Invariables include MODAL AUXILIARY VERBS, non-gradable adjectives and adverbs, most of the determiners, and all CONJUNCTIONS and PREPOSITIONS.

variation *(n.)*
Differences of linguistic features such as pronunciation, grammar and vocabulary that exist in different VARIETIES of a language. *See also* VARIABLE.

variety *(n.)*

A version of a language used in a particular set of circumstances; a version of a language that includes linguistic variables. The concept of variety partly assumes that a STANDARD form of a language exists. Three broad forms of variety can be identified.

The variety may be that of a particular level: standard or non-standard, DEMOTIC or hieratic, HIGH OR LOW, FORMAL OR INFORMAL, depending on the language user and the nature of the occasion and the audience. The variety may be influenced by region, nation or ethnicity, for example, the scouse DIALECT of Liverpool, BLACK BRITISH or Australian English.

Some varieties are specific to particular professions or subjects, for example, the languages of science, the law or tabloid journalism.

Social background or status can be a factor in most varieties. *See also* BIDIALECTALISM; DIGLOSSIA.

verb *(n.)*

One of a large, varied, open class of content words; a word that is usually the minimum requirement of a sentence or clause; a word that denotes the occurrence of an action or the existence of a condition or state. Verbs have more grammatical categories than any other class of words. The categories are: FULL (lexical), MAIN, AUXILIARY and MODAL AUXILIARY; PHRASAL (phrasal auxiliary, phrasal prepositional and prepositional); REGULAR AND IRREGULAR; FINITE AND NON-FINITE; ACTIVE VOICE AND PASSIVE VOICE; INDICATIVE, IMPERATIVE and SUBJUNCTIVE MOOD; PAST, PRESENT and FUTURE TENSE; PERFECT and IMPERFECT in ASPECT; singular or plural in NUMBER; third person or other PERSON.

verb phrase

Two or more verbs functioning as a single VERB; a single verb alone. In a phrase of two or more verbs, the first verb often indicates the tense:

> is deciding, has decided, will decide

the last verb is the main, or lexical, verb:

> could have been lost

and verbs preceding the last verb are auxiliaries:

> might be found.

A verb phrase can be finite, as above, or non-finite:

> to be closed, having been opened

verbal *(adj.)*

1 Of, pertaining to, or derived from a verb. In linguistics, the word 'verbal' is used in this sense only.

2 Of or pertaining to words; consisting of words. In linguistics, this meaning is usually expressed by the word LEXICAL to avoid confusion with definition (1) above.

verbal adjective

An alternative term for participial adjective. *See* ADJECTIVE.

verbal noun

An alternative term for GERUND.

verbalize *(v.)*

1 To form a verb from a word from another class.

>   downgrade (from *down*, adverb and *grade*, noun)

>   encircle (from *circle*, noun)

>   straighten (from *straight*, adjective or adverb)

2 To use a word from another word class as a verb.

>   to *carpet* a floor (from the noun)

>   to *forward* a letter (from the adverb)

>   to *black* someone's eye (from the adjective)

verbless clause

A clause that does not contain a verb. Some constructions without a verb can be seen to function as clauses, or elliptical clauses, rather than as phrases.

>   *Anxious about her missing friend*, she telephoned the police. (Being anxious about her missing friend, she telephoned the police. Because she was anxious about her missing friend, she telephoned the police.)

>   *If in doubt*, do not drive. (If you are in doubt, do not drive.)

>   *Without a moment's hesitation*, he dived into the river. (Without hesitating for a moment, he dived into the river.)

vernacular *(adj./n.)*

The NATIVE LANGUAGE or dialect of a speech community. The word is sometimes used to imply a difference in status between a local, or vernacular, language and an international language such as English; or the difference in status between minority, vernacular, languages and the

NATIONAL LANGUAGE of a country. *See also* OFFICIAL LANGUAGE; PATOIS.

vocabulary *(n.)*

1 The entire sum of words in the standard variety of a language; an alternative term for LEXICON. The qualification 'in the standard variety of a language' is necessary because, although a two-volume DICTIONARY will have over 500,000 definitions, a much greater number of words will be omitted. Many thousands of regional dialect words and hundreds of thousands of scientific words are not recorded in standard dictionaries. The scale of the omission is this: by the year 1950 over 750,000 chemical compounds had been formulated and over 250,000 flowering plants had been identified; all the compounds and plants were named. The vocabulary of scientific, or special, English grows at a faster rate than that of standard English.

2 The sum of words known or used by a person; a personal lexicon. A personal lexicon can be roughly divided into an active and a passive vocabulary. An **active vocabulary** consists of those words that are used and understood by an individual. A **passive vocabulary** consists of words that are not normally used and are only partly understood by an individual, for example, words that the individual may come across in print or broadcast material.

3 The range of words in a particular book or other text. By this definition, vocabulary overlaps with REGISTER.

4 (a) An alphabetical list of words, with definitions or translations, in a textbook or foreign-language publication; an alternative term for **glossary**.

(b) A set of words used to explain the meanings of, or define, other words; also known as a **defining vocabulary**. Dictionaries, for example, use defining vocabularies to explain the meanings of the citation forms, or headwords, at the head of each entry.

vocal cords

Two folds of muscle and tissue in the larynx; also known as vocal folds or vocal flaps because they resemble flaps rather than cords. The rapid opening and closing of the folds creates the vibration patterns that produce speech sounds and vocalizations.

vocal tract

The physiological features used in producing speech sounds and vocalizations; the trachea, larynx, vocal cords, pharynx, mouth, tongue, teeth, lips and nose.

vocalization *(n.)*

An utterance considered as a vocal sound or sequence of sounds rather than as a word or words. The term is sometimes applied to the wordless babbling of infants. Some interjections – *Oh! Ah! Ugh!* – are vocalizations that have been standardized as words. *See also* INTERJECTION; PRELINGUAL.

vocative *(n.)*

The CASE of a noun or pronoun that denotes the person being ADDRESSED. In English, there is no case ending for vocatives, but vocatives in written English are usually indicated by a preceding comma:

> Climb up, Fred. I'm eating, Geoffrey.
>
> *Climb up Fred. *I'm eating Geoffrey.

voice *see* ACTIVE VOICE AND PASSIVE VOICE.

vowel *(n.)*

A speech sound produced by vibration of the vocal cords and without closing the vocal tract; the PHONEMES /a/, /e/, /i/, /o/, /u/ and sometimes /y/, and combinations of these phonemes; the unit of sound that forms the nucleus of a SYLLABLE; sometimes contrasted with CONSONANT.

W

weak verb *see* STRONG VERB AND WEAK VERB.

wh- clause

A subordinate clause beginning with a WH- WORD; a subordinate relative clause, a subordinate nominal relative clause or a subordinate adverbial clause beginning with a *wh-* word. *See also* CLAUSE; RELATIVE CLAUSE.

***wh-* question** *see* QUESTION.

wh- word

A small sub-class of words consisting of the relative and interrogative pronouns:

> who, whom, whose, what, which,

the relative and interrogative adverbs:

> when, where, why, how,

and the *wh*-ever words, some of which function as pronouns:

> whoever, whatever

and some as adverbs:

> whenever, wherever, however.

word *(n.)*

A LEXEME and any of its word forms. Concise linguistic definitions of *word* may be impossible because there are exceptions to the definitions. Leonard Bloomfield (1887–1949), the United States linguist, offered the helpful definition 'a minimum free form', that is, the smallest meaningful unit of language that can stand alone in written or spoken form. But AFFIXES are meaningful units and stand alone in dictionaries and other reference works; words can be broken into affixes and stems by hyphenation, including line-breaks – *includ-/ing* – and by spelling out the letters of a word – *s p e l l*. A spoken word is usually uttered as part of a fused word-cluster rather than a separately sounded unit. MORPHEMES and PHONEMES, too, can stand alone; an acceptable answer to the question, 'Did you say *amoral* or *immoral*?' could be '*A*'.

These distinctions trouble linguists; most language users understand what they mean by *word*. *See also* LEXEME.

word class *see* CLASS OF WORD.

word configuration

The overall shape of a word, including its length, the place of ascending and descending letters, and the presence or absence of capital letters, hyphens and apostrophes. Awareness of word configuration is clearly essential for word recognition; lack of awareness can be a factor in illiteracy and dyslexia. *See also* LEXICAL MEMORY AND SEMANTIC MEMORY.

word formation *(n.)*

Inventing new words. The main types of word formation are: ACRO-NYM, the use of an AFFIX, BACK-FORMATION, BLEND, BORROWING, CLIPPING, COINAGE, COMPOUNDING, CONVERSION, DERIVATION (1), EPONYM, HYPHENATION, NONCE-WORD, PARASYNTHESIS. *See also* LEXICALIZE; NEOLOGISM.

word order

The sequential arrangement of words in PHRASES, CLAUSES or SENTENCES. *See also* SYNTAX.

word stress

An alternative term for lexical stress. *See* STRESS.

world language *see* ARTIFICIAL LANGUAGE (1); INTERNATIONAL LAN-GUAGE.

writing *(n.)*

Writing, unlike SPEECH, is not a natural activity. Speech developed as part of the human evolutionary process, whereas writing was a deliberate invention. In the life of the individual, as in the life of the human race, the acquisition of speech precedes writing and is often unconscious or intuitive; writing, by contrast, has to be learned through formal instruction and conscious, sometimes self-conscious, practice.

Because writing is usually an individual or solitary activity rather than a social one, it is less influenced by immediate circumstances than speech. At this moment, for example, a student in New York may be writing about the potato famine in Ireland in the nineteenth century.

Writing gave language a permanence and a new mobility. The written message has a lifetime that is even longer than the paper or computer disk on which it is recorded because the message can be copied repeatedly over an indefinite period of time, and the written message, not an adulterated version of a spoken message but a fixed text, can be carried to all parts of the world.

The temporal and spatial scope of the written word allowed it to be used as a record of human activities: trade, government, religion, law, literature and so on. This status as a record, something referred and deferred to, gave writing a greater authority than speech. In a largely non-literate society, the authority of the text was sometimes inseparable from the authority of the writer; the literate élite who copied the religious manuscripts were also the controllers of religion. Even in modern, literate societies, the historian is the controller of history, and the news editor the controller of news; events that are not recorded may have historical value or news value but they are neither history nor news.

From around the middle of the twentieth century the authority of the written word began to be matched by the enhanced authority of the spoken word. British courts of law allowed audio and video tapes as forms of evidence; the House of Lords, followed by the House of Commons, agreed to have their proceedings recorded by radio and television as well as by Hansard and newspapers; scholars give greater attention than before to the linguistics of speech; schools now teach audio and video techniques as well as, or sometimes instead of, the techniques of writing.

Even so, the written word will survive in most of its forms: books, newspapers, magazines, reports, leaflets and letters. Most of these formats could be replaced by the computer disk, but the message on the disk would still take the form of writing. *See also* WRITING SYSTEM.

writing system

An agreed set of visual symbols that represent language; also known as an ORTHOGRAPHY (1). Writing systems are among the most revolutionary of all human inventions, and the invention of ALPHABETIC writing systems is one of the most influential developments in the history of communications because alphabets allow the entire resources of a language to be expressed through combinations of a few symbols.

One of the earliest writing systems, Sumerian cuneiform (Latin *cuneus*, wedge), with its wedge-shaped characters, was in use in Mesopotamia, now Iraq, from around 3500 BC. Cuneiform was adapted into the Phoenician syllabic writing system, which in turn was adapted by the Greeks into what eventually, around 850 BC, became the alphabetical system of Classical Greek.

The Romans re-modelled the Greek alphabet, and by the third century BC the Roman writing system was Classical Latin in the Latin alphabet. With the addition of the letters j, v and w, the same alphabet, and to that extent the same writing system, is used in English and most other Western languages today.

Writing systems can be classified as alphabetical, syllabic or logographic. In an alphabetical writing system, each symbol usually represents a PHONEME in the language. In a syllabic system, also known as a syllabary, each symbol usually represents one or more syllables. In a logographic system, each symbol usually represents one or more words in the language. *See also* WRITING .

Y, Z

yes/no question *see* QUESTION.

zero (*n./adj.*)
A term used to indicate that a linguistic unit is missing from a context in which the unit could appear. The concept of zero is a conventionalized way of noting, and partly explaining, the omission. It also lends a consistency, or an illusion of consistency, to elliptical or irregular constructions. *See also* ZERO ARTICLE; ZERO PLURAL; ZERO RELATIVE PRONOUN; ZERO SUBJECT; ZERO THAT CLAUSE.

zero article
The omission of the definite ARTICLE *the* or the indefinite article *a* or *an* before an uncountable noun.

> He bought fish, fruit and milk

and the omission of an article before a plural noun:

> Newspapers, magazines and books are on sale at the kiosk.

Although the term 'zero article' is traditionally applied to examples like these, it would be more accurate to define the missing word as the indefinite DETERMINER *some*.

zero plural
A NOUN that is not inflected to show the plural but has the same form for both singular and plural:

> caribou, deer, moose, sheep; cod, salmon, trout; hay, wheat; series.

See also NUMBER; PLURALE TANTUM; SINGULARE TANTUM.

zero relative pronoun
The omission of a RELATIVE PRONOUN from a relative clause.

> She framed the picture [that] she had painted.
>
> She is someone [whom] I admire.

zero subject
The implied SUBJECT of a verb in the imperative mood; the implied subject of a verb in a compound sentence. The zero subject of an imperative verb is usually *you*, and this is confirmed when the reflexive pronoun *yourself* or *yourselves* appears as the object of an imperative:

[You, singular] Take care of yourself.

[You, plural] Just look at yourselves.

But the zero subject can also be the indefinite pronoun *someone* or *everyone*:

[Someone] Answer that telephone!

[Everyone] Leave the building immediately.

Zero subjects are also implied in some compound sentences:

She went home, [she] watched the six o'clock news, [she] ate supper and then [she] listened to some tapes.

zero *that* clause
A relative clause or a nominal relative clause from which *that* has been omitted.

We know [that] you are honest.

See also CLAUSE.

zeugma *(n.)*
A figure of speech in which one word refers to two contrasting words or phrases in a sentence. The single word is often a verb, and the two contrasting words or phrases are the object of the verb. The effect of zeugma is similar to that of anticlimax: absurd, sarcastic or satirical:

He lost his memory and his handkerchief in the accident.